6/22

THE
LIGHT
SIDE
OF
LITTLE
TEXAS

UYLESS BLACK

LEA COUNTY MUSEUM PRESS
LOVINGTON, NEW MEXICO

THE LIGHT SIDE OF LITTLE TEXAS
BY
UYLESS BLACK

Available at Amazon.com

Log on to www.UylessBlack.com
and communicate with author

Or go to Blog.UylessBlack.com

Additional works by Uyless Black are available
at his Web and blog sites

Lea County Museum
103 S. Love St., Lovington, NM 88260
email: leacomuseum@leaco.net
www.leacountymuseum.org
575-396-4805

Library of Congress Control Number: 2010941943
ISBN 13: 978-0-9787663-4-4
ISBN 10: 0-9787663-4-2

Cover & Book Design by
Arrow Graphics, Inc.
info@arrow1.com
Printed in the United States of America

To author Mark Twain and son Tommy

*With thanks to the fine
horseman Ed Black for his
contribution to Chapter 4*

Recent and upcoming books by Uyless Black

See pages 240-241 for essays and other books

Lea County Museum Press
The Light Side of Little Texas

SAMS
Teach Yourself Networking in 24 Hours

IEI Press
A Swimmer's Odyssey: From the Plains to the Pacific
The Nearly Perfect Storm: An American Financial and Social Failure
    (available 2012)
The Deadly Trinity (revision available mid 2013)
Networking 101: An Introduction to the Internet and Social Networking
    (revision, available 2013)
My Capital, My America (available 2014)
Cold Wars, Hot Wars and America's Warm War (available 2014)

TABLE OF CONTENTS

Introduction vii

Notes for the Reader ix

1. Name that Name 1

2. Little Texas at Mid-20th Century 13

3. My Lips are Sealed 30

4. Shearing, Branding, and Breeding 54

5. The Tadpole Puddle 72

6. The Hunter and the Hunted 82

7. Cornered by a Stud 94

8. The Carnival 107

9. Confessions of a Southern Baptist 118

10. Water Life 125

11. Little Texas Music 101 140

12. The Christmas Cantata 150

13. Idle Minds 159

14. The Dog Catcher 173

15. Buzz Off! 183

16. Duds for Dad 192

17. Lost in Lea County 202

18. The Real Heroes 211

19. Thus Far, it's been a Good Life 218

Credits 230

Readers' Comments 233

INTRODUCTION

———◆———

New Mexicans, including myself, have a *thing* about Texas. This *thing* is based on one reality and one fantasy. Reality: the state of Texas is geographically larger than New Mexico. Size is an important factor in many ego contests dealing with self-worth and Texans love to talk about the size of their state. It's part of their God-given bragging rights. I am often reminded by my Texan friends about the relatively small size of my home state (and New Mexico is the fifth largest state in the Union).

The second thing is about fantasy: Any accomplishments we New Mexicans claim, Texans say they did them earlier and better. At the same time, they lay on layers of exaggerations about the feat, well beyond what any reasonable liar should claim.

Texans don't give much credit to New Mexico, but they should. Among many other positive attributes, we have more mountains and fewer people than the Lone Star State. Texans love mountains; they come in droves to Ruidoso, Taos, and Santa Fe to get their mountain fix. If you go to New Mexico's mountains during the ski season you will find great populations of reverse snowbirds—they are not Virginians, New Yorkers, or any other significant assemblage of East Coast gringos. Mostly, they are Texans.

My explanation about New Mexico's neighbor to its east and south could lead you to think I take the gloves off when Texas comes into the picture. Perhaps the best way to put it is that I consider Texas to be an amiable sparring partner. I like the state well-enough. And its bravado—taken in small does—does no harm. In general, I like Texans, and I especially like the idea that my parents were born in Texas, but moved from the Lone Star State to the Land of Enchantment.

This book is about a part of America that is surrounded by Texas on two of its sides. It's not in Texas, but in New Mexico. It's called Little Texas. The Texans who read this book will understand why it is so-named.

Notes for the Reader

Use of Direct Quotes

The use of direct quotes can be a touchy issue in a book dealing with an undocumented past. For this book, my use of quotes is based on being present when a conversation took place or on my parents' and brothers' recollection of a conversation. While we have good memories, my brothers, parents, and I cannot remember the specific words and associated profanities uttered during my childhood, teenage, and later-year experiences. I place dialogue in quotation marks as a tool to re-enact conversations. They are not verbatim reconstructions but they convey the spirit of the exchange. The dialogue in Chapters 16 and 17 are abridged conversations taken from recordings.

Mark Twain Quotes at Beginning of each Chapter

One of my favorite writers is Mark Twain, a man who had an amazing ability to express complex ideas with simple prose. As you may have noticed, I have dedicated this book to him and my son Tommy. I begin each chapter with a quote from one of Twain's writings and the last chapter has some of his thoughts at its end. The Credits section at the back of the book directs you to the source of each quote.

Style and Grammar

Writers are discouraged by critics and writing teachers from using clichés in their prose. I bow somewhat to this convention, but not completely. I have done a disservice to my reader if I compose a book that is designed to reflect the everyday discourse of our lives, yet excludes well-worn phrases from my descriptions. Such an approach sullies the flow and style of the narrative. However, a point is reached where excessive use of clichés makes for trite prose. My approach attempts to strike a compromise between the two extremes.

The chapter "Little Texas at Mid-20th Century" is written in the past tense, as is most of the book. However, many of the buildings described in this chapter are still standing, as are the churches and other institutions residing in the buildings. Fortunately, or unfortunately—depending on where one chooses to spend one's time—the saloons and bars I describe did not have the staying power of the churches and they are described correctly in the past tense.

The ranch in this story was operated by my Dad and my step-mom Mary, who owned the ranch when Dad came aboard. In the eyes of a child, I viewed this ranch as Dad's, and my story is told from this perspective. I thank Mary for marrying Dad and providing a venue of several summers for a child to experience a wild world of creatures, critters, and wonderful adventures.

Let me Hear from You

I look forward to your comments about this book. For more information about my work, go to www.UylessBlack.com and Blog.UylessBlack.com. At either site you can send me correspondence.

1

Name that Name

*When a teacher calls a boy by his
entire name it means trouble.*

—Mark Twain

Shortly after I was born in 1939, my fortunes in life went downhill. This descending slide was not due to an accident; nor was I a sickly child. I suffered none of the problems one might expect from a kid starting off on the wrong foot. The problem was my name, a seemingly harmless aspect of one's life.

I was given an odd name, one that was difficult to pronounce, and if pronounced correctly, was most likely misspelled. I was not given a name like Bill, Joe, or Frank. I was given a name appreciated by a genealogy expert.

As I lay semi-comatose in my newborn state at the hospital, my parents attempted to settle on what my name was to be. They placed my name onto a birth certificate but this submission represented the first of several entries. I didn't know about these alterations at the time because I could not yet read. It came to my attention later.

Let's get my names on the table. My original birth certificate shows my name as Uylsses Harold Black. My amended second name is Ulysses Harold Black. My third and final name is Uyless Delton

Black. The first name is spelled differently in each version and my middle name is no longer Harold.

At that early stage of my life, the name changes were not a big problem. I did not know about them until I chanced upon my birth certificate when I was older. The difficulty arose because I was not called by my name, but by my initials, U.D. Not only was my name in disarray, my parents didn't use it—preferring some unnatural letters instead. Thus, I began my life with a moniker handicap.

Errors at the Hospital

The first problem with my name occurred because of an error. The hospital where I was born, the Lovington, New Mexico General Hospital, misspelled my first name as Uylsses when recording the event of my birth into their records. Evidently, the person-in-charge of registering births at the hospital was not versed in Greek mythology or the American Civil War. Perhaps the hospital personnel had a mental block about how to spell the name Ulysses or for that matter, Uyless. I have encountered hundreds of other people with the same problem. I can count on one hand the number of people who have spelled my name correctly on their first attempt.

Eventually, my birth certificate was changed to correct the misspelled first name but the change itself was also incorrect. It was now Ulysses but was supposed to be Uyless. Shortly, I will explain how I became Uyless. For now, I need to explain the Harold part of my name; it has a more interesting origin and history.

Harold?

Years ago, I asked several people why the name of Harold was entered on my birth certificate. Logically enough, I first turned to my mother to clear up the mystery. After all, if anyone would know the details of a baby's name, it would be the mother of the baby.

As I handed Mom my birth certificate, I asked, "Mom, I noticed the name Harold is entered on my birth certificate. Who is Harold and why was I named after him?"

Mom, "That was a long time ago son. I seem to remember the hospital mixed-you-up with another baby named Harold. I think the hospital entered parts of Harold's name on your records and parts of your name on his records." (Giving Mom her due, she was almost 90 years old when I posed this question to her).

Great. In addition to the hospital exchanging the names of Harold and Uyless, maybe they also exchanged the bodies of Harold and Uyless. At this point, I suspected I knew the reason I did not look like my parents or my brothers. Somewhere in the world, there could be a person named Harold lurking about, bearing a striking resemblance to members of the Black family. My brothers teased me with the tale that I was not really a member of the family—that I was adopted. Their taunt was too depressing to contemplate.

What made the matters worse was the fact that my brothers had ordinary names. They were, in order of their births and resultant pecking orders: David, Ed, Ross, Jim, and Tom. Followed by Uyless? It made me an outlier.

Before leaving the mystery of the Harold name, I wish to state I have nothing against anyone named Harold. No offense is intended to the Harolds of the world, but name one great "Harold" who lived in this world? Oh sure, there was a king in ancient England named Harold. I think his complete name was Harold the Mediocre. Have you heard of any great athletes named Harold; any presidents; any great writers? Anyway, in hindsight, I was relieved to discover Harold was not to be one of my permanent monikers, although admittedly, Harold is an easy name to remember.

My Final Name

How did I end up with the name of Uyless Delton Black? Because I was named after a person whose name was Uyless Devoe Sawyer, but who was known as U.D. Mr. Sawyer was a close friend of my parents and they wished to honor him by naming one of their sons after him. As you can see, I was only partially named after this man— really only 1/3.

I was as curious about the name Delton as I was about the name Harold. I asked Mom, "I noticed the name Delton is entered on my birth certificate as my final, official middle-name. I thought I was named after Uyless Sawyer, whose middle name was Devoe, not Delton. Who is Delton, and why was I named after him?"

My mother's reply, "As I recall, when I was asked by the hospital personnel to provide your name for the birth certificate, I didn't know the exact name of your namesake."

What! How can a mother name her son after a person whose name she does not know? The whole idea borders on the surreal or at least something from Dear Abby. "Uh, Mom, I'm not sure I understand. You didn't know the middle name of Mr. Sawyer, yet you gave me his middle name?"

Mom responded, "Yes. As you know, Mr. Sawyer was known by his initials, U.D. When I was asked by the hospital personnel to provide your name for their records, I told a nurse you were to be named after U.D. Sawyer, and of course, everyone in Lea County knew U.D. (Writer's note: But they didn't know his name.) That was the end of the matter for me, as I didn't see the birth certificate. Your Dad signed it and he never read anything he signed."

The hospital naming guru struck again. I seemed to have a naming albatross draped around my tiny neck. I was being set up for all sorts of problems, to which I was blissfully unaware—until later in my life.

Crisis in the First Grade

At age 5 years and 9 months, my name created an identity crisis in my life. I was to attend school for the first time, at the Lovington, New Mexico Elementary School. In those simple and innocent, pre-metal detector times, it was unnecessary for a child to be accompanied by parents or bodyguards to school—even on the first day. Mom instructed my brother Tom to walk me to school and to make certain I was registered (i.e. deposited) in the correct classroom, that of Ms. Shackelford, the first grade teacher. Tom was a seasoned veteran for this chore; he was in the third grade. As such, he had been through the registration ropes. On a September morning in 1945, Tom escorted me to school, located about a mile from our home.

I recall our walking into Ms. Shackelford's classroom as if it happened yesterday. I recall Ms. Shackelford as clearly now as I saw her then. The following conversation took place.[1]

Tom, "I'm here to register my little brother for school."

Ms. Shackelford, "What is your name?"

Tom, "Tom Black."

Ms. Shackelford, "What is the name of your little brother?"

Tom, "U.D. Black."

Little brother, "Is not!"

Tom, "Is too!"

Little brother, "Is not! My name is U.D. Sawyer."

Tom, "Is too! Be quiet!"

Little Brother, "Is not! Not! Not! I was named after U.D. Sawyer. So, I *am* U.D. Sawyer!"

Clearly, my brother and I were at an impasse. It was obvious I had not been schooled in the custom of a child taking on the last name of his parents or I had ignored this part of my education.

Tom then handed my prospective teacher a note, which I suspect came from Mom. She looked it over, and muttered my name, "Uyless Delton Black? My word!" Next, turning to me, she declared, "U.D., hereafter you are U.D. Black."

For my entire conscious life I had been under the mistaken impression that I was U.D. Sawyer. With one sentence, Ms. Shackelford gave me a new identity. Her directive marked the end of my relationship with the name of Sawyer. Fine by me. Mr. Sawyer was my last name namesake no more. I liked having the same last name as my Mom, Dad, and brothers. If I had the same last name as my family, I might actually be a legitimate member of the family—not adopted after all.

Under Developed

As time passed, I came to resent carrying around a moniker my playmates could ridicule. As I entered my school years, some of the older children in town nick-named me _under developed_. It seemed to fit; I was very small for my age and did not begin my growth to a height of six feet until my later high school years. I began to think of myself as under developed. My playmates called me "the little midget." In later years, I learned their taunt was redundant, but at that time, I was too little schooled in the nuances of the English language to debate their claim.

Crisis on the Stage. The crowning blow to my under developed image happened one night when I was eight years old. A magician had traveled to our town to put on a magic show. His act was held in an auditorium in one of Lovington's school buildings and he bedazzled the audience. Adults and children alike were drawn to his tricks and fun.

At the end of his act and to climax his show, the magician put a turban on his head. With his assistant playing exotic music on a record player, he appeared to levitate a rope into space without touching it, raising its end toward the ceiling of the stage—a cobra snake responding to a flute. It was impressive but the audience suspected the rope was connected by a hard-to-see thin thread. And it was; the thread and the attached rope were drawn upward through a pulley secretly operated by the assistant.

The magician wanted to substantiate his rope-raising feat. He claimed the rope was not held-up by anything at all; that it was suspended in midair and capable of holding the weight of a person. But not just any person. He challenged the audience, "To demonstrate my magic to you, I invite a midget from the audience to come up on this stage and climb this rope."

Ha! Ha! His challenge brought forth laughs and good-hearted jeers. The audience knew he was pulling their legs—except for one little boy. I was under the impression I was a midget and therefore a candidate for climbing the magician's rope. In those days, I didn't realize the term midget had negative connotations. Today, I gather it cannot be used to describe a small person, only items like cars and servings at French restaurants. At that time, I thought midget simply meant someone who was little. Enough said. I headed down the aisle toward stardom.

What can I say about my walk onto the stage? The crowd, such as it was, went wild. Even my brothers, who were scattered through the audience, thought my confrontation with the showman to be funny. Yours truly had no clue whatsoever. Without realizing it, I had called the magician's bluff.

The challenge worked. The magician was taken aback—if only momentarily, and he laughed along with the audience. What else could he do? He then exposed the pulley system he had devised to raise the rope. He was slick about his exposed anticlimactic act.

In place of another rope trick, he ended his act by demonstrating how to fold a road map correctly the first time, which also got a lot of laughs. I didn't see the humor of this part of his act but I had never attempted to fold a road map. For the grand climax, the magician presented the road map to the midget as a token of his appreciation for the midget's contribution to his act. A road map? Even for a midget, the gift seemed small.

A Dubious Gift

For the remainder of the school year, I was called "The Midget." Even at my young age, it didn't take a long time to realize the term was being used in a derogatory manner with regard to my vertically-challenged stature. After all, other little kids in my class were small for their age and no one called them under developed or a midget. All of this misery rained down on me because of one reason: my initials, U.D.

I made it past elementary school, into junior high, and even through high school. I kept the name U.D., even though I didn't like it. My midget handle faded away and I graduated from high school sporting an above average height. Luckily, U.D. came to mean just U.D.

But in the back of my mind, I had always wanted a real name. My decision to do away with the initials U.D. came about during my senior year in high school. I was given a set of cuff links as a graduation gift. In those days, cuff links were an important part of a young man's wardrobe and I had begun a cuff link collection, thanks to my Dad and brothers passing-off their used and ugly sets. As I opened the gift and viewed my loot—my very first set of virgin cuff links, I noticed they were engraved with fancy lettering. I read the initials "V.D." on each cuff link. That was it! I had had it with U.D. and I was not going to wear a set of cuff links around town suggesting I was a diseased ex-midget.

I was incensed, and taking a clue from the name on the jewelry box, I took the cuff links back to the local jewelry store—well, the only jewelry store in town. There, I confronted the engraver and awaited his explanation.

His defense? He said he had engraved my initials using Latin letters. Yes, Latin letters! Why a hack jeweler was dabbling in Latin lettering in the backward plains of southeastern New Mexico remains a mystery to me.

But he had me over a barrel. The letters may have been properly inscribed. I didn't know Latin. Living in the boondocks of New Mexico, I barely knew English. Defeated, I took the cuff links with me as I left the store. They became an invisible part of my cuff link collection. To this day, I am convinced the jeweler made a mistake but didn't want to give me a new set of cuff links at his own expense. My erudite friends have informed me the letter "V" was once part of an old version of Latin. Who knows? Perhaps my jeweler was also an anthropological linguist.

Underwater Demolition Black

From the time I leaned to swim in water tanks on our ranch, water sports became my preferred past time and swimming pools became my favorite playgrounds. I took to the water, and with each summer, I became a better swimmer. Since my childhood, I had one goal in life: to be a frogman. Watching war movies of Underwater Demolition Team (UDT) swimmers (now called SEALs) and confident of my swimming prowess, I knew I was destined to be a great frogman. And I had some sterling initials go along with my job. UDB of the UDT—has a nice ring to it, don't you think?

Each summer I trained to meet my goal, swimming thousands of laps, many of them with weights tied onto my hands or legs. I became a fine swimmer and when duty called, I was ready. I was one of six men selected from 120 applicants for UDT training in my U.S. Navy OCS class and I will recount my UDT experiences another time. For this story, it turned out the only instance in my life when I actually wanted to use my initials as my name was the instance when I could not do so. After learning I had been selected for the UDT program, I was called into the office of one of the frogmen who had evaluated me. We had a talk.

"Mr. Black, congratulations. Not many men are selected from OCS for UDT. I wish you well."

"Thank you Commander. I will do my best."

"I'm sure. … Um, you told us during your interviews you are called U.D., correct?"

"Yes sir."

Glancing down at some paperwork on his desk, the Commander said, "Here's some advice. You're going to be harassed during your training. I suspect if you show up and tell the instructors you are Ensign U.D. Black, you are going to be selected for special treatment. I recommend you report to UDT as Ensign … Ulysses … eh. … Ulssee … or. … say, I think your first name is misspelled on my report."

Why should I have expected my name to somehow magically help me in life? Why break a record of 22 years of miserable name experiences? My pathetic initials and my miserable first name were once more a giant pain in my ass. For the zillionth time, I explained my name.

For most of my life I had fantasies of going to frogman school with the moniker of Underwater Demolition Black. If you've got it, flaunt it. In your face man! But no, taking the frogman's advice, I reported to UDT training in Coronado, California as Ensign Uyless Black.

Using my Name

Time marched on. So did my life, as well as my dealing with initials. With some desultory exceptions I had resigned myself to being known as U.D. Then, in my later years, an opportunity presented itself to rid myself of this so-called name. I had entered a new profession and almost all my encounters were with strangers. I could now discard the initials albatross and begin to use my first name, Uyless, with my new business associates and acquaintances. In addition, my book publishers preferred my full name to my initials.

Great. I was certain I would have a much easier go of it; no V.D.s, no under developed jokes—just plain and simple Uyless—a real name like my brothers.

I can guess you know where the final part of this story is going You can't? Ok, try to pronounce my name. If you pronounced it as U-less, congratulations. Your feat places you in a very small population who pronounce my name correctly on their first attempt.

I had exchanged one set of name problems for another. At least, people could pronounce U.D. Uyless was another matter. Even worse, it was unusual when a person spelled Uyless correctly. Here is a sampling of the various spellings of Uyless I received in my mail in less than a year after I took it on as my mark: Euless, Ulis, Oless, Eulis, Uless, Olis, Ules, Uylless, Ulyssesses, Ulysses and so on.

My name problems never stopped, they just took on different forms. As one example, I began to be called Useless—especially by those who had come to know my social skills. When all was said and done, it was a troubling turn of events.

Naming Our Son

In my late twenties, my wife and I had the good fortune to have a son. Unlike his father, I decided he was going to have a name with pizzazz—no wimpy Harold, no confusing Uyless. I lobbied with my wife to have him named Pitch. Alternately, Coal. Third choice, Blue.

Had I gone mad? Pitch Black? Coal Black? Blue Black? Looking back on this part of my life, I admit I was immersed in the hippy mores of the late sixties and involved with the counter culture. I was impressed by parents who pushed the name envelope by labeling their children Picabo, Chastity, and Moonbeam. To this day, I would like to meet Picabo Street—because she is a great skier but especially because of her name.

An off-beat name for my son did not pass muster with his mother. My wife insisted on a common, simple name. I relinquished but I still think the name of say Magic, or maybe Tiger, could have helped my son make his way through life.

And as it turned out, our son is named Thomas (Tommy) Delton Black. Tommy is from my brother Tom; Delton is from me, courtesy of an uninformed clerk at the Lovington General Hospital.

I continued to harbor visions of a glorious name for Tommy, even if I had to use his initials. Yes! T.D.B. for Touch Down Black. I schooled Tommy during his childhood on the game of football and he loved it. I was certain he was going to be a football star; I could see the headlines, "T.D. Black scores more TDs."

My son did not follow his dad's love of football. Early in life Tommy discovered rock and roll, and became a musician. Today, his interests in football and TDs are nonexistent. In deference to our houseguests last Christmas, Tommy watched the first football game of his adult years. By the way, our son owns a record label called Pitch Black, which provides some vindication to my attempts to tag him with an unusual name.

The Past Becomes the Present

My name continues to confuse strangers, as well as my friends and relatives. They are no longer certain if they should call me U.D. or U-less. That's ok, I answer to either. And to make matters easier for new acquaintances, I have adopted the practice of asking them to just call me "U." That's it; what could be simpler? I often call myself U, which creates some interesting situations when I answer the phone, "Hello, this is U."

Nonetheless, at this point in my life, I no longer have the energy to enter into yet another explanation of the pronunciation and spelling of Uyless or the "real meaning" of U.D. Nowadays, when I am asked my name, I try to avoid using it.

An example of my resolution is the occasion when I eat out and must wait for a restaurant table, "Can I take your name sir? We will call you when your table is ready."

I respond to the waiter, "Yes, my name is Harold."

---

[1] Please see the front matter in this book for my convention on using quotes.

2

LITTLE TEXAS AT
MID-20TH CENTURY

*Good breeding consists in concealing how much we think of ourselves,
and how little we think of the other person.*

—Mark Twain

Now that the history of my name has been chronicled for the ages, let's set the stage for the remainder of this book: Life in the 1950s on a small country town and a county located on the flat, dry prairies of New Mexico.

Lea County lies in the southeastern corner of New Mexico. It is surrounded by Texas on its southern and eastern borders. Lea County old timers recount an attempt by Texas to annex Lea County in the early 1900s. Not that it would have made much difference to the county natives because Lea County is quite similar to Texas. I once heard a Lea native joke, "Lea County is more like Texas than Texas is like Texas." Many people refer to Lea County as "Little Texas."

New Mexico and Lea County were once part of Texas, but eventually became independent lands. As the Lone Star State made its way to statehood, New Mexico was partitioned away from Texas.

The position of the county in relation to the U.S. and New Mexico is shown in Figure 2-1. The county encompasses over 4,000 square miles of land; it measures 117 miles north to south and 40-48 miles east to west. It rests on the *Llano Estacado*, the Spanish name for *staked plain*. The Llano is known as the "largest level plain of its kind in the United States" and "one of the most perfect plains regions of the world."[1]

The Llano is big. It exceeds the size of seven of the original thirteen states. As a mesa of 50,000 square miles, spreading over West Texas and East New Mexico, its terrain is flat.[2] Until I ventured into the hills of central Texas during my childhood, I had not viewed a rise in the ground of more than three or four feet high. With no mountains or hills to impede construction, most of the roads in Lea County are straight as an arrow.

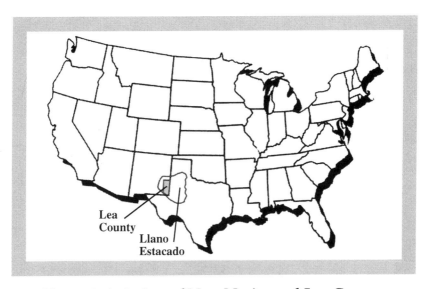

Figure 2-1. A view of New Mexico and Lea County.

The county is dry, at times semi-arid, with no natural forests. Except in towns and the immediate vicinity around a rural home, trees are few and far between. The horizon is visible for many miles. Lea County relatives visiting my home in Virginia's Shenandoah Valley, a place of abundant foliage, tell me they experience claustrophobia when traveling on Virginia's tree-lined highways. A Freudian-related malady no doubt; I suspect they suffer from tree envy.

The County's Blue Bloods: Cowboys and Oilmen

At mid-20th century, Lea County was a typical American rural enclave and its county seat, Lovington, was emblematic of a small country town. A blue collar community, without claim to blue book registers or blue blood breeding, the county citizens made their living tilling the soil, raising cattle and sheep, and working in the oil fields.

Horse breeding was also a common industry among the ranchers; principally Quarter Horses—the workhorse of the Southwest. Naturally, cowboys were abundant in Lea County. In those days, pointy-toed boots, Stetson hats, and big belt buckles were as common a sight as today's Nike shoes, backward-worn baseball caps, and the absence of belts ... with the associated pants clinging precariously to teenage buttocks.

My parents came to this part of the country from Texas. Dad arrived around 1910; Mom in the early 1920s. They met in Lea County and made this part of America their home for the rest of their lives. They went into cattle and sheep ranching, and horse and child breeding. I don't know how many horses Dad raised. His children count was six, I being the last one to come along.

Shortly after Mom and Dad married, oil was discovered in Eddy County, an area west of Lea County. Two years later, in 1926, the liquid gold was unearthed in Lea County. By mid-century, oil had become a major player in the county's economics. As part of the famous Permian Basin, the county became a prolific source of crude oil; it was one of the richest fields in the United States. The oil well equipment changed the landscape of the county. Its rural setting of prairie grass pastures, interspersed with sagebrush, cotton fields, sheep, horses, and cattle was now accentuated with drilling derricks, tanks, and refining plants.

Five major communities populated the county, as shown in Figure 2-2. The largest was Hobbs, with about 15,000 people. Some people in the county, especially the citizens of Hobbs, called Hobbs a city because it was larger than the towns of Jal, Eunice, Lovington, and Tatum. Hobbs paid little attention to the other communities in the county, in the same way Texas ignores New Mexico and the United States ignores Canada. Other smaller communities were scattered throughout the county. One was Maljamar, a small burg sitting on top of enormous oil pools. Another was Crossroads, where my parents met and courted.

I have noted with an "X" the location of our family ranch, a place we will visit during our exploration of this part of the country. I have also noted other cites that will be players in our tale.

Lovington was populated with about 8,000 people. As mentioned, it enjoyed the distinction of being the county seat. The county court house was situated in the middle of downtown Lovington on the courthouse square. Small commercial buildings surrounded the square. They housed many of Lovington's retail stores and several of the offices associated with county matters.

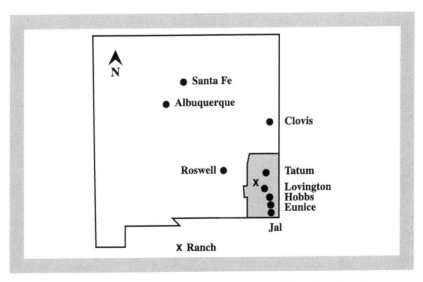

Figure 2-2. Towns and cities noted in this book.

A World War II memorial commanded the southwest corner of the square. As a boy, I spent many hours at this memorial; not because I was a patriot but because the site included two WW II cannons.

The cannons were included in my top ten list of things to do and see in Lovington.

The nine other entries in this list included the local swimming pool, Jake's Drug Store, the county jail, the school building's sliding fire escape, my BB gun and bicycle, my friend's motor scooter, the Katty Korner Kafe, the Saddle and Smoke House Bars, and any extant frogs or tadpoles populating Lea County's rare, endangered rain puddles.

On second thought, make that eleven; I also include the movie theatre, which ranked very high in this list. Anyway, the courthouse still stands but the WW II memorial is gone, replaced with a Vietnam veteran's memorial.

An Abundance of Churches, Bars, and White People

Churches were plentiful throughout the county. The majority of these buildings housed Baptist worshipers and my parents were non-practicing Southern Baptists. For myself, I was a semi-Southern Baptist, and attended a First Baptist Sunday service for two reasons: After my youthful sins got the better of my rather somnolent conscience, or after I discovered my current girl friend was going to church that day. As you might expect of a young boy, these reasons were related.

The Catholic faith was not yet represented in Lovington, nor was there a synagogue for the Jewish faith to meet and worship. I met my first Jewish person my Freshman year in college at the University of New Mexico in Albuquerque—at least as far as I know.

Although northern New Mexico experienced a rich history of Jewish immigration in the 18th and 19th centuries, a Spanish legacy has dominated that area for hundreds of years. Thus, the northern part of the state was (and is) predominately Catholic. Not so for Lea County and southeastern New Mexico. Most of the church-going crowd was made up of Baptist, Methodist, Church of Christ, Presbyterian, and Assembly of God folks.

Churches and bars competed with each other for the town's prime real estate and clientele. (Service stations were a close third). My favorite bar—to watch from the window or to sneak in and steal a peek—was the Saddle Bar. I liked going there to check-out the action and admire the barstools, which were made of western saddles.

A close second in my bar rankings was the Smoke House Bar. This saloon had a couple of unique characteristics. First, its fixtures included a shuffleboard, a popular game with the beer-drinking population. My Dad was a fine shuffleboard player and occasionally traveled to nearby Eddy County to match his skills (and gambling money) with other players.

The second unique characteristic pertained to the bar's chairs. During the fall months of the year, some of the Smoke House seats were constructed of bales of hay. This furniture made for an odd sight to a newcomer. In my late teenage years, two of my college buddies ventured down from Albuquerque to visit. I took them on a tour of Lovington's bars, but we eventually settled-in at the Smoke House. My city slicker friends were quite impressed by the Smoke House's eclectic interior design.

The hay bales were installed during the cotton-picking season because the increased clientele of cotton pickers exhausted the saloon's chair and stool inventory. To solve this problem, the bar owner paid a visit to the local feed store to stock-up on additional fittings. After the cotton pickers left town, the owner transferred the hay bales to his pastures to feed his cattle—the modern notion of dual-use furniture.

White, Brown, and Black

The majority of Lea County citizens were white. A few African Americans and Mexican Americans resided in Hobbs and Lovington; even fewer in the other communities. The blacks were restricted to living in ramshackle housing in a section of the town called "the other side of the tracks." The schools were integrated during my freshman school year (1953-1954) but I cannot recall conversing with a black person until I was in junior high school. Even though school integration proceeded smoothly, it is fair to say mid-20th century southeastern New Mexico exhibited certain characteristics of a "southern" society. Lea County continued to be segregated—if not in law, then in practice.

Fortunately, my parents were color blind and culturally neutral. I cannot recall Mom or Dad expressing a negative opinion about blacks, Chicanos, Jews, Catholics, Muslims, or even Methodists. I was living in an era when many people condoned unconcealed prejudice, so I am grateful to my parents. They kept my mind as untainted as was possible in those days.

Cotton Picking Season

Cotton was a major crop in the county. I spent some of my childhood summer days picking cotton, which ranks very high in my list of undesirable jobs. The work was mentally numbing and physically exhausting—the backbreaking position of kneeling and stooping to reach the plants made for a long, arduous day. The cotton bolls were not fond of being picked and protected themselves with sharp stickers. I used gloves to protect my hands but most of the veteran pickers went barehanded.

During the cotton-picking season, laborers traveled from Mexico to pick the county's cotton. The day before the cotton-picking season began, the streets in downtown Lovington were populated with white people. The next day, the streets were inundated with Mexicans— with a few white skins sprinkled among the brown. After the season ended, and the laborers had returned to Mexico, the white folks came out of their homes and businesses to reclaim the streets and the picked-clean cotton fields.

The Uniqueness of the Communities

Chain stores and franchises were quite rare in Lea County, or for that matter in New Mexico. During those days, each business was unique in its physical appearance and the way it conducted its operations. The minor exception in Lovington was a drug store displaying the Rexall sign in its window. In hindsight, I suppose it was part of a chain but it had no resemblance to the bland, monotonous franchises that homogenize today's urban landscapes.

The other two drug stores, Jake's Fountain, and Peck's City Drugs, were not affiliated with any later-day Rite Aides.

Each store in Lea County was a unique merchandising world unto itself—a tiny universe, separate and apart from other capitalistic goings-on in the town and county. To cite some examples, let's stay with the drug stores and later, the variety store.

While they sold the same wares, the three stores were different in appearance and atmosphere. Jake's smelled of food; Peck's smelled of preserved pills; the Rexall store smelled of freshly printed magazines. As a young boy, after playing in odorous oil-permeated fields; after hours of hoeing, painting fences, and picking cotton in hot, dry, sun-drenched pastures, I looked forward to visiting those stores. I looked forward to experiencing their fanciful ambiences. Escapes, pure and simple.

Escapes? Fanciful ambiences? In drug stores? Yep. My childhood preceded Disneyland, television, video cell phones, computers, video games, iPods, kid-specific DVD players, talking books, and talking heads. Truth be told, I suspect my threshold level for being entertained was very low; certainly lower than youngsters today—who routinely ignore the playground gyms at McDonalds. Most kids my age were in the same boat as I: Without external stimulation, we made up our own Disneylands. (But oh, what I would have given for an hour or so in a McDonald's playground gym!)

Upon entering Jake's Fountain on one of those hot summer afternoons, I immediately felt the cool air conditioning—gradually but every so thankfully—changing my hot wet shirt to a chilled limp cloth. As my skin cooled, I walked farther into the store, toward the fountain, where I smelled Jake's hot dogs, vanilla extract; and marshmallow syrup. I was thankful to be closed-away from oil field smells. Nothing but cool air, the tang of a cherry Coke, and the taste of a hamburger. Heaven on Earth.

When traveling across the United States and to other parts of the world, I often reminisce about the towns and merchants of Lea County, each with their own personality. Even though Lea County's local merchants consisted of the modern-day McDonald's and Walmarts, these stores maintained their own dispositions. Yet they somehow managed to sell us what we wanted at an affordable price, and at the same time, helped keep our senses keen and vibrant.

The Prototype Toys-R-US. The variety store was named Plummer's, also owned by a local family. When I was a young child, a visit to Plummer's was a journey to a make believe world, although I imagine a modern kid would be under-whelmed by the store's toy inventory. Plummer's devoted only twenty feet of shelf space to toys and games—a miniscule fraction of such space in a Toys-R-US store today. But the road to satiation must begin somewhere, usually with an initial, modest approach to consumption. Over indulgence can follow later.

Communications

The telephone was a popular communications tool, but was used sparingly because of the cost of long distance calls and the sharing of the line with other parties. In my first home in Tatum, the phone was fixed to the wall in the corner of our living room. The phone had a hook on its side by which to hang the earpiece. A separate "mouthpiece" for speaking was attached to the phone. I knew what "on-hook" and "off-hook" meant long before I learned about these terms during my college classes in telecommunications.

As mentioned, while living in Tatum, we were connected with a party line. After moving south to Lovington, Ma Bell upgraded our phone to a black, dial-up instrument, and we progressed to a private line service. Local exchange codes were numerals for the future; our telephone number was the simple four-digit 4101.

In rural Lea Country, if a family had electricity, they listened to the radio. But in certain parts of the county, electricity had not reached some of the homes. We had electricity at our home in town but none at the ranch. There, we used a wind charger, and later, a gas-powered generator for our electrical power.

Another form of communications, television, did not appear until the mid-to-late 1950s. Even then, the poor reception discouraged most people from buying a TV set. The nearest transmitting station was Roswell—yes, of UFO fame. By the way the crow flies (see Figure

2-2), the transmission was 70 miles from Roswell's TV tower to Lovington's TV sets. In retrospect, Roswell's resident aliens may have beamed our TV transmissions to us.

Country was Cool

Listening to music was a popular way to spend leisure time, and like Barbara Mandrell, I liked country when country wasn't (yet) cool. Dancing was a favored pastime for many families in the rural areas of the United States and Lea County public dances were highly attended. My grandmother taught my Mom how to dance. In turn, my Mom taught me the two-step, the waltz, and a funky dance called "Put Your Little Foot Right Out." (After leaving Lea County, I never danced it again). Mom's lessons were essential to my successful navigation of Lea County's dance floors.

I carried my fondness for dancing into my adult years and discovered I was often in demand at parties. Not because of my looks and social graces but because I knew how to lead a female across a dance floor. Thank you Mom; thank you Grandmother Rogers.

My favorite dancing place in Lovington was the second floor of an animal barn; the first floor contained cattle and sheep pens. Located on the county fairgrounds, logically enough, we called the building the Bull Barn.

The monthly Barn Dance was a big event for the county's dancers. A live band provided the Barn Dance music. It consisted of a guitarist, a fiddler, a drummer, and sometimes, a bass player. They played standard country and western fare: Bob Wills and his Texas Playboys; Hank Williams; Eddy Arnold. The band kicked-off their music at 8 PM, and as an evening of dancing progressed, the mixture of music, sweat, whiskey, and barnyard fragrances brought forth fine two-step performances from the dancers—accompanied by associated aromas. All in all, a pleasant melding of sounds, sights, and smells.

The folks at the Barn Dance were well behaved; many were prominent county citizens. I recall the crowd was sober and docile— even friendly. Most of the dancing couples were husbands and wives but a few of the dancers were intimate dating pairs whose two-step intertwinements were accepted as pre-wedding foreplay to post-wedding play. Their machinations were the prototype steps to dirty dancing, but with a honky-tonk style.

Everyone inside the Bull Barn talked and laughed according to the age-old protocol of "getting along with your neighbor." Idle chatter mostly. Passing the time until the next set of music started. Then, back onto the dance floor to shuffle around a counter clock-wise ring of couples; circling about the Bull Barn in two-step unison.

Fired-up by the songs with a fast tempo, I took pride in dancing my partner and myself around the floor faster than the other dancers. Circling past the band, coming back around to the band again, and again ... and again. Executing an occasional lightning-fast 180 degree switch to dance backwards for a while, as the two of us continued around the larger circle. An occasional collision with another couple, but rebounding onto the next vacant place on the floor. Human electrons prancing around a musical nucleus.

Even today, through an aging prism, I can hear, see, taste, and smell the Bull Barn scene of music, dancing shadows, whiskey, and sweet sweat. Light cascading from the bare 100 watt light bulbs hanging on black cords above the floor. Evanescent clouds of smoky dust, faintly visible through the light, kicked-up by cowboy boots, billowing faintly around moving dancers. Laughter, and a yell here and there. A scene bathed with undulated moods of friendly haze and loud yet muted noises.

As mentioned, arguments and fights were rare at these festivities; amiability was the prescribed mode of behavior. Not so for the rodeo dance—the after-affair of the day's rodeo contests.

Rodeos and Rodeo Dances

I recall watching horse races when I was a child, between the ages of four and five. Before moving to Lovington and also to our country ranch, Dad built our home (my first) on the outskirts of Tatum where we had access to open pastures. My family and our friends spent many hours racing Quarter Horses on this range.[3]

Horse races were not considered an integral part of a rodeo because the expansive terrain required for a race was beyond the bounds of a rodeo arena. But the other horse-associated contests took place at the rodeo show ground.

The rodeos of the 1950s have not changed much from today's matches shown on ESPN. The rodeo managers are smart enough to know they should not tamper with a good thing. Thus, the contests remain the same, as do most of the rules. If my Dad and brothers were still physically capable of riding in a modern rodeo, they would find their favorite events of calf roping, the cutting horse contest, and steer wrestling to be the same now as they were fifty years ago.

The Lea County Fair and Rodeo was a big event each year. The fair was held at the fair grounds (and site of my favorite place to dance, the Bull Barn). The rodeo was held at the Jake McClure Arena, named after a native son, who once held the world's calf roping championship title.[4] The fair and rodeo attracted large crowds, maybe as many as several hundred people!

The parade was the most popular event of the week. People came from miles around to watch the parade and applaud its participants— who were mostly horses, cowboys, and cowgirls. Miles of horses and their riders paraded down Main Street, interrupted with an occasional high school band, or a rare decorative float. The only other parade exhibits competing in number with the horses were trucks and fire trucks; favorites of the crowd, especially the children. Figure 2-3 contains a picture of part of this parade, taken in the late 1940s, as it makes its way down Main Street.[5]

The evening dances held after the conclusion of the rodeo were similar to the Barn Dances. Two-steps, Put Your Little Foot, and waltzes were the ordained dances for the evening. But the rodeo dance participants like to drink and fight. A few of the Barn Dance dancers attended the rodeo dances but most of them stayed away because the crowd was usually raucous. Rodeo dances seemed to invite fighting. The brawling had no logical explanation, except for the possibilities the fighting cowboys had been reading their own press, or had watched too many western movies.

Figure 2-3. A typical parade scene: scores of horses, cowboys, and cowgirls.

The Pool Hall

Another hangout was the local pool hall. Dad was a frequent pool hall customer, although he preferred spending his time at the domino tables, located in front of the hall. Another frequent customer was Troy Fort, who like Jack McClure, was a world championship roper. Troy often came into the pool hall with his spurs on his boots. The spurs were so much a part of Troy's every-day clothing he forgot he was wearing them.

Unlike some parts of the county, the pool hall and its customers did not carry an unsavory reputation; respected citizens frequented our pool hall. The Music Man's retort about the sins of pools halls would have fallen on deaf ears in Lea County. A man who shot pool in southeastern New Mexico was as respected as a man who bowled in north Jersey.

Sports

The popular sports in Lea County were football, basketball, and track and field. A few people played baseball and softball was a popular sandlot game. Swimming was popular in the summer and this sport became an important part of my life. Golf and tennis came along later, but in these early times these sports were considered insufficiently macho for a cowboy's consumption. I recall a solitary forlorn tennis court posited behind the high school building. Profusions of weed and sage brush compensated for the absence of a net; a testament to the "popularity" of tennis in my town.

The county featured two golf courses; one in Hobbs and the other in Jal. The Jal course had sand greens—perhaps a contradiction in terms. Kathy Whitworth honed her skills on the Jal course before she went on to become professional golf's most prolific winner, and a famous golfer (even beating Sam Snead's record for wins).

Kathy and a few other extraordinary girls were exceptions to the practice of the boys' almost exclusive access to Lea County's sports facilities. Physical education classes and some intramural contests made up the girls' athletic programs. Female inter-city (well, town) sports programs did not exist.

To this day, the memories associated with my basketball days come back to me when I enter a basketball arena. My mind has stored these experiences intact, without alteration. As I enter the arena, they appear to me, ready for reminiscence. I can still smell the freshly painted varnish of the gym floor. I can still taste the Doublemint gum I put in my mouth while I was suiting-up. I can still see the crowds, the players, the referees, and the cheerleaders. ... especially the cheerleaders.

A few years ago, I paid a visit to Lovington and dined at one of the local, non-chain cafes. After finishing the meal, I walked to the cashier's stand to pay the bill. A photograph of a Lovington Wildcats football team was hanging on the wall, next to the cash register. It was the 1951 high school team and my brother Jim was in the picture. I asked the café manager why the picture was displayed. She replied its presence generated conversation among many of her customers who knew members of the '51 team. Some customers knew the team members' children and grandchildren.

In relating this anecdote to you, it is not my intention to disparage big cities and the anonymity that comes with their large population. But I doubt an old picture of, say, the Hollywood, California High School football team would engender much interest or talk at the local Hollywood McDonald's.

Raising the Bar of Affluence

With the discovery of oil, some of the ranchers and farmers in Lea County and East Texas became wealthy. In regard to my family, Dad had sold the mineral rights to his land before the oil was found. Fortunately, he became a successful rancher, which helped assuage the loss of oil royalties.

The income from the oil industry was transferred to many county enterprises. One recipient of this wealth was the school system. The schools were expensively built, beautifully equipped, and staffed by fine teachers. The Lovington school system had pristine, even immaculate campuses, with separate buildings for band, chorus, driver education, crafts, and agricultural studies. Unlike many schools in America today, the Lovington school system was guided by a practical, savvy Board of Education, whose members were successful businessmen and ranchers.

Figure 2-4. Members of the Board of Education.

Looking through my high school year book, I came across their picture, shown in Figure 2-4. It appears one of the requirements for a position on this august body was wearing cowboy boots. Many people in New Mexico wore boots and I carried this habit back east when I moved to the Washington, DC area. I would have drawn less attention if I had worn a set of clown shoes. Many people stared at me as if I were from another world (perhaps I was). I am certain they wondered what I had done with my chaps, spurs, and lariat (rope).

My newly found Yankee buddies regaled me with jokes about "dumb country clothes." Eventually succumbing to peer pressure, I traded my boots for penny loafers and even wore them on a visit to Lea County. My hometown friends and relatives gave my footwear a second look but no one made a comment on my new style. Nonetheless, I suspect I was one of the very few people in Lea County sporting these strange and ill-functioning shoes.

It's a Small, Small World ... No More

When I visit Lea County, I'm struck by the smallness of the dwellings in which we lived. Even the expensive homes of the 1950s, those still standing, are modest houses, when compared to those we live in today. I suppose we need more room now because most of us are overweight.

I suspect most of our possessions today would dwarf what we had sixty years ago. Our houses are bigger; we have more of them. Our beds now come in Queen size, King size, and Over size. Multiple cars per family is not a luxury, it's a necessity. We have more clothes, more shoes, more TV sets, more medicines, more phobias, more diversions—well, more of everything. Lowe's displays this very message on its parking lot marquee in Coeur d'Alene, Idaho, "We have more of everything."[6]

I also suspect events unfold much faster today than they did a half century ago. I don't mean we are driving faster cars or flying in faster airplanes. I mean we are doing more things and often doing them more quickly. Fast food restaurants are given their name for a good reason.

Our attention span seems to be shorter. TV clips have conditioned our minds to think in sound bites lasting a few seconds. Today's credo could be, "I want more of everything and I want it faster."

More of everything, and as fast as possible, is not necessarily an unwarranted desire. I visited East Germany before the wall came down. I traveled through poverty-stricken barrios in the Philippines. I toured villages in Vietnam, during and after the Vietnam War. The people in those places would be happy as larks to realize the meaning of the phrase, "More of everything." As they say in Lea County, "We have it pretty good."

On the other hand, perhaps we should recognize that more of everything, and everything faster, does not unto itself translate into a contented existence or a better life. For my mental well-being, I try to keep in mind a statement by Henry David Thoreau in his *Walden*, "After all, the man whose horse trots a mile in a minute does not [necessarily] carry the most important message."

It is time to move on in our journey of recollections about life in New Mexico and Lea County. A fine place to start is Tatum, New Mexico, where I spent the first five years of my life.

---

[1] National Oceanic and Atmospheric Administration, *Climate of Texas*, Ashville, NC; National Climatic Data Center, 1982.

[2] *El Llano Estacado*, by John Miller Morris, Texas State Historical Association, 1977, p. 2.

[3] Advancing the bragging rights of New Mexicans, it is New Mexico (The Ruidoso Downs), not Texas that runs the richest Quarter Horse race in the world. Source: Flynn, Kathryn A., Editor, *New Mexico Blue Book 1999-2000*, Compiled by Staff of Office of Secretary of State, 1999, pp 289-310.

[4] According to the Lea County Cowboy Hall of Fame, Lea County has produced more Rodeo World Champions than any other county in the U.S.

[5] Source: Lea County Electric Company, and Mauldin, Lynn C., *Lea County New Mexico: A Pictorial History*, The Downing Company Publishers, Virginia Beach VA, 23462, 1997.

[6] I was more impressed with the advertising honesty of a small store merchant I encountered in St. John, Virgin Islands. His store sign read, "We have almost all you need." Can you imagine this slogan being used by the big-time merchants? Hardly, it's much too modest.

3

MY LIPS ARE SEALED

---·•·---

A slip of the tongue would be
the most you get from me.
—*Mark Twain*

My lips are sealed. I don't recall the first time I heard this saying but I remember it spoken when I was a child. The sentence was confusing. After all, if the speaker's lips were sealed, the speaker would not be saying anything.

Like most children, I interpreted words and phrases in a literal way. I didn't posses sufficient skills to understand the nuances of my language. But as I came into contact with more adults, I learned to deal with their varnished obfuscations.

Notwithstanding my ignorance, I was a quick study and early in my life I put into practice the idea behind the term, my lips are sealed. On occasions, I also practiced the antipode to this cliché, my lips are not sealed. Granted, I was inconsistent about the employment of this term. I took a *realpolitik* approach to situations in my life regarding talking or not talking: What worked best for one situation might not be the best approach for another.

To set the stage for this story, you may recall I was born in the Lovington General Hospital but I lived the first five years of my life in Tatum, a very small town in Lea County. During this residency, Dad held the job of Lea County Deputy Sheriff. He was hired for this position by the county's elected sheriff, a man whose name I do not recall. Shortly after Dad was hired as a deputy sheriff, my Uncle Joe, Dad's brother, was elected to County Sheriffdom, and replaced Dad's initial benefactor. Lucky for Dad and his family, as well as Uncle Joe, my father was on the Lea County sheriff payroll for ten years.

Although Uncle Joe performed his sheriffing duties from Lovington, the county seat of Lea County, he didn't solve crimes or rescue people and other animals throughout the county; it was too large. Divide and conquer was the idea of the Lea County Sheriffs, so Dad's jurisdictional realm was the Tatum area. Given this responsibility, he traveled within the northern parts of Lea County to perform his duties. Take a look at Figure 2-2 in chapter 2 to orient yourself with the landscape under discussion.

Physical Skills

People who choose law enforcement as their occupation in life are usually confident of their capacity to deal with others' aggression. They recognize they will be required to counter violence with their own physical strength. Good cops are not above kicking ass. My Dad fit this mold perfectly.

Figure 3-1.
Dad in his younger days.

Figure 3-1 shows my father as a young man. He looks healthy enough and although his physical powers are not evident, he was prodigiously strong, loved to box, and looked for opportunities to show his skills. When a small carnival came to Tatum, New Mexico in 1935, Dad took advantage of an offer to fight one of the carnival's main attractions. As told to me by my mother and brothers—I was hovering around in a waiting-to-be-born-queue—the following events unfolded on a hot summer day in Lea County.

Sideshows at these early carnivals featured a variety of attractions, such as a bearded lady, a flame eater, a sword shallower—folks who did not use standard templates to write their job descriptions. For this event, one of the attractions was a wrestler. According to my family (hence family legend), he was a large, powerful man who walked around the entrance to the carnival tent, grunting and strutting in front of potential customers, the local folks.

The carnival barker announced, "Ladies and gentlemen, I will pay two dollars for anyone who will step into the ring for three minutes with my wrestler—and avoid a pin. All for two dollars!"

Against the advice of Mom, Dad responded, "I'll take the challenge—if your wrestler will also box with me for one minute, and remain standing up."

I've been told the carnival barker could barely contain his glee, "One minute! (And thinking, *You local lads are full of it.*) Sir, I must warn you. Our wrestler is also a skilled boxer, and he doesn't use gloves."

Sensing the crowd's interest in a local boy trying to make good and seeing an opportunity to fatten the sideshow ticket sales, the barker replied, "OK, come on up here. Let's get started! And folks, line up here for the tickets. Ten cents will gain you a place for the contest."

After an agreement was reached, Dad and the wrestler stepped into the ring and began their wrestling match. The two grappled with each other for a few moments and the wrestler, using superior techniques, twice succeeded in taking Dad down to the mat. But he could not pin my father; he was no match for my Dad's strength. Even with two take downs on Dad, the first part of the contest ended in a draw. My brothers told me Dad had put up a good fight and the best part was yet to come.

They started the boxing match, and wasting no time, the wrestler lunged at Dad with ineffectual punches. It was clear the man was a full time wrestler but a part time boxer. Dad easily deflected the man's blows and countered with a right hook to the wrestler's head. He crumbled to the floor and lay motionless on the mat—unconscious. His wrestling and boxing for the day had ended. Dad collected his appearance money from the carnival barker.

The wrestler's lips were sealed! So were those of the barker. Yes, I know this story is supposed to be about my lips and their sealed or unsealed nature. But you must admit the saying fits in rather well with this part of the story.

From the many stories I've heard about Dad's boxing strength and skills, I gather he possessed a Rocky Marciano hook, and throughout my youth, I heard many stories of Dad felling his lesser opponents with one or two punches. Dad never laid a hand on me—never came close—but I knew about his reputation and during tense moments between us, I kept a safe and prudent distance from this man.

In my pre-teenage years, television finally reached Lea County. Nonetheless, Dad would not allow a TV set in our house until his sons had graduated from high school and left home. Without fail, he followed the heavyweight championship fights on the radio. If the welterweight and middleweight bouts were broadcast into Lea County, he also followed them—because of Sugar Ray Robinson. I listened to many of these matches with my Dad and learned to admire Sugar Ray's elegance and power. He became one of my childhood heroes.

I was the sixth and last of my parents' children to leave the household. On my first trip back home during my Freshman year in college, I entered the back door to our house, walked into the living room and found Dad, sitting in front of a new television set, watching *Friday Night at the Fights.*

The Sheriff's Sleuthing

When our family members get together, we often talk of Dad's sleuthing exploits in and around Tatum. As a child, I thought of him as a great detective. I didn't know about Sherlock Holmes. If I had, I would have equated my Dad with Mr. Holmes because both were good at their jobs. My Mom and brothers told me about his exploits and I also recall a few of his adventures. Let's take a look at some examples of how Deputy Sheriff Jim Black practiced his trade.

Gasoline Theft. A local service station owner was losing his gasoline from theft. During off-hours and at random times, the robber pilfered the gas from a reserve tank, located to the side of the station. Dad compiled a list of suspects, including the ne'er-do-wells of the town, but he had no hard evidence on anyone. To snare the thief, Dad dyed the petrol in the tank. It was slightly off-color but not noticeable to the casual eye. He also instructed the service station owner to sell the gas in the other tanks. Therefore, the spiked petrol would be found only in a thief's vehicle.

Each morning, the owner checked the level of the tank to determine if a night visitor had stolen any fuel from the doctored tank. A few days later, the owner contacted Dad; someone had siphoned gas from this tank. Dad checked the gas tanks of his suspects and caught the thief red-handed.

Grain Theft. Another theft involved the sacking of sacks of grain. A farmer north of Tatum complained to Dad about losing his feed to theft. According to this man, someone had been sneaking into his barns while he was away and were making off with this important animal food. Basking in his gasoline thief victory, Dad borrowed his entrapment ideas from the gasoline case, and doctored the farmer's feed inventory; he put a small amount of rice into each sack. The rice could not be detected unless a suspicious person examined the grain very closely. On the next heist, he paid visits to his list of suspects, checked their grain and found his entrapment material dispersed among the thief's grain. Later in my life, Mom told me the looter was also involved in stealing cattle. During the same time he was stealing grain, he was making off with his neighbor's cows, the subject of Dad's next exploit.

Cattle Rustling. The cattle rustling story is one of my favorites about Dad's detective skills. Kevin Costner could have used it in his movie, *Open Range*. The rancher west of Tatum was also losing his cattle to theft. He operated a ranch encompassing about 10,000 acres. Not a big ranch in Lea County but sufficiently large to allow a clever rustler, sight unseen, to filch a cow or two.

The rancher and Dad suspected the thief was killing the cows and butchering them for food. Selling the critters would have been foolish because of the rancher's brands on the side of each cow. As was the usual routine, Dad checked out a number of suspects. One man who ran a small spread nearby had several cow hides stored in his barns. The brands were cut off; obviously, a suspicious situation. Still, Dad had no evidence to prove the suspect's guilt.

Dad once again placed an identifying mark on the victim's inventory. A tiny brand, invisible to a casual observer, was put on the bellies of the victim's cattle. Later, when another theft occurred, he paid a visit to the suspect's ranch. Sure enough, one of the suspect's hides displayed the telling brand and the cattle rustler was arrested.

The gas, grain, and cattle thiefs were not sophisticated offenses, but I was impressed with Dad's detective skills and his clever methods to solve these crimes. I secretly wished his exploits were known to the world. As a young boy, I fantasized listening to them on a weekly radio program, "This week, follow the exploits of Deputy Sheriff Jim Black, as he breaks the Gasoline Thief Conspiracy, and saves the grateful victim five gallons of precious petrol." I was confident his other exploits could be chronicled with equally exciting stories.

Capturing a WW II Prisoner of War. My favorite tale of Dad's sheriff days is about a German prisoner of war (POW). During WW II, a German POW camp had been constructed near Roswell, New Mexico, 70 miles west of Tatum. On a hot summer day, a prisoner escaped from the Roswell facility. He walked and hitchhiked over 100 miles south, then east, then north as the authorities looked for him. He was spotted; he disappeared; he was spotted again; he vanished again—making seemingly random attempts to find his way to Germany. Probably unknown to him, he was inadvertently making his way back to the prison camp, as shown in Figure 3-2.

Dad received a phone call from Uncle Joe with information on the prisoner's location. The wandering POW was last seen in the Lovington area, apparently headed north, toward Tatum. Dad was involved in a hot criminal case and could not be diverted to look for the fugitive. But time was short; the escapee could be passing through Tatum at any time.

The Tatum sheriff department of one person presented a problem: Deputy Sheriff Black could not be in two places at the same time.

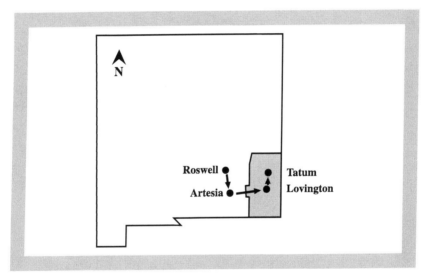

Figure 3-2. The prisoner's journey.

Hmm. Sitting in Dad's living room was the answer to his difficulty: My brothers Ed and Ross. They could be deputized as teenage sheriffs and formed into a posse to capture the German soldier. From my five-year old perspective, the situation was more exciting than the mystery programs broadcast on our radio—even better than my fantasy about Dad's Deputy Sheriff Show.

I was enthusiastic about the manhunt but I was not being deputized for the single goal of finding and confronting an escaped prisoner of war. Naturally, my brothers were not as enthusiastic as

I. If Ed and Ross had possessed one ounce of sense, they would have argued with Dad that they were teenagers, legal minors in the eyes of the law, and could not be employed as sheriffs:

Dad, *Boys. I have a chore for you.*

Boys, *Yes sir!*

Dad, *I want you to capture an escaped German soldier prisoner of war. He may be armed and dangerous.*

Boys, ... pregnant silence, followed by, *Sorry Dad, we're ineligible. You need to brush up on child labor laws.*

But being teenagers, they were too ignorant to possess these valuable legal facts, which should have been stored away for emergency use. And being Jim Black's sons, they did not argue with Jim Black. Anyway, in an urgent situation, such as an escaped prisoner of war, all citizenry must become soldiers, including boys.

Dad drove Ed and Ross to the Lovington-Tatum highway intersection. He dropped them off with instructions to stop all northbound cars and search them for the elusive German. For this assignment, Deputy Sheriff Black gave his Assistant Deputy Sheriffs exactly one ... pistol? ... rifle? ... can of mace? ... vial of tear gas? ... BB gun? ... slingshot? ... pea shooter? No; one flashlight. It constituted the newly appointed deputies' arsenal.

My locally inclined (AKA country bumpkins) brothers had a slight problem with their assignment: How were they to know they had encountered the German? Ed and Ross had never seen a German. Did he look like Hitler? According to the photos in newspapers, German soldiers resembled their leader: A sub-human countenance, accentuated with a cowlick and a funny-looking moustache.

Dad's directions to his pubescent deputies might have unfolded something like the following conversation. My bothers don't recall the exact instructions given to them by Deputy Sheriff Black. Regardless of the specifics, Ed and Ross agree the orders contained these elements, "Stop each car coming into town from Lovington. Ask each passenger the following question, 'What is your name and place of birth?' A German probably won't understand enough English to respond. But if he does answer your question, he'll have an accent and you'll know the man is the escaped prisoner."

Sons, "What if he says nothing?" (Writer's note: His lips are sealed!)

Dad, "Assume he's the German."

Sons, "Yes sir, we understand. Then what?"

Dad, "Then what! Why arrest the man."

Sons, "With a flashlight?"

The boys' response reflected a practical concern. Implicit in their question were several thoughts: He's a soldier; we're not much more than overgrown children. We're armed with a flashlight; for all we know, this man may be carrying a German Lugar pistol or one of those bayonets we see in the newspaper pictures.

My point in inserting this hypothetical dialogue into a true story is to emphasize the scene, regardless of the dialogue among the parties, must have bordered on the surreal. Any set of directions or orders to my brothers, any dialogue between them and Dad had to be weird. And any manner in which you or I might choose to create the scene, it will remain Kafkaesque.

Cutting Dad some slack about this matter, he was away from the roadblock for a short time. Additionally, his other case was nearby. Still, he was gone for a while; Ed and Ross were indeed alone and, except for the flashlight, they had no way to defend themselves.

Fortunately for my brothers, they did not encounter the German. Unfortunately for the German, my father arrested him a short time later at the roadblock where he found the fugitive as a passenger in a car. The man offered no resistance and the family who picked him up on the Lovington-Tatum highway was not aware of the news about the escaped prisoner. It turns out the German spoke passable English and sure enough, Dad discovered his identity because of the German's accent.

Because Tatum's small jail was full of Tatum's deadbeats, Dad brought the German back to our home. Dad called Mom to alert her she was about to have a guest. *(Guess Who's Coming to Dinner?)* Mom relayed the news to me, with orders to straighten up one of the bedrooms in which several of my brothers and I slept.

A German soldier. In the middle of WW II. In the middle of Lea County. And soon: In the middle of my home and my bedroom! I pictured a menacing German warrior, wearing the "Nazi" helmet and boots (in my mind, all German soldiers were Nazis). I wondered if he would have any German stuff on him. I was a great admirer of stuff but could only dream what German stuff looked like.

Quite the opposite image emerged as the poor soul entered our living room. I recall his countenance sixty years ago as if it were yesterday. Reasonably enough, I was greatly disappointed. Expecting to be greeted by a Germanic version of Attila the Hun, the man who came into my home and bedroom was a disheveled ragamuffin. A sunburned, dehydrated, exhausted, hungry, and dirty adult waif.

I can't remember Dad ever handcuffing his prisoners. He didn't cuff drunks or thieves, and the POW walked into our home with his arms swinging at his sides. Yet Dad carried handcuffs in his car. I remember them well, because they held a certain adventuresome fascination for me. As I placed the huge metal lockets around my tiny wrists, I thought, *What sort of man has to be handcuffed? A killer? A kidnapper?* ... the only two crooks whom I suspected might warrant handcuffs. In hindsight, I think Dad refused to cuff his prisoners as a matter of pride. Given his physical prowess, that pride was well placed.

Anyway, Mom assumed responsibility for the prisoner. She led him to our bath room to let him wash-up. She then directed our "guest" to the bedroom where clean clothes awaited him. Next, she prepared a meal for him.

Although the German spoke limited English and was obviously a foreigner, he did not resemble Hitler. He was a nice-looking man. He was unfailingly polite and seemed grateful for our kindness. He did not match my stereotype of the barbaric German monster that had been fed to me by the newspapers and radios.

After Mom's ministrations, Dad drove the prisoner back to the POW camp in Roswell and my brief fanciful encounter with a WW II soldier came to an end.

Big Trouble Today

In today's society, the acts of my father deputizing his two teenage sons for roadblock operations to catch a fugitive seems so out-of-place it borders on the unreal—not to mention, the unlawful. We can only imagine the wrath and indignation spewing fourth from scores of government agencies, single issue pressure groups, and media pundits. Dad's 1945 actions in modern times may have led the courts to take away the custody of his children.[1]

Perhaps not. It could be that the reaction of our society to the Black Family roadblock would depend on how the story was "spun" by the local and national TV shows. Dad might have been hailed a hero on one program, and a villain on the next. For certain, my brothers would have been in a winning situation—perhaps gaining an appearance on a Wheaties cereal box.

Giving Dad his due, Ed was fifteen years old; Ross was thirteen. During America's Revolutionary and Civil Wars, boys of those ages served in the army; many of them were on the front lines. WW II and the Normandy landing witnessed seventeen-year-olds participating in battles. Moreover, in 1945, we had not yet begun to develop the cocoon of security around our young that now pervades our society.

Paramedic, Doctor, Nurse, Ambulance, Hospital, and Candy Striper

I recall a car accident episode during my Dad's sheriffing days. The mishap required Dad to perform the duties of a paramedic, a doctor, and an ambulance driver. In addition, our home filled the role of a hospital, where my Mom assumed the responsibilities of a hospital nurse, a hospital kitchen cook, and a candy striper.

I often accompanied Dad on his sheriff-oriented rides—probably because of my impressive five-year old conversation skills. On the day of the accident, I was riding with Dad on the highway leading to Northern New Mexico, toward Clovis, site of the famous Clovis Man. I don't recall how Dad learned about the accident; my recollections begin at the accident scene itself where a car had turned over. No one was killed but three people, two men and one woman, were lying or sitting on the side of the highway. The woman had a lot of blood around the top of her head and face; a man appeared to have a broken arm. It was an ugly scene.

Dad had me stay in the car as he took care of the victims. He spent a few moments tending to them; then he checked-out their car. Next, he escorted them to our vehicle, where the two men were placed in the back seat, and the woman in the front seat. I was also sitting in the front seat between Dad and the injured lady.

Dad drove us to Tatum. He didn't take the wounded people to a hospital because Tatum's medical industry consisted of one doctor. He drove them back to our home. (*Guess Who's Coming to Dinner?*)

Mom took over the medical chores. She cleaned the accident victims and dressed their wounds. That finished, she prepared a meal for all parties. After the meal, Mom allotted them beds for the evening. Dr. Smith eventually made his way to our home to amplify my parents' treatments.

The victims stayed the night and Dad made arrangements for transportation to their destination and for a tow truck to pick up their car. The next day, they thanked us and left our home. We never saw or heard from them again.

Looking back on this event, the rescue and care of the car accident victims seems primitive. Today, with mobile phones, GPS, and helicopter ambulances, most victims have access to care within minutes of an accident. On the other hand, I am sure the victims were pleased with my parents' free paramedic, ambulance, doctor, nurse, and hospital services—not to mention the nonhospital food served up by Mom. The adage, *necessity is the mother of invention*, is an appropriate phrase to describe my parents' care of the accident victims.

The Drunk Vagrant

On another summer day, Dad had again taken me along for a ride while he performed his duties. This trip took us out of town— a very short trip, because Tatum's boundaries did not quite span multiple time zones. The town's signs, "Welcome to Tatum" and

"Thanks for Visiting Tatum" could have been nailed up onto the same post on the highway leading into and out of Tatum, but on opposite sides of the sign.

We encountered a hitchhiker east of the Tatum city limits, attempting to leave the county. I suspect hitchhiking was not illegal in Lea County; I recall seeing lots of hitchhikers during my childhood. Nonetheless, Dad eased the car behind this man. He appeared to be drunk. He wasn't going far; he could hardly walk. As he careened down the side of the highway in front of our car, Dad kept the vehicle moving at a snail's pace just behind him.

After a few moments, Dad honked the horn. The sudden noise startled me but had no effect on the drunk. After a few more toots, Dad got out of the car, and walked to the tottering man, who was still proceeding, albeit slowly, toward the great state of Texas.

I watched Dad talk to the man and take a bottle from his hand. As a five-year old, I was not versed in the spirits department but I concluded the bottle had alcohol in it. If so, I am certain its volume paled in comparison to the amount of booze in the drunk's body.

Dad collared the man and walked him to the car. He placed him, along with his suitcase, in the back seat. Dad didn't handcuff him or take away his suitcase. I suppose in those innocent days there was little fear of a drunken man doing much harm to anyone.

Nonetheless, the drunk was a seedy looking man. He was bearded;[2] his swollen eyes were red; his clothes were dirty. His looks in my direction were not friendly; his stare and scowl frightened me. I would have preferred he still be on his way to Texas, which deserved him more than my fair state.

As we proceeded into town, Dad stopped the car at an old house with a windmill in its side yard. As a courtesy to some friends, Dad sometimes checked-out this property and made sure the windmill was in working order. Dad left the vehicle and walked to the windmill.

Because the booze bailiff was on a break at the moment, the drunk saw an opportunity to become even drunker. I was watching Dad examine the windmill, and from the corner of my eye, I was also watching the drunk. As soon as Dad was engaged in his examination of the windmill, the man opened his suitcase and pulled out … not a knife, not a gun—no tool for making mayhem—just another bottle of liquor.

He took some swigs of the stuff, and quickly (for a drunk) returned the bottle to the suitcase. He had been looking my way as he undertook these operations. He knew I was a witness to his transgression. Next, as they say in today's jargon, he made me an offer I could not refuse, "Sonny, don't tell your old man about my other bottle. I won't make no trouble if you keep quiet."

Trouble? Did he have a gun or a knife hidden on his person or in the suitcase? Was he going to fight my Dad if I spilled the beans about his hidden cache? I was confused and not eager to push the envelope about the drunk's definition of trouble. I responded with a meek nod of my head and, "OK."

This episode is my first example of my using the phrase, "My lips are sealed." I didn't utter those words but my acquiescence conveyed the same meaning.

I found myself as an unwilling conspirator with a total stranger—a repellent drunk—against my own father. I didn't like the situation but I was intimidated by the drunken man. Dad returned to the car and we continued the trip to Tatum. I remained silent about the drunk's other bottle.

Upon reaching Tatum, Dad searched the man, including his suitcase, and discovered the contraband. The drunk was placed in Tatum's tiny jail, a small concrete box. The stand-alone building resembled a dungeon more than a jail, as shown in Figure 3-3.[3] It had no faucets, showers, or toilets (just a large jar). Small windows provided some light and limited ventilation, but I imagine the jail was hot in the summer and cold in the winter.

Dad pushed the drunk into the jail. He locked the jail door and his son breathed a big sigh of relief. My departing thoughts were, *He deserves that jail.*

Nonetheless, a depressing feeling of guilt entered my gullible mind. Thanks to the few church services I had attended, I remembered sermons dealing with, "We are all rotten to the core." As a church-goer, my threshold tolerance for guilt was probably lower than non-church going five year old boys. Mom didn't help either;

Figure 3-3. The jail.

she was pretty adept at conducting lengthy culpability seances focusing on my guilt—with the goal of my admitting to crimes against our household. As a consequence of this propaganda, I wanted to confess to Dad about my holding a secret with the alcoholic cretin. I did not. My lips remained sealed.

By the way, can you imagine the jail scene I just described in the present climate? In today's society, a single-issue group would be picketing the jail, demanding the man be released from his cell because of its inhumane conditions. I can see it now, picket lines formed and marching around the small hut, the protesters carrying signs of, "Free the Tatum One!"

The Katty Korner Kafe Incident

I began to resent adults who recruited me into their conspiracies and then asked me to keep quiet about them. The drunk was one example. The cook at the local greasy spoon was another. The Katty Korner Kafe was Lovington's answer to McDonald's—without the merry employees and sparkling counters. Two men comprised the personnel staff; one worked the counter and cash register (the maitre d'); the other cooked the burgers and French Fries (the chef).

The Kafe was tiny, consisting of a counter with three or four stools and a couple of small tables. The even smaller kitchen was separated from the main dining room by a wall and a swinging half-door. The door was kept open for a number of reasons: The customers could see the chef in action, the chef could communicate with the maitre d', and the greasy ether emanating from the grill could more easily escape the kitchen to lodge inside the lungs of the diners.

Their food was not only palatable, it was delicious. The cook's irresistible recipes were forerunners to the modern fast food chains. Consider these examples demonstrating how the Katty Korner Kafe was ahead of its time: The hamburgers were laden with fat; the fried potatoes were covered with a greasy sheen … somewhat oily looking. Everything coming off the grill was covered with so much salt and pepper it was difficult to detect the color of the underlying food. To accentuate the four star dining, cigarette smoke modulated the greasy air drifting in from the kitchen. My kind of kafe!

Fortunately for my health, I had an ongoing battle with Mom about consuming the Kafe's food. On rare occasions, she would allow me to eat at the Kafe, usually during a trip to the movie theatre. The Katty Korner Kafe was conveniently located next to the Lea Theatre (at an angle to two intersecting streets—thus, its name). More often than not, I had to be satisfied with a bag of popcorn. But on wonderful, limited occasions, I was given a quarter for the purchase of one hamburger, one order of French Fries, and one Coke. A visit to the Katty Korner Kafe was a big event in my life.

During one of these special treats, I had placed my order and was sitting at the counter, sipping my Coke, idly watching the cook fulfill his job description. He was quite efficient as he went about his job. He gave me confidence in his craft: Sporting a stubby beard, dangling a cigarette in his lips, with hair falling into his eyes, he nonchalantly tossed hamburger patties into the air. Without fail, they landed back onto their allotted places on the grill. Really, quite impressive.

Hmm. Make that *almost* without fail. On this occasion, with one other customer in the kafe, the cook made a slight error in one flip and the patty landed on the floor. There it lay, awaiting an answer to two metaphysical questions. Question One: Would the hamburger patty transfer grease to the floor or would the floor transfer grease to the patty? Question Two: Which of the two Katty Korner Kafe customers was destined to eat this piece of meat?

The answer to the first question was never answered. The second question was easy to answer: Not me. From my perspective, the patty was destined for the sandwich of the *other* customer. After all, it was I, not he, who witnessed its aerial experience.

The cook took a quick look at the floored hamburger patty. Its position didn't faze him for a second. He simply picked it up and placed it back on the grill. But his cover was blown. Just as he completed the transfer, he looked into the dining room and beheld an eight year old kid who had been a witness to his culinary exploits. He was surprised to see me staring at him. I was equally surprised to see him looking at me.

But without ado, he put his finger to his lips to signal me to be quiet. Then he motioned with his hands that the wayward patty (pointing to it) was scheduled for the other customer (pointing to him). He finished-off the classical My Lips are Sealed protocol exchange with placing his finger to his lips again.

Caught in another adult conspiracy! All because of a hamburger patty. And what was I to do? Complain to the management? The management consisted of the two men in the kafe. Should I warn the other customer he was about to eat a dirty hamburger patty?

"Excuse me sir, but I just noticed the cook dropped your hamburger meat on the floor. He asked me not to reveal his mistake, but I feel it is my moral, eight-year old duty to warn you."

First, would this stranger believe me? Second, I tried to avoid confrontations with adults. Even with only eight years of experience with them, I knew they could be pretty nasty when aroused or threatened. Third, if I ratted on the cook, I was certain I would become *persona non grata* at the Katty Korner Kafe. No more Kafe hamburgers for me.

I made a momentous decision: To hell with the cook, his conspiracy, and the Katty Korner Kafe. I got up from my stool, placed a nickel on the counter for my Coke, headed for the door, opened it, and yelled, "Hey mister, the cook dropped your hamburger on the floor!" I then slammed the door and ran toward the Lea Theatre—without my cherished hamburger and fries.

Within a few seconds I had made a decision that—this time—my lips weren't sealed. I'm not sure what tipped the scales but I had been thinking about my unwanted conspiracy with the drunk and how I had deceived my Dad—a guilt trip warranting another Sunday visit to the First Baptist Church. I also recall part of my decision took this fact into account: Jake's Fountain, just down the street, made a delicious hamburger.

Encounter with My Guardian Angel's Six Shooter

As an eight-year old boy, I lived part of the year at my Dad's ranch in the summer (See Figure 2-2 in "Lea County at Mid-20th Century"). Mom and Dad had divorced in 1945, and their children split their time: Winter in Lovington with Mom; summer on the ranch with Dad and his wife Mary.[4]

Bill and Wanda, two of Dad's hired hands, were a married couple. Bill performed the ongoing chores of a ranch hand. Wanda was the cook and maid for our household. These people were my pals. I liked them and they liked me. Wanda had helped me out of a mess when I attempted to kill Dad's pet wildcat, recounted in my story, "The Hunter and the Hunted." Bill participated in this conspiracy to keep me out of trouble. Wanda also took care of my ailments, once nursing me back to health from severe sunburn, recounted in my story, "The Tadpole Puddle." She was my surrogate mother and guardian angel.

Bill and Wanda were a loving couple; they often flirted and teased each other. But they could also be volatile and short-tempered. One moment they would be joking and laughing. The next, they would be yelling at each other, angry about a slight beyond my understanding. I was baffled by their behavior. When they were not in each other's company, they were as even-tempered as our milk cows.

One lucky day, I was selected to accompany Bill and Wanda to town to pick up supplies. This privilege was not taken lightly. Dad's sons were allowed one trip into Lovington during the summer for the purpose of getting a much needed haircut and paying our respects to Mom. I was to be treated to two trips this summer.

We left the ranch for our journey into town; Bill was driving the pickup; Wanda sat on the right side; I was seated between them. The trip started uneventfully. I don't remember any notable events for the first few miles. But before we reached the paved highway to town, Bill and Wanda began another quarrel. Shouts, yells, insults, profanities, and spit spewed back and forth between them. Finding myself in the middle of yet another of their fights, I hunkered down in the seat, deciding to wait it out. Truth is, my options were limited. We were in the middle of nowhere, at least ten miles to town.

Suddenly, Wanda opened the glove compartment of the pickup and pulled out a pistol. The scene unfolded as follows.

Bill asked, "Wanda, what the hell are you doing?!"

Wanda pointed the pistol toward her husband, "Shut up! Stop the pickup, you rotten son-of-a-bitch!"

I remember the weapon quite vividly; it was positioned directly in front of me, a few inches from my face. The gun was a long-barreled six-shooter. I had seen it several times before this incident when Bill took me on pasture chores; we practiced shooting at fence posts. One thing was certain; this spat between Bill and Wanda was not like the others.

I cannot speak for Bill and Wanda but the situation was tense for me. I knew a lot about guns. I knew about their mechanics and how to shoot them. I knew a pistol, with the hammer pulled back, was very easy to fire. Wanda had cocked the gun.

Some memories never leave us; they remain sealed in our minds, virtually intact. Wanda's hand on the pistol handle, her thumb on the hammer, her finger on the trigger, the veins in her wrist, my contracting sphincter. These images are as vivid now as they were then. I wanted to close my eyes and put my hands to my ears because I was certain a very loud noise was about to erupt a few inches from my head.

Bill made two wise decisions. (1) He shut up. (2) He stopped the pickup. Wanda then ordered him out of the vehicle, "Get out you dumb son-of-a-bitch. And start walking."

Bill made two decisions, one wise, and the other not-so-wise: (1) He got out of the pickup. (2) He started walking. … *back* toward the ranch, behind the pickup. His choice of directions was not what Wanda had in mind, "You dumb son-of-a-bitch! I meant walk in front of the pickup. How can I keep this gun on you if you're behind me?"

I think Bill assumed the question was Wanda's way of passing time, because the answer was obvious. Once again, he was wise not to challenge her … and her gun. I also kept silent but I had concluded Wanda considered Bill to be a son-of-a-bitch of assorted varieties. She had made her feelings about this matter quite clear.

Bill reversed his direction and continued a slow walk to a point about twenty feet in front of the pickup. Wanda ordered, "Stop!"

Bill made another wise decision. Actually, he made two wise decisions. (1) He stopped. (2) He then initiated a serious groveling routine: Many, "I'm sorry." Several, "I'm real sorry." Several, "You know I love you." Followed by a number of, "It won't happen again."

Even for an eight-year old, the scene was pathetic. Of course in hindsight, it's easy for me to believe it was pathetic. The truth is, the loaded and cocked gun was pointed at Bill, not me. My friend was simply executing the ideas of the cliché I cited earlier: *Necessity is the mother of invention.*

The supplications lasted quite some time. My fear and excitement gradually turned to boredom. Here I was, in the middle of nowhere, witnessing a forerunner to a soap opera; a slow, plodding melodrama. No one was killed or wounded.

Amazingly, after Bill's incessant pleadings and promises, as well as facing-down a gun, he seemed no worse for wear. Eventually, he was allowed back into the pickup. Wanda put away the pistol and we continued the trip to town. The remainder of the journey was devoted to the adults convincing the boy to remain silent about their argument.

Wanda asked me, "Do you remember shooting your Dad's pet wildcat?"

I replied, "Sure."

Wanda asked, "Do you remember what I did?"

I replied, "Sure. You took the gun into the house and told me to be quiet about my shooting the wildcat, else I would be in lot of trouble. You said your lips were sealed."

Wanda responded, "If you tell your Dad about Bill and me fighting, we will get into a lot of trouble."

I replied, "That's OK. My lips are sealed." I was happy to protect my two friends.

I never told Dad about the roadside argument between Bill and Wanda. To the day he died, I remained silent. Looking back on the happening, I wish I had shared the story with my father—of course, after Bill and Wanda were far away from his wrath.

Running Away from Home

During one of our summer days on the ranch, my brothers Jim and Tom had been giving me a hard time. As with most older-younger brother relationships, my brothers were usually tolerant of, or indifferent to me. But on this day, they resorted to performing the preordained, genetically determined roles of older bothers: Pains in the ass.

In fairness, I must say in my brothers' defense that I was also a big pain in their asses. I often played tricks on them and set up stunts at their expense. They countered my mischief with taunts—mostly to even the playing field of sibling rivalry.

They were not abusing me physically. They performed the obligatory mocking chants, emphasizing I was not a real member of the Black family, that I was adopted. This scorn was their favorite because they knew it was at the bottom of my list of preferred scorns. I could handle almost any "sticks and stones" abuse, except the suggestion I was not a bona fide member of the family.

Finally, I could take no more of their banter. I went to my room and pulled out some clothes from the chest. Taking a clue from a Mickey Rooney movie, I attempted to tie the clothes into a knapsack.

My brothers were watching my packing scene. After I had completed tying my clothes in a bundle, I threatened to run away. My warning brought fourth more jeers from my tormentors. That did it. I picked up my knapsack and took-off for town. My destination was Mom. Jim and Tom did not impede my exit; they practically pushed me out the door.

They committed a serious error in banishing me from the house. They had not thought through the strategic implications of their tactical warfare. Even though I was a very small person, I would still be missed at the dinner table.

More mocking and derision followed my leaving the main grounds of the ranch. My brothers followed me as I walked into the pastures, miles away from another house, and miles away from Lovington and Mom. I could hear their yells fade away as I headed toward my destination of emotional ointment.

The fact was, I was not sure about the route to Lovington and Mom. I knew the roads by casual observation but not by actual navigation. I didn't have much confidence in making it to my destination anytime soon, and although I thought I could find Lovington, I was not sure when I would arrive. I was also thinking I should have stopped by the kitchen on my way out of the house.

Carrying the knapsack in my arms was awkward and tiring. Taking another clue from Mickey, I found a mesquite branch, draped the knapsack over it, slung it over my shoulder, and continued my trip.

I had been walking for a couple miles, still wondering if my departure from the house was a sound decision. I was hoping I would not encounter wild, large critters; I wasn't much bigger than an adult coyote. It was late afternoon and I began to think about the upcoming night; I was becoming discouraged and frightened.

I then saw Dad's pickup appear on the horizon, returning from a trip to town. Surely, there must be a patron saint for run-away boys because I was about to be rescued from a difficult situation. I watched Dad as his pickup came closer to where I was standing. He had an amused look on his face, but for the life of me, I could not see any humor in the situation. He was almost laughing when he said, "Son, where are you headed?"

"Town."

"Why?"

"Jim and Tom are picking on me. They won't leave me alone."

Dad seemed neutral about my gripe. He was an old hand at listening to sibling complaints. But as a former sheriff, I suppose he was disposed to get to the facts of a case. He responded, "Well, what did they do to you?"

"They told me I was adopted."

Case closed. Dad's smile turned to a frown. He replied, "Hop in. We'll get this situation straightened out."

I was allowed to take the next scheduled trip to Lovington—personally escorted by Dad—where I attended a movie, imbibed in a feast of popcorn and candy, and visited Mom. My brothers were allowed … well, nothing. After receiving a thrashing from Dad, they were restricted to the ranch. I was witness to the whipping and this aspect of the battle with my brothers left me regretting I ran away. I could have sulked in any number of places around the ranch.

It is prudent to consider the possible consequences of one's actions. Precipitate acts may produce unhappy consequences. Sometimes the actions should not be undertaken. A wrestler should not box with a boxer. A German prisoner of war should not attempt to reach Germany from Roswell, New Mexico. A drunk should not ask a boy to betray the child's father. A sleazy cook should not feed his customers dirty food. A husband should not argue with a volatile wife who has a pistol within her reach. A little brother should exercise discretion about tattling on his older, larger, and stronger brothers.

Still smarting from bruised butts and bruised pride, the boy's older brothers might seal the lips of their tattle-tell sibling. I began to think about the consequences of my ratting on Jim and Tom.

During my return trip to the ranch, sucking on lollipops, my thoughts turned from my recent adventures in town to my brothers. As I neared the ranch, I asked myself, with a momentary dread, in what way would they try to get back at me?[5]

This story has a happy ending. My brothers did not seal my lips. I think they were skittish about the possibility of any more encounters with Dad regarding their recent taunting. Being the youngest and weakest of the family, I sometimes took on the behavior of a human Switzerland: mediation and conciliation to avoid pummeling. I offered them some candy, leftover from my brief vacation. Naturally, they accepted and no more was said about the matter. The remainder of the summer was relatively peaceful. I didn't suspend my pranks. My brothers didn't cease their retaliations, but we kept these sibling activities among ourselves.

---

[1] Would his doctoring ploys be considered today as illegal entrapment? I suspect he could not get away with searching a citizen's gasoline tanks, sacks of grain, and cowhides without a search warrant.

[2] No offence intended to bearded men and women, or to the Society for the Prevention of Insults to Bearded People. I too have a beard. But fellow bearded brethren, we must admit that the term "clean-cut" has connotations of being well-groomed, good-looking, honest, forthright, without fat, without sin, *and* without facial hair.

[3] This photo was taken recently, but the jail remains as it was in 1945, *sans* prisoners. I ventured inside and discovered four beds in two cells, each about 8 x 5 feet. The jail is now closed to humans. It is relegated to the incarceration of rusted bunk beds, old bottles, and decades of dust.

[4] In his later years, Dad moved into town. After assorted spouses had died-off, Mom and Dad found themselves as very close friends. At separate times, they also lived in the Good Samaritan Home in Lovington, recounted in "The Real Heroes," and "Duds for Dad" later in this book.

[5] I was certainly thinking those unhappy thoughts but in not such an articulate manner. I have paraphrased from Joseph Conrad to convey the magnitude of my misery. Conrad said in his book, *Victory*, "I often asked myself, with a momentary dread, in what way would life try to get hold of me." The quote, with my modification, described my feelings on the ride back to the ranch.

4

Shearing, Branding, and Breeding

And what is any joy ... without companionship?
—Mark Twain

The hot summer day was ending. The disappearing sun had left a residue of orange across the horizon. The Mexicans' campfire was burning with branches of mesquite, casting flickering shadows on their nearby tents. Several men were sitting around the fire, roasting freshly slain mutton on their open spit. One of the men was playing a Spanish tune on his guitar and another accompanied him, singing a flamenco chant. Gradually, the others joined the concert with high-pitched gritos and noble attempts to sing harmony.

A meal followed, as did red wine. The music kept on. The Mexicans exchanged roles, sometimes playing the guitar, sometimes eating, sometimes drinking—but always singing.

As the sunset surrendered to the night and the orange horizon disappeared, the campfire became the source of light for the Mexicans' supper. This gradual change—from a sunlit day to a campfire night—gave the scene a sense of containment and isolation. Solitary and secure, but open to eyes peering in from the distance.

The night's repast was short-lived. The Mexicans were tired after a full day of shearing sheep. Gradually, they drifted off to their tents, and for some, to a couple of blankets under the stars.

A few men stayed around the campfire, telling tales in Spanish. Occasionally they tried some English, in deference to their eight-year old guest—who was captivated by the strangeness of the Mexicans, their music, and their plaintive flamenco yells. He was grateful for their kindness and attention.

An idyllic setting? I thought so. I've just described the few hours that Mexican sheep shearers enjoyed after a hard day of labor at our New Mexico ranch. I was smitten by the Mexicans and my recollection may have been colored with time. I suspect I have interjected a romantic aura into my memory about those evenings. But I do recall the music sounded fine to me. Some of their chants were even on-key … at least to my ears.

I have not altered the facts about the campfire scene nor my reactions to it. The Mexicans cooked sheep for their meals—Dad gave them a mutton each day. They drank wine, played music, sang, and took me in as their comrade.

Oh yes, for a brief time I was the "the eyes peering in from the distance," until a Mexican saw me observing them from behind a mesquite bush. Thus discovered, they invited me to join their supper—and I returned to their campfire each evening they were at our ranch. For a few days each summer, these men were my friends and companions.

"Firewood"

Cooking with mesquite wood is an "in thing" today. Famous chefs use mesquite in their pizza ovens. An abundance of this wood grows in New Mexico's Lea County and was used in campfires during those nights on the ranch. But around our house, where the Mexicans camped, mesquite was not plentiful; scraggly mesquite bushes were available for firewood, but not larger trees. To supplement the mesquite, the Mexicans used cow chips on their fire.

Manure smoke waffling over mutton would have diminished my appetizing supper scene, so I excluded it from the introduction to this story. Consider the more accurate sentence, "The Mexicans' campfire was burning with branches of mesquite and pieces of dried cow chips." A dose of fact tends to diminish the romantic intent of the introduction.

Now that I have thrown a bit of water (well, manure) on my campfire scene, let me tell you about sheep ranch life—as well as cattle branding and horse breeding—in Little Texas during the 1950s.

Life on a Ranch

As it is today, ranching was a vigorous life in the 1950s. My Dad, our hired hands, and my brothers arose early to start a long day and toiled away at their many tasks until late afternoon. They fixed barns, tended herds of cattle and sheep, repaired windmills, dug postholes, painted miles of wooden fences, and hoed weeds in Dad's gardens and orchards. Hundreds of other tasks made up the routine of our life on the ranch.

Hard work was the staple of the day for the ranch hands, except for one person—the writer of this tale. During the summer in which this story took place, I mentioned I was only eight years old. As such, my jobs around the ranch were not strenuous.

I was tasked with gathering eggs from our hen house each morning. I also slopped the pigs, feeding them our table scraps and corn; sometimes grain. I helped my brothers cart fresh milk from the milking pen to the kitchen.

Occasionally, I was given control of the cow's teats, to try my hand at the art of milking. It took several tries before I succeeded in coaxing a tiny drop of milk from the cow's udder. Doing my futile attempts, I received an occasional look from the cow. She would turn her head in my direction as if to question the competence of the small amateur manning the pumps. (*Lay off kid. If you're going to fondle my udder, stroke with authority.*)

During the day, Dad sometimes had me hoeing, weeding, and painting fences. But other than a few strenuous tasks during our branding and shearing times, I was left to my own. Consequently, I was often alone, because other people were not around the house. The big people were busy tending 32,000 acres of land containing ten windmills, thousands of fence posts, and hundreds of sheep, cattle, and horses.

Sheep Shearing

Wool shearing on our ranch occurred each year in the late spring or early summer. Shearing too early would leave the sheep without protection from the cold weather; shearing too late would leave them vulnerable to the heat of a New Mexico summer.

We ran about 2,000 head of sheep, not a large operation, but not small. It was big enough to justify the hiring of a sheep shearing crew—my Mexican friends. The crew brought a rather elaborate shearing machine with them. The contrivance was powered with a gas engine supporting 6 to 10 shearing stations. A forceful motor, a shared conveyor belt, and individual clutches allowed each shearer to engage his shears as he chose. Manual shearing was obsolete; it was too slow and tiring.

Some of our fleeces were shipped to the Pendleton Mills to make coats, jackets, scarves, and blankets for our family. Each year, Pendleton sent us a catalog from which we chose the items to be made from our own wool. I often wondered how Pendleton kept our wool separate from the wool of other ranches. Wool pretty much looked the same to me, regardless of where the sheep came from.

The Hercules of Sheep Sharers. During the late 1920s and through the 1930s Dad earned some of his income by shearing sheep. Before sunrise, he would depart the family ranch on his pony, carrying his hand shears, water, and sandwiches in a saddlebag. After riding to another ranch, he would shear sheep, sometimes staying several days.

My father was the Hercules of sheep shearers. I am told he once sheared 105 sheep in one day. Another source claimed the number was just under 100. And not with electric shears; with hand shears. Either figure is extraordinary, considering the daily output from an average motor-driven shearer was 50 to 60 fleeces.

On this occasion, Dad was out to set a record and stayed at the job without taking breaks. To rekindle his energy, he would occasionally gulp down a quart of buttermilk. Buttermilk? You bet. Try it; there's as much protein in buttermilk as there is in any health food gooey. And buttermilk is fine stuff; salty and thick; a ranch hand's milk shake.

My father used a very sharp set of shears. He did not so much clip the wool as cut through it, making long sweeps across the sheep's belly, sides, and back. He trimmed the head and legs with quick pruning actions.

As Dad grew older, he left the shearing to the hired hands. I recall his clipping a few sheep during the shearing season, perhaps to keep his style tuned. But he cut-down his cutting as his physical powers diminished. To this day, when I return to Lea County, I still hear stories about Dad's shearing prowess.

My job during the sheep shearing season was to pick up the fleece as it was removed from the sheep and carry it to a platform holding a large burlap sack. It was a big task for a little person. If I fell behind, one of the shearers would take a break from his station and scoop up enough wool to allow me to catch up with the operations.

The Mexicans accepted me as part of their sheep shearing crew and were willing to lend me a helping hand. I expect my status was enhanced by the fact I was the ranch owner's son and my father was footing the bill for the shearing operations. But I think the shearers took a liking to me; I surely did to them.

The wool sack platform was about seven feet high; the sack was of the same length. The man at the platform accepted the sheared wool and dropped it into the sack. He then tapped it down to allow space for more wool. After the sack was full, it was tied-off, pulled from the platform, rolled onto a tractor's power lift, and transported to a barn to await shipment to the wool mill.

In addition to carrying the wool to the platform, I was also the official wool sack compactor. The man at the platform would lift me up and deposit my body into the sack where I would stamp the wool down toward its bottom. This operation completed, the Mexican lifted me from the sack to allow me to continue my wool-toting tasks.

After I had handled a few fleeces, my arms, hands, neck, and face felt as if I had dipped them into a vat of lanolin. For good reason, the substance is also called "wool fat." Before long, I forgot about the slippery substance and after the workday, soap and hot water took care of this minor inconvenience.

Branding[1]

Our ranch ran about 500 head of cattle—again, not a large operation, but not small. The branding operations took place during the summer. The exact dates were determined by Dad's reading the signs of the moon. He believed the moon affected the amount of bleeding a calf would experience as a result of the dehorning and castration operations.

Our cattle were branded before they were sold. A cattle inspector examined the brand on each animal to make sure it belonged to the proper owner. Thus, branding guarded against cattle rustling. Even so, stealing cattle was not a thing of the past. A few years later, my brother Jim often lost cattle to rustlers at his northern New Mexico ranch.

Male calves were selected for branding, castration, and dehorning. The heifer calf was not dehorned. She needed her horns to protect her future off-spring from predators, such as coyotes. Dad also sold cattle to other ranchers; some resided in the mountains of northern New Mexico. In that part of the state, horns were important to the cow's defense against mountain lions.

The list below provides a summary of a calf's two-minute adventure in the branding corral:

1. A calf was brought into the pen.
2. It was roped.
3. It was flanked (thrown to the ground).
4. Its horns were removed by a pincher-type tool.

5. Its testicles were removed by a knife.
6. It was branded on its hip with a red-hot iron.
7. It was vaccinated (against black leg, and hoof-and-mouth diseases).
8. The resulting wounds were covered with a medicine.
9. The calf was released from the corral, possibly thinking, *On the whole, I'd rather be a dog.*

During these events, dust clouds floated through the corral, kicked-up by the cowboys who were roping and flanking the calves. The smell of dirt blended with the stench of burning hair and seared skin as a cowboy pushed the branding iron into the flank of a braying animal. The calf's eyes were wide-open, staring—pleading—at the brander in wretched panic as the man held the blistering iron to the calf's skin.

The cutting of the horns and testicles released more smells into the corral—the sweet fragrances of blood and fresh flesh. The crowning olfactory sensation was the application of a foul-smelling medicine onto the bleeding head and crotch of the calf.

Everyone was sweating; the cowboys had cakes of dirt smeared on their faces and shirts. Levi's were spotted with calf blood and urine; the latter liquid sometimes sprayed out of a panicked, pain-ridden animal. No one cared, although nasal fatigue was not a bad condition to experience if a person was odor-impaired.

The smells were not offensive to me. I liked them—they were part of the branding landscape. The only smell I found offensive was the medicinal "dope bucket." Its smell was unlike any thing that had ever passed under my nose, and I never became accustomed to it. To make matters worse, the dope bucket's odor was immune to nasal fatigue.

Unfortunately for me, the dope bucket was my primary responsibility. No riding the horses in the corral to corner the calves; no flanking the calves; no removing their horns; no cutting-off their balls—none of the glorious cowboy chores. The lowest, dirtiest job in the entire operation fell to yours truly; a fitting example of the human pecking order in action.

The Worst Job in the Branding Corral. My job in the branding corral was to carry a large bucket of medication/disinfectant to the downed calf, arriving at the animal just as it had been liberated of its horns and testicles. As mentioned, the bucket was dubbed the dope bucket. And I complain again: My task was the worst job in the corral. The bucket was heavy and contained a thick, foul-smelling, black tar-like substance. It was called "dip".

Dip was a greasy semi-liquid I applied to the lacerated, vacant areas on the calf's body—those area previously occupied by horns and testicles. If the branding iron had burned too deeply into the calf's skin, I also placed the concoction on this part of the animal.

The dip consisted of a mysterious ingredient called criso, iodine, another mysterious substance called Formula 62, probably petroleum jelly, maybe motor oil, and other obnoxious components. In addition to providing a primitive means to combat infection, the dip kept flies away from the open wounds.

The only advantage of manning the dope bucket was to ward-off flies. These insects were attracted to the branding pen like a pig was to slop. They were hungry, thirsty, stubborn, and ever-present; except near the dope bucket and me.

During these events, I was in the company of six to eleven people in the corral. We were adept at parallel processing and usually worked with two to four calves simultaneously. One or two cowboys were on horses roping the calves; one or two others were flanking them. If our neighbors helped us, several more people were branding, dehorning, castrating, and vaccinating. After which, I applied the dip.

An observer of the branding corral would witness calves running to-and-fro, trying to avoid the rope; calves fighting the flanker's take-down; calves lying on their sides, undergoing the rituals of branding. The branding corral presented an unseasoned observer with a scene of controlled bedlam. As I charged across the pen with my dope bucket, I was sometimes knocked to the ground by a horse, calf, or cowboy. By the end of the day, I had more dip on my body than I had placed on a calf.

I had no concern; the more dip on me the better. The foul mess made me part of the process. I was actually doing grown-up chores, and for a few days, these men were my companions. In a sense, I was their equal! But in hindsight, I suspect I was as much a nuisance as I was a contributor. No matter; they never said one word of discouragement. If I got behind, one of them would grab another dope bucket and assist me in my role of bovine nurse until I caught-up with my duties.

The branded calves were moved to a pasture with their mothers. They were not touched again unless they developed screw worms. Formula 62, the elixir of life for cattle, was also used to rid the animal of these worms. In November, the cattle were shipped-off to the slaughter pens. We kept a few for our own consumption, taking the meat to a butcher plant in town for cutting and storage.

Culinary Delights of the Branding Corral

Let me sharpen your appetite by listing several of the harvests reaped from a branding session or slaughtering some of the calves for food. The items for consumption were: calf's testicles, calf's intestines, calf's brains, and calf's necks. Not hungry? Fine, I will substitute other names for these culinary delights. They are known respectively as mountain oysters (or calf fries), son-of-a-gun, brains, and sweetbread. You may wonder why brains are called just brains. I wonder too, as this part of the menu has no alternate name.

As a child, I took the English language literally. Therefore, I was puzzled by the name "mountain oysters." Mountains and oysters did not exist in Lea County. A rose by any other name is still a rose. A testicle by any other name is still a testicle.

Whatever their names might have been, and regardless of their mission in life, the calves' testicles were put to good use: We ate them. After all, they were a rich source of protein. The dining took place in the corral where we performed the castrations, or at the house, usually for the noon meal.

After a testicle was removed from the animal, the cowboy tossed it into a nearby bucket of water. During the day, if he wished to have a snack, he retrieved a testicle from the bucket and placed it on the branding iron fire. The intense heat quickly cooked the meat. When the skin popped off the gland, the cowboy knew it was done. He then popped the popped ball into his mouth—biting, chewing, and swallowing a very tasty treat. Try it, you might like it.

One of my other jobs was to carry the bucket of unconsumed mountain oysters to the house, about 200 yards away from the branding pen. During my journey, I recall I glanced down at the testicles occasionally, just to make sure they were still there, that they had not somehow sprung legs and jumped out of the bucket. For some strange reason, I had a feeling they might be alive.

Yet, even in those young times, I knew the function of testicles. As I looked at them, they lay on the bottom of the pail. Passive and inert; a bucket of defunct glands. I was thankful we humans didn't practice castration on our young males—especially at my age in life, because I belonged to this part of the population. The pecking order problem again.

As an undersized eight-year old boy, the bucket, heavy with water and testicles, was difficult to carry. On one of my trips, I dropped the bucket and it tipped over, spilling the water and calves' balls onto the ground. I hurried to recover them before anyone saw my accident. I frantically picked up each testicle and attempted to wipe the dirt away—to no avail, the dirt was now mud. I tried cleaning each ball on my pants in an attempt to remove the mud—to no avail, the gland's soft tissue seemed to capture the mud in its folds. I even blew on the testicles, in a futile attempt to dislodge the mud. Thus thwarted, I placed the testicles back into the bucket and lugged them to the kitchen. Our amused cook rinsed-off the mud and prepared the mountain oysters for our noon meal.

On the Job Experience

Perhaps because of my ranch experiences, I am fascinated by what people eat—or do not eat. I'm sure our selections are dictated partially by culture and habits. In addition, I know from personal experience that acquiring a taste for unknown foods is a matter of experimentation, and at times, a strong stomach.

As a young 20-something-year old, while in the U.S. Navy, I spent one week at a Japanese inn near Mt. Fuji. I signed-up for the "Japanese Plan," which meant I consumed nothing for seven days but raw fish, raw octopus, raw eel, rice, a strange green moss-like plant, salt-like broth—and after the second day of this diet, immense amounts of sake. The Japanese vacation represented one of my more unpleasant gastronomic experiments. But then, my palate was parochial and I had never eaten raw meat of any kind. Since those times, my tastes have changed and I now look forward to raw oysters and clams. Maybe that earlier diversity of ranch fare made me willing to experiment with food later in my life.

Studs and Mares

The breeding time for a horse depended entirely on the mare being in heat. A mare goes into heat every 18-21 days; they are most receptive to a male's advances on their third day of heat.

One of Dad's favorite studs was named Wompus McCue. For several decades, the grandfather of this horse, Peter McCue, held the world record for running the fastest quarter-mile—an extraordinary achievement.[2]

Wompus was a beautiful, powerful, and mean animal. He stood just over 15 hands high and weighed about 1,350 pounds (one hand is about four inches). A height of 15 hands is not especially tall but Wompus possessed a powerful and massive physique. He was the only coal black horse we owned—not one white marking on any part of his body. His black countenance matched his personality. I hated the horse because he almost killed me, a tale I relate in my story, "Cornered by a Stud."

Wompus produced approximately 250 colts from our mares, and the mares brought to the ranch by other people. Many of his off-spring were of a fine disposition but others, like their father, were mean and ornery. My brother Ed was very active as a result of Wompus' activity, as he broke the colts sired by Wompus.

We bred our mares in a reserved pasture near the ranch. Wompus was placed in the field with about 50 mares and nature took its course. If Wompus and we were fortunate, his sexual activity would net almost one colt per mare. The time required for Wompus to make his rounds of all the mares was about 2 1/2 months.

This time could have been reduced if Wompus had been more efficient. Brother Ed said, "He tended to hang around some of his favorite mates and stay for seconds."

I heard this comment one day when Dad, my brothers, and a few neighbors were watching and managing one of Wompus' matings. It was an intriguing idea, but I wasn't exactly sure of its complete meaning, as I had not yet had an opportunity for a "first."

Anyway, today one-on-one breeding has been replaced with artificial insemination. A single ejaculation can be used to produce nine colts. This practice is certainly not as much fun for the horses but it is more rewarding to their owners. I am certain Wompus would not have been happy with this practice.

Dad derived part of his income by renting his stallions for breeding, thus collecting stud fees. This operation entailed coaxing the stud and mare to copulate in a corral; a much safer and more structured environment than the open pasture. All horses were given a test for VD. The stud or mare owner could request the certificate, although merely stating the horse was clean was usually sufficient for both parties.

The mare's owner left the horse at our ranch for a few weeks or months. Ed knew how to examine the horse's ovaries to determine the state of her cycle. The mare's owner allowed us to determine the best time to mate the horse to our stud.

The breeding followed a precise, controlled procedure:

- Both horses were led into the corral.
- The mare was placed in a breeding chute or her rear leg movements were restrained with a rope. This restraint was insurance against the mare kicking and injuring the stud. Even in heat, a mare might kick if she were frightened or if the stud was too aggressive.

- The stud might be muzzled, depending on his nature. Some males bit into the neck of the female during mounting and copulation—holding on during the ride, so to speak. After all, the stud had no hands.
- Their genitals were washed-down with soap and water to reduce any chances of infection.
- Under control of a halter, the stud was led to the mare.
- The horses were given leeway to begin their mating ritual—feeling with the stud's nose and mouth, and snorting, smelling, neighing for both horses—which led to copulation.
- If the courting was successful, the stud mounted the mare and consummated the sexual act.

After the breeding, our mares were returned to the Horse Pasture to await the birth of their colts. The other mares were reclaimed by their owners. These pregnant females became the owners' responsibility. Dad did not provide a colt delivery service.

Dad derived part of his income from selling horses. Ed broke and tamed each horse to the extent the pony would accept a rider. Any additional training was the responsibility of the new owner. The horses were sold to local citizens or bartered at a horse auction in Clovis, New Mexico.

Bulls and Cows

We bred our cows during June and July, resulting in March and April births. The timing for the births took advantage of warm weather and the new grass in the pastures.

Our Bull Pasture was named appropriately enough—the bulls lived there. But during the breeding season, they were herded to several other pastures where the cows awaited their arrival. For this move, a well-trained horse was essential. Each cowboy used his mount to keep the bulls organized and moving in the correct direction. Ed was the most gifted horse trainer in our family; he usually rode the best trained pony.

As a general rule, the bull-to-cow copulation ratio was 1:25. That is, one bull serviced 25 cows. Older bulls were given a less vigorous schedule; for example, a 1:12 ratio. The cows might have preferred a bull-to-cow ratio of 1:1, but they were not consulted on the matter.

At times, we kept the old and young bulls in separate pastures to prevent the old males from injuring their younger colleagues. Notwithstanding this cautionary practice, the bulls usually got along with each other. Like horses, they often paired-up to become buddies. A notable exception was the time they were placed in the cow pastures for breeding. Like most males, they fought each other for position in the copulation queue. A dominant bull was able to impregnate more cows than its competitors—thus ensuring its genes would be passed on to the next generation.

During this time in the breeding season, the bulls looked like battling sumo wrestlers. They used their massive weight to fight, pushing other bulls around the pasture. If the opportunity presented itself, a bull would gore its horns into the neck of the other bull.

I was given few warnings about my wanderings around the ranch. But Dad was adamant on one topic: I was to stay out of the bull pasture, as well as the pastures where breeding was taking place. Bulls can be territorial. As well, it's dangerous to be near them when they are fighting. Even on a horse, a cowboy must be careful not to place himself and his mount between the bulls. Astride a horse, my brother Jim attempted to break up a fight between two bulls and found himself the object of their wrath. Luckily, his (savvy) horse took control of the situation and moved away from the battle.

Some bulls were not discerning about their choice of mates. Ardor would get the best of them and a bull (the mounter) would attempt to mount another bull (the mountee). Sadly for the mounter, if he probed for a convenient orifice on the mountee too aggressively, the search could result in broken pride and a broken penis. Alas, the Wayne Bobbitt of bulls was no longer of any use and its job description had to be rewritten. The bull was removed from the envied list of bulls that serviced cows to the ignoble list of bulls that appeared on dinner plates. As a result of their accident, these animals were slaughtered for their meat—which made for delicious steaks.

Dad's Rescue. After the breeding was complete, the cows were left to their own, and we looked forward to the births of their calves. As the time approached for the births, Dad or our hired hands visited the pastures to check on the progress of the pregnancies, as well as the births. I accompanied Dad on one of these trips. He drove the pickup slowly through a herd of cattle, looking at each cow, and checking out the newly born calves.

We came across a potentially soon-to-be mother cow that was in trouble. The baby calf was only partially birthed; the angle of its body in the mother's birth canal prevented the mom from pushing the baby completely out of the canal. Both animals were in danger of losing their lives.

Dad and I saw the struggling cow at the same time. I remember calling out, "Dad! Look!"

He answered, "I see her son," as he pulled the pickup closer to the cow. He stopped the vehicle, exited the cab, and walked to the rear end of the mother. He pushed the baby calf around a bit, then put an arm and hand inside the canal. He succeeded in repositioning the calf just enough to allow the mother to expel the small animal and complete the birth. The calf was alive; so was the mother.

The mother appeared to be dazed but I was no judge of bovine post operation moods. The other cattle surrounding Dad's rescue operation seemed oblivious to the recovery of one of their pasture mates. Some looked our way; others continued with grazing and feeding their new calves.

One animal surveying the scene was far from oblivious to what had just happened—an eight-year old boy. I was in awe of Dad's salvage; his unhesitating actions; his thrust into the mother cow. His response to the dangerous situation.

Dad's arms and hands were covered with afterbirth. As he walked back to the pickup, he wiped his hands and arms on his pants. It didn't matter to Dad. He was performing a routine chore and was accustomed to the procedure and the afterbirth. We drove back to the house, where Dad washed and changed clothes.

Bucks and Ewes

In addition to Dad's stallion, Wompus, I placed another animal on my list of despised animals: male sheep. To be fair, not all male sheep, just one specific contrary buck who made a habit of attacking me when I ventured into his pasture. I did not mind avoiding bulls or Wompus; they were big, strong creatures. But a sheep? After all, aren't sheep noted for their humble and docile natures? Not necessarily, and I learned a strong buck could be as formidable as a bull.

Figure 4-1. A big buck and a big bully.

Once, a big buck subjugated a bull during a confrontation in one of our pastures. The bull could not counter the buck's continued ramming of its side. It would not answer with butts of its own because a bull's head is not designed for ramming (an occasional gore, but not continuous ramming). Eventually, the buck kowtowed the bull, forcing it to move to another part of the pasture. Very impressive and scary as well. You can understand why I steered clear of bucks.

Before I was born, my mother was also harassed by a big buck, named Jack, shown in Figure 4-1. This animal butted most people who did not confront its bullying behavior. Mom was a peaceful sort, so Jack would often pick her out for ramming practice. (He stayed away from Dad). On an early morning in the 1930s, Mom was carrying a chamber pot from the house to the outhouse. You may have seen movies depicting life in the West before bathrooms became commonplace. Many households kept a chamber pot in the house to use during the night.

Jack was nearby as Mom made her way to the outhouse. He spotted mother and started her way, ready to administer a butt to her butt. But Mom was tired of Jack's butting. Just as the buck lowered his head to initiate his first ramming action, Mom tossed the contents of the pot in Jack's face. Her defensive move stopped the buck in his tracks. After Mom's retaliation, Jack left Mom alone. Who said sheep are stupid?

Lambing. Our sheep were pasture-bred. In November, the bucks were let out into the pastures with the ewes. If the matings went well, the lambs were born in April, an ideal season for the fleeceless babies. With the ewes in heat, a buck sheep was assigned a daunting task: copulate with 75 to 100 ewes in a short time. A mere two days in the pasture with the sheep could result in 75 to 100 impregnations—and we hoped, as many lambs.

During the gestation period, we spent many hours in the pastures checking on the well being of the sheep. If a prospective mother looked underfed, haggard, or otherwise handicapped, she was transported to the shelter of our lambing barn to await the birth of her baby.

After the successful births, the new sheep became part of the inventory for the shearing operations and their job description required them to submit to an annual fleecing. Many of the male sheep were castrated. Those displaying exceptional fleeces were fortunate enough to escape the knife. They would live to pass their genes and fleece to the next generation. They had to earn their keep by working a few days each year—during the breeding season. Nice work if they could get it.

Oh yes, the sheep testicles were also considered a delicacy. We consumed them, just as we did the mountain oysters. They too were called oysters—not mountain oysters—just oysters. We concocted another fine menu item from the sheep, thanks to our French immigrant neighbors. In their old country, the tail of the lamb was cut off, skinned, covered with meal, and fried in hot oil with seasonings that no one in Lea Country had ever heard of. The taste of deep fried lamb's tail, accentuated by the French touch, was delicious beyond description.

Many years ago, I read a passage in a book by Fredric Manning titled, *Her Privates We*. As I wrote the story you have been reading, I was reminded of this quote. I thought of my Mexican friends at their campfire and my companions in the branding corral:

> Men are bound together more closely by the trivial experiences they have shared, than by the most sacred obligations.

---

[1] This part of our story is titled "Branding." It is a convenient catch-all word. The term is used to describe one act, or the acts of branding, dehorning, and castrating.

[2] Records show the horse was timed with five stopwatches; electronic timers were for the future.

5

THE TADPOLE PUDDLE

You never see a frog so modest and straightfor'ard as he was,
for all he was so gifted. And when it come to fair-and-square
jumping on a dead level, he could get over more ground at one
straddle than any animal of his breed you ever see.
—*Mark Twain*

Rain was a rare event on the dry prairies of the Llano Estacado. It was a subject of discussion before, during, and after its occurrence. A rain related conversation often unfolded as follows:

"Well, it looks like rain."
"Yep, we sure need it.
"Yep."

"Well, it's finally raining."
"Yep, we sure need it."
"Yep."

"Well, that was a real good rain."
"Yep, we sure need it."
"Yep."

These dialogues reflected the taciturn conversations among Lea County ranchers and farmers. Their brevity did not discount the importance of their subject because rain was essential to their livelihood. Of course, rain is vital to most parts of the earth. But rain was (and is) rare in this part of the world, so it received a lot of attention.

When a rare rain cloud visited Lea County, it often brought water to the earth in a huge downpour. We called these rains thunderstorms because they were accompanied by spectacular flashes of lightning and loud clashes of thunder. As the savage storm moved slowly across the flat spaces of southern New Mexico the lightning's startling, sudden radiance captured short-lived images of cactus, yucca, mesquite, and sage. The luminous landscape, suspended in light for a second or so, accentuated the raw beauty of the Llano Estacado.

Because the dry earth was unable to soak up a huge downpour, a deluge could cover a countryside's entire plain. The result of this enormous inundation of water was a huge lake, spanning for miles over the horizontal prairie. No streams. No gullies. No torrents of water overflowing the riverbeds; just one large and level sea, often flooding peoples' barns and houses.

Relief could not be obtained by building on a hillless landscape. The ranchers and farmers were as vulnerable to a rare rain storm as beach dwellers were vulnerable to a rare hurricane.

Figure 5-1. A prairie lake.

An idea of the situation can be gained by a look at Figure 5-1. This rainstorm occurred in the Tatum area in the 1940s, creating a lake of about one-half foot in depth; one that spanned several miles across the smooth landscape. The lake was short-lived. The thirsty earth adjusted quickly, and drank-in the precious liquid. Any remaining water not consumed by the soil rapidly evaporated into the air.

A Limited Partnership

Like the Pavlovian subject responding to a stimulus, the earth acknowledged the water and brought forth a fantastic display of flowers and foliage. The once dry, barren land was soon covered with blossoms. The formerly brown prairie was colored with a vast, stunning multicolored floral arrangement, courtesy of Mother Nature.

But for a few days only. Before long, the flora sought recluse from the harsh sun. Hoping for eventual regeneration, the plants shed their seeds, pollen, and petals. They fell to the ground, or were transported to other soils by critters and wind. Afterwards, conditioned by millions of years of evolution, the foliage retreated into the ground to await another rare soaking.

Lea County was not completely flat. Small hollows and recesses punctuated an otherwise uniform terrain, providing temporary reservoirs—small puddles—for the rain water. Temporary, because the dry ground absorbed the precious water and the dry air soon desiccated any liquid remaining in a puddle. Whatever the cause, dry earth or dry air, the surrounding land soon returned to its dehydrated state.

My Security Blanket

When the storm's electrical show was in full force, the younger brothers in our family were required to remain indoors and watch the rainstorm from a door or window. I thought I was safe from lightening if I watched the rain with something in my hands that did not conduct electricity. I was ignorant of the physics of this idea but I respected the awesome force of lightening. The reverberations from nearby strikes persuaded me to remain in our safe house.

I was told rubber was a fine insulating material. Consequently, I came up with the idea of grasping a piece of this material as I sat at the door watching the lightning storm. My favorite insulator, my electric security blanket, was a small rubber drain stopper used in our kitchen sink. My brother Tom and I shared this electrocution avoidance tool as we sat at our living room door, enthralled and frightened by the storm. He held one side of the drain stopper; I held the other. Somehow, through a tiny piece of rubber, divine intervention, or the laws of physics Tom and I escaped the lightning bolts.

Adventures on the Ranch

Living on a cattle and sheep ranch during the summer was an uninterrupted adventure, from the time I arose in the morning, until the time I dropped off to sleep. The diversity of activities available to a child would have made a (future) Disney World an entertainment piker. The variety of mammals, birds, insects, and reptiles captured my interest every waking moment of the day.

Added to my youth was the fact that I was also little. These two factors—being young, and being small—meant I was not part of my father's hired hands brigade, the big people who labored to keep the ranch profitable and in working order. With the exception of some minor daily chores and more arduous jobs during calf branding and sheep shearing days, I was free to do as I pleased.

My Dad, my stepmother, my brothers, and the hired hands were too busy to worry about an eight year old child. I was miles from town and miles from the nearest neighbor. I was out of harm's way, unless I created the harm. Any parent reading this story knows you cannot protect a young boy from himself—unless you establish a twenty-four hour watch on the kid.

Like many children, I was drawn to the role of protector of the ranch's life forms. If I came across an injured bird, lamb, rodent, or for that matter almost any living thing, I would do my best to save it. I viewed the ranch land as my private game preserve.

I was not one of those kids who liked to dissect frogs, cats, or dogs. I was the critter social services worker. But I drew the line with poisonous snakes. If they had the misfortune to cross my path, I killed them without hesitation. Also, I was not fond of large buck sheep, my Dad's stud horse, and his wildcat. In other chapters, I explain the reasons for my animosities.

New Members of my Game Preserve

One summer afternoon, we had the good fortune to receive a huge downpour from one of those rare thunderstorms. The next morning, as I left the house to begin my day, I came across a big rain puddle about 50 yards from the house. Well, "big" depends on one's perspective; the puddle looked big to me, but I imagine it was only twenty feet of so from one edge to the other.

As I examined the puddle I discovered it was populated with tadpoles—new members of my game preserve! I knew about tadpoles. I knew they were baby frogs in disguise and would soon become regular frogs. Frogs were also on my list of protected species. Even more, I enjoyed watching frogs swim and leap. I considered the frog to be an amazing critter because it performed so well both in and out of the water.

Plus, I liked capturing frogs and watching them watch me as I kept them prisoners inside my cupped hands. I was impressed that their capture never seemed to upset them. They maintained their precapture frog-like demeanor, nonchalantly accepting their encasement. After opening my hands, they often just sat there for a while. Then, in an instant, they would leap away with a thrust so powerful that it pushed my hands back toward my body. Powerful creatures. Cool amphibians.

For this day, my initial fascination and delight gave way to the realization the tadpoles might not live to become frogs. The equation did not look promising:

The sun was already up in the sky + The sky had no clouds = A very hot day was a certainty. Translation: A short life for the puddle and its tadpoles.

The Rescue Operation

My solution to this equation was simple: Transfer the tadpoles to one of our water tanks. The strategy was straightforward: Use a bucket to scoop up the water from the puddle and of course, the beleaguered tadpoles.

I would carry these buckets of water to the nearest tank, located in our lambing barn, about 300 feet from the puddle. (This shelter was used to house pregnant sheep.) In the middle of the lambing barn was a small metal tank, which always contained water—an ideal refuge for my tadpoles.

Time was short. Hundreds, perhaps thousands of wannabe frogs were in danger of permanent consignment to tadpole purgatory. I had to begin my rescue effort immediately. Running to the tool shed, I fetched a bucket and started transferring the water and the tadpoles to the water tank.

My rescue operation was slow going and laborious. As I scooped up the water, the tadpoles often swam around the bucket, avoiding my attempts to capture them. In addition, with each scoop, the puddle became muddier, making my efforts to locate the tiny amphibians more difficult. The trek to the water tank was not an easy journey. The bucket was heavy and I sloshed water on the ground as I made my way to my destination, sometimes spilling unlucky tadpoles along the way.

Despite the obstacles, I stayed with my job. If such a condition can exist in a child, I was a driven eight-year old. I was determined to retrieve the tadpoles and deliver them to the water tank before the puddle dried-up.

The task became an impossible effort. I discovered the seemingly small puddle was not really a puddle. As I labored throughout the morning and into the afternoon, other terms besides puddle came into my mind—sea, lake—larger bodies of water. I was not strong enough to carry big buckets of water the length of a football field. Yet, if I left the bucket partially filled, I knew it would take a long time to finish my task. But I had no choice in the matter. I was committed to my mission.

Just before lunch, Dad, my brothers, and the hired hands came in from the pastures and other places where they had been performing their chores. A few visited my puddle to check-out what I was up to. After I explained the tadpoles' precarious situation and demonstrated my life saving operation, they silently walked away— perhaps hoping I would soon grow up and help them with the practical problems of ranch life.

Dad dropped by during the noon break, "What are you up to son?"

Son, "Saving frogs Dad."

Dad, "What for?"

What could I say? If he didn't know the answer to his question, how could a child enlighten him? Perhaps I could have offered, *"You see father, the land on which you are standing is really my land. It's my game preserve. Not 'game,' as in killing, but 'preserve," as in saving. My job is to save the critters who live here … with the exception of snakes, buck sheep, and your mean stud and wildcat."*

Nope, it would not have worked. First, Dad was an avid hunter. Second, he had little empathy for creatures. Third, I was eight years old, and had absolutely no capacity to articulate such a clever response. So, what was my answer?

Son, "Eh. Oh, I dunno. Just seems like a good idea."

He listened to my lame explanation. Turning away to walk to the house he advised, "Well, put a hat on son."

My brother Jim provided the only positive feedback and one suggestion. He noted the sheep barn tank was a conventional metal container. He thought the frogs would have trouble getting out of a tank with vertical sides. He suggested I place some large blocks of wood in the tank to act, as he said, "… as artificial lily pads." The tadpoles, now transmogrified into frogs, could climb onto these small floating islands, leap out of the tank, and make their way to frog suburbia.

I don't know if his view was correct and I have not conducted research on frogs' abilities to leap or climb from metal tanks. But his idea seemed reasonable, so I found several pieces of wood and placed them onto the tank's water.

Abandoning the Rescue

The tadpole rescue became one of my more miserable experiences on the ranch for that summer. The situation was hopeless. I simply could not capture all the tadpoles. The round trip journey to and from the water tank was exhausting. To make matters worse, failing to clothe myself properly, and forgetting Dad's advice about a hat had resulted in serious sunburn to my face. The big people did not notice my plight until midafternoon, when our cook came out of the house to smoke a cigarette and saw me laboring away in the distance.

She walked over to my place of operations, surveyed the scene, as well as my exhausted, red-skinned countenance and put an abrupt end to my mission. I didn't protest. I was tired, near ill, and disappointed with my efforts.

My feelings about the tadpoles were mixed. I knew I had saved many of them. But as the puddle became smaller, I also knew many more were doomed, unless they were very fast bloomers. Nonetheless, my *Save the Tadpoles* operation was over. The cook took me back to the house for some sunburn ointment and a much needed nap. By the next day, the puddle was almost gone. The rain puddle, once a formidable body of water, was now a small pathetic pond of mostly mud. My treasured amphibious urchins were history.

Music to my Ears!

Following supper a few days after the rain, our family and hired hands were sitting on the lawn outside our house—the only patch of green grass in the thousands of acres on our ranch. On most evenings, we escaped from the house to our front yard in hopes of finding refuge from the evening's dry, windless heat.

I was playing mumble peg (a game of throwing a knife into the ground at different angles) with my brother Tom. Dad had fired up his harmonica. Listening to Dad's tunes, the others engaged in idle talk. We had settled in for a pleasant interlude before turning in for the night.

Gradually, as Dad played his music, the air around us began to resonate with frog croaks. Initially, the volume was modest; we could detect the direction of each croak. Shortly, several croaks were heard. Then many, soon cascading into a cacophony of frog music. Before long, we were surrounded by croaks from hundreds, perhaps thousands of frogs. In a few minutes, the croaking became so loud we could barely hear Dad's harmonica. We were in the middle of a concert! A near-deafening acappella performance of croaks, intermingled with the plaintive and increasingly faint sounds of Dad's harmonica.

Those croaks were music to my ears. I was sure they came from my tadpoles, now fully functioning frogs. My tadpole refugee program had worked!

The croaks were not music to Dad's ears. After a few moments of competing for the musical stage with a huge population of amphibians, he stopped playing his harmonica. We also ceased our activities and turned to Dad, who had never interrupted his music in the middle of a song. He reminded me of those pianos that use paper rolls to play a song. Once he started his tune, he finished it.

Something was bothering him and I knew what it was. He glanced around, looking toward his barns, tanks, and pastures. He looked in all directions, as if he were doing a series of sonar pings—trying to assess his competition for the evening's entertainment.

After this pause, he fixed his eyes on his youngest son and asked, "Where did all those frogs come from?"

Taking a clue from Moses, a frequent subject in my Sunday school classes, I wanted to say, *"They came from me Dad. I am the savior of frogs. Think of me as a Lea County Moses, leading my tribe of tadpoles from the troubled puddle to the sanctuary of a local sheep water tank. The sounds you hear confirm the tadpoles' flight from an endangered puddle to their promised water."*

Of course, I did not think those profound thoughts at all. I offer them to establish myself as the articulate hero of this tale. But I share with you that I did feel a great deal of pride in listening to the frogs drown-out my father's harmonica performance.

I dared not bask in my glory by offering a wise-ass response of any kind. Dad did not tolerate flippancy from his sons. And I knew many of the croaking frogs came from other puddles; I was only a co-producer of the amphibian concert.

In addition, Dad was staring at me during his question and my father was not a man to be trifled with. I uttered not a word but as I looked up to my father's face, he was smiling at his son.

6

THE HUNTER AND THE HUNTED

*The proper office of a friend is to side with you when you are in the wrong.
Nearly anybody will side with your when you are in the right.*

—*Mark Twain*

I spoke earlier about the chores and tasks required to keep a ranch in operating condition. Although ranch life in New Mexico was a hard way to make a living, it was not all work. After the chores were completed, Dad allowed his sons to participate in several rest and relaxation treats: swimming in one of our water tanks; fishing from small ponds located next to our windmills; listening to Dad play his fiddle or harmonica; roping calves in our small rodeo arena, and going hunting.

I learned to swim in one of those tanks and we did a lot of fishing from the ponds. Dad had stocked some of them with catfish. And we boys hunted every day, just after we stopped working and before the evening meal.

Hunting Jackrabbits for the Cats

The most common prey for our hunt was the jackrabbit. This critter was a very unpopular animal with ranchers. It ate the pasture grass used to feed our stock. It presented a big problem, because grass was a precious resource in the semi-arid plains of southeastern New Mexico. We hunted rabbits for another reason. My stepmother Mary had a penchant for collecting cats and the cats needed food, such as jackrabbits.

Collecting cats? It's a strange way to describe taking care of pets. But the phrase is accurate because Mary had scores of cats. Some of them were tame and lived with us in the house. But most of the cats were not domesticated—semi-wild really—and roamed around the ranch.

Because the wild part of her feline population refused to be counted, no one knew how many cats were in Mary's collection. They could be seen throughout the day, darting around our house, the barns, windmills, and sheds. They wouldn't come near us, nor could we approach them. That is, until we showed up with four or five dead jackrabbits. Then, the place was crawling with friendly cats.

On most of the jackrabbit hunts, I was the designated gun bearer and game fetcher. For the gun bearer tasks, I was responsible for loading the guns. I was also allowed to shoot the ordnance under the eyes of my older brothers or hired hands. From the bed of the pickup, with a .22 rifle, I could easily pick off a rabbit several hundred feet away.

As the game fetcher, I was responsible for retrieving the animals. This part of the job entailed my jumping from the pickup to snare a jackrabbit that had been felled by a shot from one of our rifles.

Unlike my brothers and Dad, I was not an avid hunter. My father hunted for many years, sometimes traveling to Northern New Mexico, where he rode his horse into the snow-covered, mountain wilderness, searching for deer, elk, or bear. One of my brothers was a talented bow-and-arrow hunter. He stalked coyotes, deer, and even fish. Another brother was a remarkable marksman, and could hit a coin as it was tossed into the air.

I had been exposed to hunting since my early years; I was acculturated to the hunting ritual.[1] My earliest recollections of the booty of hunting are reflected in Figure 6-1. I learned later that 15 people organized this antelope and coyote hunt. The spoils are evident by a casual look at the bodies strewn across the car. It appears my father is explaining some of the nuances of the hunt and it appears I am taking it all in.[2]

As a young boy, I liked to hunt and shoot game. But eventually, I must have experienced an aberration in my family's DNA strand. I exhibited one problem with the hunting affairs: An inordinate amount of empathy for the rabbits. I knew they were not domesticated animals and I knew they damaged our grass and some of our crops. When I first started hunting and I was the shooter, I was thrilled when I bagged one of them.

But occasionally, a rabbit was only wounded. As the designated retriever, I would leap from the pickup and run to the downed animal, pulling it off the ground by its long ears. I learned quickly that an injured, frightened jackrabbit is a pitiful sight to behold.

When I picked up the hurt, yet conscious animal, it would usually cry. The cry sounded like a squealing human baby, and I recall it as vividly today as I did over sixty years ago. Try that out on an eight-year old boy. The experience will make a reluctant hunter out of any but the most callused child.

Yet I was not (and am not) against hunting— especially certain critters. But given immunity from Dad's wrath, I would have gladly shot his prize stud (an ill-tempered, dangerous horse) and one of his prize sheep.

**Figure 6-1.
Dad explains the hunt to me.**

Enter the Ram

If I made the mistake of wandering into the sheep pasture, Dad's treasured ram would attack me. Trust me, taking head butts from a territorial ram is not a pleasant way to stroll through a meadow.

To this day, I can feel the helplessness of this encounter. The never-ending butts were just that: tenacious and never-ending. As I picked myself up, the ram would "ram" me back into the turf. He seemed content to keep me contained. I got up. He put me down. I got up again; he put me down again. As long as I stayed-down, the ram was content. When I tried to get up, he butted me back down.

Now that I am on turf far away from this animal, our encounters seem trivial and harmless. And I suspect they were. The ram never hit me with much force. He never inflicted anything close to pain. In fact, he seemed to be playing with me. I never felt threatened, just considerably inconvenienced. He levied just enough thrust to keep me in my place … and I suspect his place as well.

I finally decided to stay down. It turned out to be a good choice. The ram became bored and drifted-off to other parts of the pasture.

Enter the Wildcat

I didn't care for another critter living on the ranch, a wildcat.[3] Dad's "pet" wildcat was a pain in my ass. For starters, it was not tame. Tame animals can be petted. Not this animal; petting it ran the risk of being scratched and bitten. To compound matters, during the late afternoons I usually roamed the area around the ranch house and barns (my private game preserve). During this summer, the wildcat stalked me. It was the hunter and I was the hunted.

The wildcat had chosen me as its prime prey. It never stalked any of the large-size people at the ranch; just me. From its place of hiding in a bush it would often jump onto my back or chest. Making growls and snarls, it would then run away, looking for another convenient bush for its next point of attack. The wildcat weighed half as much as I, a scary situation for a child.

If I were lucky, I might spot the outline of the animal behind the cover of the bush, as it waited for me to pass by. Thus sighted, I would take a different direction to my destination. But often as not, its attack was a complete surprise, and for a moment or so, it scared me out of my wits.

The animal was not attacking me for a kill, possibly because I was too big, or my shouts and actions frightened it away. Nonetheless, it seemed to like the game—it kept coming back for more.

As a sign of its visit, the animal occasionally left scratches on my skin. I'm reminded of guest logs placed in the lobbies of hotels, funeral homes, and wedding receptions. Visitors record their signatures in these books to prove they paid a call on the place, or were present for a ceremony. My body was the wildcat's sign-in book.

The term son-of-a-bitch (SOB) was not permitted in my vocabulary. Dad could swear. His sons could not. Notwithstanding this fatherly proscription, I heard the term often from Dad, the ranch hands, and my brothers. As the summer progressed, SOB entered my thoughts about one subject: I wanted that son-of-a-bitch wildcat dead. As I found myself avoiding parts of my former territory; as I discovered my domain on the ranch was being usurped, I began to utter SOB under my breath. The nemesis to my reign wasn't a mere wildcat. He was a son-of-a-bitch. Because the wildcat was increasingly intruding on my territory and scaring the hell out of me, it ceased to be a wildcat in my mind. It had become a son-of-a-bitch. Killing a cat is one thing. Killing a SOB is another.

Looking for Help

Like any normal eight-year old, I sought help from my parents. Mom was not at the ranch, as her presence would have made for a crowded master bedroom. Mary, my stepmother, was a horsewoman (a deft barrel racer in rodeos), but definitely not a housewife. She didn't cook, sew, wash dishes, clean house or perform any of other supposed female duties. For these tasks, Dad hired a cook. The cook's job was to feed us and keep the house and clothes in order.

Mary was as good a cowboy as you could find. She dressed like a cowboy, talked like a cowboy, walked like a cowboy, and rode horses like a cowboy. Could she ever ride horses! But it is fair to say Mary was not versed in parenting skills. I think she uttered four or five sentences to me during the first month I was at the ranch. She was a cowgirl, focused on her horses, cats, and Dad. I'm amazed as to how well she took the inundation of Dad's kids into the ranch during the summer. She was always polite to me. I recall that as the summer wore-on, we had some laughs together. But I gathered she did not know how to talk to children. I didn't mind; I had no interest in her either.

So, I couldn't talk to my Mom and I didn't want to talk to my step mom. My brothers were not paragons of empathy; they were off my list of counselors. As the summer unfolded, I grew more frustrated with the wildcat. I finally decided to talk to Dad about my problem.

I was a bit scared of my father and was reluctant to approach him. Dad was a taciturn person and physically imposing. As I said in earlier chapters, he was known throughout the county for his brevity of manner and fighting skills. I had heard of Dad knocking a person unconscious with a single swing of his fist, without so much as uttering a word to the man.

Dad never laid a hand on me. Throughout my life with him, he treated me fairly and with consideration. Nonetheless, seen through the eyes of a child, he had an aura of silent enmity, and I viewed my father as a powerful and somewhat daunting person. Knowing his reputation and his overall demeanor, I was reluctant to talk to him.

But the wildcat situation had me in dire straits. I came to believe I had no other choice but to have a discussion about my problem with my father. Our conversation unfolded as follows.

"Dad, I need to talk to you."

"What about son?"

"The wildcat. He jumps on me almost every afternoon. I'm scared of it."

"Has he ever hurt you?"

I would have been ashamed to say the minor scratches on my chest and back constituted anything injurious. I didn't mention the marks and answered, "No sir."

Dad concluded the counseling session, "Seems to me the wildcat won't hurt you. When he jumps on you, just shoo him away." Dad walked away to tend to more pressing matters.

I should have mentioned that the damned animal often knocked me down during his jumping routine. But I concluded my help session with my father was not going to be of any real help, and I should have predicted the outcome of my talk with him. Dad usually left his children to their own devices to solve a problem. My problem was Dad's pet.

The Hunted becomes the Hunter

I was losing the freedom to walk around the ranch house, as well as the barns, gardens, and orchards—my turf, my game preserve. The wildcat was holding me prisoner in my own territory. The incarceration affected most of my waking moments. I became scared to venture outdoors. With this fear, also came anger.

I'm not by nature an aggressive person; never have been. But many years ago, I developed this sense of: *You leave me alone, I'll leave you alone*. Perhaps it came from my being little for most of my life and hoped playground bullies would indeed leave me alone. From those rough times on the playground and in other parts of my life I developed a resolve to "hang in there." But I also know that I developed another sense of: *Enough is enough*. I still have these traits in my personality.

Anyway, for this story, I finally said, in both anger and fear, *enough is enough!* So, I came up with a solution: I decided to take off my hat as the ranch's unofficial game warden and became its unofficial game hunter.

We had several .22s, .30-.30s, shot guns, and pistols in our house. This arms cache was not locked up and household members were knowledgeable in the proper use of each gun. I was restricted to the use of .22 rifles. The other guns were too powerful for me to fire without assistance from an adult or my brothers.[4]

I selected one specific day to execute my solution: The big people were on the ranch's pastures—away from the house, performing their chores. On this opportune afternoon, I took one of the .22 rifles from its place, loaded it, and walked into my game preserve—the preserve now under assault by the wildcat. But the stalkee had just become the stalker. The hunted was now the hunter.

What a sense of empowerment I had! I will never forget the exhilarating sensation I felt on that summer day. It was not the decision to shoot something in general that gave me this sense of elation. My excitement came from my decision to shoot something specific: the wildcat. I had killing on my mind; revenge was in my gun sights.

I'm certain my self-satisfaction came partly from the realization I was trying to deal with a situation which had been out of my control. As I've gone through life I've discovered I deal with adversity well, as long as I'm actively involved in trying to make things better for my situation. I become disconcerted when I don't take action or when I don't know what action to take. Many people can live with these ambiguities. So can I, but my preference is to put them to rest, so that I can rest.

As I ventured into the yards around the house to stalk my prey, it became evident he was also stalking me—just the situation I wanted. Walking through Dad's orchard in the front of the house, I spotted the cat in a bush to my right.

I had the rifle loaded, with the safety off. I would have preferred the wildcat to be positioned to my left, because I was right-handed and it would have made for an easier mark. No matter, I was a good shooter, and as I saw the outline of the wildcat, I raised the gun and drew a sight on it.

At about the time I pulled the trigger, the cat moved downward and forward in the bush. I was aiming for the head, and as the shot went off, I think the bullet went just over his shoulder. It might have hit the shoulder.

The end result was the near destruction of one of Dad's bushes as the wildcat snarled, growled, and trashed around. I thought he was fast when he had attacked me. The cat was even faster on this occasion. He turned on the afterburners as he catapulted himself from the bush.

He ran toward a dirt water tank and its surrounding bushes—about 100 feet from my first assault. I pursued, and after running about 50 feet, stopped and took another shot. The cat was running like hell but not executing any evasive zigzag motions (no wonder we humans are higher up on the food chain than lowly wildcats). But he was moving fast and my shot missed, passing over and hitting some dirt beyond him.

I pursued the wildcat to the water tank. I rustled around the bushes, excited that I had it on the run. I had turned the tables on my predator. I was on a hunter's high, ready to do-in my prey. To this very day, I find it difficult to describe the elation I felt during those moments. I was free! I could claim-back my game preserve.

Enter my Guardian Angel

Because the big people were far away from the house, I assumed my shots would not be heard. I was a kid and I had not thought this through. I was focused. My plan was that if I killed the cat, I would bury its carcass. No one would ever know. The perfect murder!

Sometimes, eight-year-olds are protected from their folly by an especially designated guardian angel. In this case, it was the ranch cook, Wanda. I had forgotten about her. Wanda had been sitting in her bunkhouse on the other side of the main house, and upon hearing the shots, she walked to the front yard to investigate. As she came into my view, I was foraging around in the bush by the water tank, still looking for the wildcat. I spotted Wanda and began to return to the reality of the moment, leaving the fantasy world of the big-game hunter.

Wanda was a lively, high-spirited woman and the wife of one of the hired hands, Bill. She liked me and I liked her. We had become confidants over the past few weeks and I often told her about my adventures with the bugs, birds, snakes, and other wild life I encountered. She became my surrogate mother during that summer. But I had not shared my plans for the wildcat hunt with her. I thought Wanda would disapprove. In hindsight, I am sure she saved me from a father's wrath.

Wanda approached me and asked, "Honey, what in the world are you doing with that gun?"

In my excitement, I blurted out, "Shooting a wildcat!"

As soon as I uttered this statement, I knew I had blown my cover. During my excitement, I had lost my composure.

"Any luck?"

" I might have hit it. I'm sure I scared it."

"Your Dad is awfully fond of that wildcat."

Oh? I had never thought of my Dad as a person who would show affection toward a pet. He hardly demonstrated warmth to his horses, by far his favorite animals. But the situation began to permeate my immature mind. Yes, my father would not take too kindly to my shooting his pet. But, as I said, I was not entirely obtuse about the matter, as I intended to bury the body, so no one would find it. I certainly did not think Dad would grieve over a missing varmint.

The situation had changed. With the cook's intervention, I began to have reservations about my solution to the wildcat problem. My fear of the wildcat was replaced with my fear of Dad's knowing of my recent safari. I didn't know what to say to the cook. Instead of explaining my well-justified plan, I responded with an embarrassing silence. I was certain she would be obligated to tell my father about the incident.

It is not without good reason that I called Wanda my guardian angel. She came up with a solution to my new fear, "Let's keep this to ourselves. We take the gun back to the house. If anyone heard the shots, we'll tell them we were doing some target practice. If the wildcat is hit, your lips are sealed—it might have been shot by a neighbor—who knows? I wouldn't mention your wildcat hunting to anyone … not even your brothers—especially not your brothers. If you do, I think you may be in for a big whipping. As for me, my lips are sealed."

Enough said. My lips were also sealed. Luckily, as it turned out, no one else heard the shots. And Wanda? I bet from her perspective, she thought my shooting an innocent critter was wrong. But she was my friend, and she protected me from a father's certain wrath. As Mark Twain said, "The proper office of a friend is to side with you when you are in the wrong." I was very lucky to have Wanda as my friend.

Free at Last

The wildcat didn't show itself around the ranch that day, or the next, or the next. I had frightened it away or killed it. He was gone! I could now walk through my preserve without fear of being attacked by the animal.

During the next few days, usually during supper, Dad would bring up the subject of his wildcat or rather the subject of the absence of his wildcat. He wondered what happened to it. The people at the table offered some opinions on the matter (except the game warden, whose lips were sealed). One of the hired hands suggested the cat was more wild than tame, and anyway, it probably ran away to find a mate. As he told the story, he glanced at me, and then the cook, who was tending the table. Dad seemed to accept this possibility.

Who was this hired hand? He was Bill, the husband of the cook. As he talked to Dad about the fate of the wildcat, as I watched him glance at me, then his wife, I realized he had become my second guardian angel.

I never told Dad about my shooting at his wildcat. I had forgotten about the episode until I started writing stories about my youth and began thinking about my adventures on the ranch.

I wish I had told my father this story before he died. He had a keen sense of humor and I think he would have liked the story about my battle with his wildcat. Nonetheless, I would have waited until he was in his older, less formidable years. Because who knows? Dad may have loved that SOB.

---

[1] Don't mistake me for an anti-hunter zealot. I'm a proponent of (controlled) hunting. In our present over-populated country, hunting is a reasonable way to keep humans and the hunted wildlife in an acceptable balance.

[2] I also learned later that a bounty was paid for each pair of coyote ears sent to a government office. The reward was $2.00, plus the hunter's satisfaction of exterminating an animal that attacked his livestock.

[3] The terms wildcat and bobcat are used synonymously in this story.

[4] I recall an unexpected recoil from a 12-guage shot gun shot. It knocked me back a couple feet. My gun buddies (Dad's hired hands) let out a laugh about my surprise. But they were not mean about my deficiency. They then told me more about the recoil of guns' firing and about sightings. Thanks to these men, I became a fine marksman.

7

CORNERED BY A STUD

The horse has too many caprices, and he is too much given to initiative.
He invents too many ideas. No, I don't want anything to do with a horse.

—*Mark Twain*

At last, you are going to learn why I hated Dad's stud horse. Notwithstanding this scoop, the explanation is going to be difficult to write because I must explain why I *don't like horses* in general. There, I said it. And my confession was not as difficult as I thought it would be. But then, I am making this statement to my computer and a word processing program—not to my family and other horse lovers.

If an acquaintance learns I spent part of my early childhood on a ranch in New Mexico, and discovers my father was a horseman, they invariably ask if I still ride. My answer: No. If the opportunity presents itself, I add I don't like to be around horses; they bring-up unpleasant memories of my past.

As I write this sentence, I have not told my family and close friends about my views on horses. After all, how many people claim they don't like horses? To say so is almost un-American and not what one would expect to hear from a person who spent some of his childhood years on a cattle and horse ranch.

Horse Lovers Galore

I have trouble expressing my attitude about horses. Since my childhood I have been conditioned—like a Pavlovian laboratory subject—to believe horses are inherently good (the animal kingdom's version of Rousseau's Noble Savage). Horses are all-American. Horses are masculine (even mares). Horses personify America and the West. And the crowning claim: Horses are often ridden by cowboys. What person in this great country can speak against such icons as the fabled cowboy and the cowboy's horse?

If DNA were a factor, I would be a supreme horseman. I am genetically disposed to adore horses, to love riding them, and to be adept in handling them. My father was an excellent rider, a skilled rodeo performer, as well as a horse breeder. I have numerous friends and relatives who made their living working with horses.

Several of my brothers are cowboys. Brother Ed is a fine horse trainer. He once owned a horse named Jeep Jr. who performed stunts in rodeos, and is shown in Figure 7-1. Brother Tom was a talented steer wrestler and roper. Brother Jim owned a couple of cattle ranches, first in New Mexico, and later in Florida.

I rode my share of horses and was around these animals a considerable part of my early life. I state this fact because I don't want you to think my role of a horse critic is taken from an uninformed viewpoint. Unlike many critics, I know my subject.

I lived in a part of America where the horse reigned supreme. Little Texans and Big Texans took to their horses like Hindus take to their cows. If I were to have spoken the truth about my feelings toward the equine creature, I would have been branded un-American and most likely, a wimp. For certain, my masculinity would have been questioned. I was well aware of this fact and kept my views about horses to myself. Also, until I was around nine years of age, horses were favored animals, ranking very high in my private poll of nifty critters.

To make matters more difficult for a horse critic living in a horse-loving country, I cannot recall hearing anyone in Lea County utter a negative word about horses in general. Of course, a person could

Figure 7-1. Jeep Jr. with Ed.

disparage an individual horse without fear of being ostracized. For instance, "Damn, that horse is dumb. I don't like it."

But to disparage the horse as a group—that was taboo. For instance, the statement, "Damn, horses are dumb. I don't like them," was bordering on blasphemy.

Old Baldy: Horse of Five World Champions

The rodeo arena: A courser's stage. The horse's rostrum. A pony's platform for prancing. And in Lovington, New Mexico, a monument for a national hero. As you might have guessed, it's a monument to a horse. Not only is it a monument, a horse is buried there! Why? Because the horse carried five men to world championship roping fame. I will let this eulogy about Old Baldy speak for itself about the reverence for horses in my childhood home.[1] Take a look at Figure 7-2 while you read this praise; it is a picture of Old Baldy.

> Baldy was the greatest. He was gentle and kind around the ranch, but not many ropers could rope off him. He had such a terrific stop that not many were able to do much more than ride him, much less to think about catching a calf ... Volumes could be written about Baldy. He was born in Oklahoma and is well known there. One roper near Plains, Texas thought so much of Baldy that he went to Oklahoma to see Baldy's brother! When arena gates open on rodeos and ropings this year (1961), Old Baldy won't be there.

As the mesquite grass turns green and soft winds of spring blow across the range, the familiar sight of Old Baldy will be missing. Baldy is laid to rest where he was most at home.

A Horse by any other Name is Still a Horse (but Elizabeth Taylor is only Elizabeth Taylor)

Is that reverence or what? Part of my aversion to horses is my distaste for society's propensity to revere things that do not warrant being revered, although I must admit that Old Baldy's press clippings are impressive. Aside from this exception (and to keep myself in a somewhat favorable light with the Old Baldy Fan Club members, as well as my relatives), let's discuss other examples of erroneous reverence: baseball and golf.

I don't consider baseball and golf as anything more than games. Yet, too often, they are described as something well beyond what they actually are. When I watch the World Series or tune into the Masters Golf Tournament on TV, I could easily mistake Jim Palmer and Jim Nance for Oral Roberts and Pat Robertson. For example, the sycophantic junk uttered by the commentators about the Masters is enough to make one ill. You would think Amen Corner is a church. As another example, Ken Burns' salute to baseball resembles a religious genuflection. I like baseball and golf but I dislike their being elevated to a status that borders on religion or heroism.

Figure 7-2. Old Baldy.

The same goes for horses. If the fantastically beautiful Elizabeth Taylor can fall in love with a horse in the movie *National Velvet*, could there not be anything amiss about the horse?[2] The critter has been given a status well beyond what an insignificant male member of the human race can ever hope to attain.

By the way, I wish Ms. Taylor had also performed in the *Black Beauty* movie. If so, with her raven hair, this stunning woman would have been named Black Beauty, not the horse. If I were the head of the movie studio where Ms. Taylor graced her presence, she could have named her price for making a picture.

As you can see, it is easy for me to lose my train of thought when thinking about Elizabeth Taylor. I will wrap up this part of my argument by stating that horses do not warrant being revered but Elizabeth Taylor does. And I was tempted to place a picture of the youthful Ms. Taylor in this chapter as a welcome change of pace, but decided against it, because the subject is primarily about horses.

To continue my discussion about horses, name a book or film about horses that is not one of complete veneration for the horse? If there is a bad-guy horse in the plot, it is rapidly defeated, culled, and exiled from the herd by the good-guy horse. (*And there, on yonder slope, the renegade stands, looking forlornly into the distance at a herd of mares and the herd's one very lucky stallion*).

My point is that, like bad people, there are bad horses. Some are gentle, kind, and smart; and some are ornery, selfish, and mean. Some are even dangerous, just like people.

Diagnosis: Anxiety Reaction

I may have forced myself to dislike horses because, during my youthful love affair with them, I was not allowed to ride a horse into the pastures of our ranch. Under the watchful eyes of adults or big brothers, my riding was confined to pens and the small rodeo arena on our ranch.

Dad did not permit me to accompany him, my brothers, and our hired hands to the far reaches of the ranch to tend to their chores. Often, they went on horseback and I was left at the ranch house in the company of my stick horse. I was seven years old, and was not allowed to ride horses unless accompanied by an older (and larger) person.

Being a resourceful kid, I made mental adjustments about my separation from the men and my confinement to a make-believe world. My rationalization, "Who cares about riding out into the pastures with those cowboys? Who cares that my Dad and brothers are riding their horses on the prairies, amongst the sagebrush, probably shooting rabbits and coyotes, maybe even shouting 'Yippie, ti, O, get along little doggie,' living the American dream, just like I see in the Saturday afternoon movies? Who cares that I am on a horse ranch but not riding horses? Who cares about spending the night at the remote parts of the ranch, camping out, and cooking on an open fire? "

The only image lacking in my fertile imagination was Roy Rogers sitting next to me by the campfire—singing *Happy Trails*, and Trigger nudging my cowboy hat playfully with his nose. It did not enter my mind that the work on those pastures was bone tiring and often boring. For example, digging fence post holes in the dry, rock-filled ground for days at a time. No matter, I recall on more than one occasion telling myself I was just as well-off back at the ranch house— that I did not like horses anyway.

Some Specifics about Specific Horses

A reasonable question at this point in my story is, "What have you got against horses, other than the fact that their reputation is better than yours?"

Point well taken. Let's leave the abstract arguments aside and get down to the brass tacks of the matter. I have four specific grievances against horses: (1) When I was four years old, I was kicked in the head by a horse, rendering me unconscious, (2) When I was nine years old, I was almost stomped to death by a horse, (3) When I was ten years old, a horse ran away with me as the rider. I fell off the horse to save myself from migrating to Mexico. (4) When I was eleven years old, I was bucked off and stepped on by a horse.

Let's hear the gory details. By the time I have finished, you might not care for horses either. To keep this tale as a short story, I will tell you about two experiences. I listed the four episodes cited above as ammunition for my argument against unbridled horse loving.

Kicked in the Head

Episode number one occurred when our family's all-time favorite horse named Cricket, an adored pet, kicked me in the head. Cricket. Who could not admire a horse named Cricket? In addition to being named after a whimsical insect, Cricket was a gentle horse, noted for her tender nature. She was a beautiful horse as well. How could I have been kicked by a lovely horse that had the credentials of a pacifist?

Because Cricket was not exactly a pacifist. She did not like people walking behind her. I didn't know this fact; my family had not enrolled me in the School of Cricket Behavior. Even more, to the time of her untimely kick to my head, Cricket was my buddy and I rode her often.

Unfortunately, one day I was wandering about in the pen where Cricket was kept and I walked behind her as she was feeding. A well-placed kick with her back leg to my head put me in a coma. I remember the kick but little afterwards. The first thing I recall was lying on the ground in Cricket's pen, with my parents and brothers looking over me. The second thing I remember was lying in my bed, with the same set of people hovering overhead.

To be fair, I imagine Cricket meant no offence. She was probably thinking, *Stay away from my rear end kid. I have a suspicious nature; what the hell are you doing back there anyway?*

I had now graduated from the School of Cricket Behavior. I never looked at Cricket again with the same affection as I did before the kick.

Cornered by a Stud

I recovered from Cricket's kick and I was still fond of horses, but I made it a practice to stay in front of them. Five years later, I began to harbor doubts about my beloved critters poll and the esteemed position occupied by the horse in my rankings. Again, the problem came about because I did not attend the school of horse behavior—specifically the School of Wompus McCue behavior—my Dad's prized roping horse and one of his favorite breeding studs.

Not yet schooled in how Wompus behaved, I made the mistake of inviting myself into his pen. As a general practice, I wandered in and out of most of our pastures and pens without concern and free from harm (except for our bull pasture—whose inhabitants were even meaner than Wompus). I petted the horses; most of them were receptive to my attention; others ignored me.

Wompus is the villain in this story. He is the reason I am emotionally detached from horses. He is the main reason for my stating, "I don't like horses." Let's cut to the chase and fill-in the details: Wompus almost killed me.

Wompus McCue was a beautiful, black-haired, powerful Quarter Horse. He stood almost 15 hands high, and weighed-in at about 1,300 pounds. In those days of the late 1940s, a Quarter Horse of this height and weight was considered to be about average; not huge, but not small.[3] The striking characteristic of Wompus' physical makeup was his muscles. He was an equine Charles Atlas. His neck, chest, buttocks, and leg muscles were as big and well formed as any horse my family owned then, or has owned since. His hindquarters were massive, laden with horsepower.

The striking characteristic of Wompus' mental make up was his bad temper. He was a mean and spiteful horse. He was also a bully. On one occasion, Wompus bit into another horse that was occupying a stall adjacent to him. Wompus would not let go of the neck of this horse, in spite of the victim's efforts to free itself.

The strength of his bite and grip was awesome. Without avail, Dad whipped Wompus with a rope to persuade him to stop his attack. Finally, Dad resorted to punching his neck with a pitchfork; only then did the stud release his bite and make a retreat.

A pitchfork! Not only was this horse mean, it was tough and stubborn.

I didn't know about Wompus' disposition. Had I an inkling of his temperament, I would have kept my distance from him. But I was enamored of horses and had no fear of them (as long as I did not venture toward their posteriors).

One morning, I paid a visit to the pen where Wompus was located. Instead of confining my hospitalities to the outside of his pen, I blithely slipped between the boards in the gate to say hello and pet this beautiful animal.

The front of the pen consisted of a wall of corrugated tin and a wooden gate. Horizontal boards were nailed to the gate's fame every foot of so, providing gaps for a little person to slink through. The two sides of the pen were closed-off by tin walls. The back of the pen was constructed of conventional wood boards, also separated by gaps.

As I crawled through the gate, the horse trotted from the back of the pen to examine me. Ignorant of Wompus' nature, I lifted my arm to pet his face and was knocked to the ground by a swipe of his head. I found myself in the forward corner of his pen— surrounded by two tin walls. I had no way to crawl out; Wompus had me cornered; he blocked possible escapes to the gate or the back of the pen.

The next few seconds were a formative experience in my affair with horses. Wompus kicked at me with his right front hoof. He hit the side of the pen, making a loud clanging noise. In hindsight, I think Wompus was playing around, something like a killer whale toying with a dolphin before the kill.

Whatever the stud's motives or intentions may have been, I was scared out of my wits and had no idea what to do. I was afraid to move, yet afraid not to move. Lacking any attractive alternative, I lay frozen in front of the stallion.

Enter the Bodyguard

At precisely the time Wompus executed what I think was his experimental kick—before he got down to some serious stomping, a twelve-year old bodyguard undertook some rescue actions.

On more than one occasion, my brother Tom had served in an unofficial capacity as my bodyguard. His job entailed chasing away playground bullies who threatened or otherwise bothered me. He did not chase them away so much as chase them down. Tom was a fleet-footed youth, and a fine fighter. The chase invariably ended by Tom overtaking and exchanging blows with the slower-footed boy. In truth, the exchange was mostly one-way: From Tom to the former bully.

Tom is also a person who shows coolness and composure in crisis situations. I am happy to report he displayed this trait early in his life—especially on the day I found myself in dire straits with Wompus.

My brother was nearby when I slipped into the pen but he didn't have time to warn me to stay outside, or to restrain my actions. As I made my way through the gaps in the gate and found myself inside the pen, he shouted, "Get out of there!" Too late. I had been felled and cornered by the stud.

Tom had the presence of mind to stay out of the pen and divert the horse's attention to himself. As soon as Wompus made his hostility known, Tom yelled and pounded the wooden gate and tin sides on the front of the pen. The noise distracted and irritated the horse; he turned his attention from the interloper to the noisemaker.

I wasted no time in taking advantage of Tom's diversionary tactics. Springing up, I sprinted to the back of the pen. As I was crawling through one of the gaps in the wall, I looked back and saw Wompus racing toward me. He was mad, irritated, heated, livid, angry—generally pissed-off. His ears were pinned back and his eyes were blazing.

I thought, "Too late you. ..." ... Adding my recently learned moniker for poisonous snakes, obnoxious buck sheep, stealthy wildcats, and mean horses, "... son-of-a-bitch!"

By the time he had made it to the back of the pen, I had slipped through the back wall and was standing safely out of his reach—out of harm's way. But I was shaken. It took a while for me to gain my composure and several days passed before I started petting and riding the (other) horses. Thereafter, horses lost their esteemed position in my private poll of favorite critters.

Life went on, and I slowly distanced myself from horses. Losing interest in them during my teenage years, I turned by attention to more attractive and gentler (two-legged) creatures. As an adult, my work and hobbies kept me away from New Mexico, Lea County, and horses.

I Sorta Like Horses

In my later years, I began to write stories about my life in New Mexico and Lea County. Horses had to be part of the tales. When I began writing the story you are reading, I called my brother Ed to obtain some background information about Cricket and Wompus. After providing me with this information, he asked what I was up to and I informed him, "Ed, I'm writing a story about why I don't like horses."

You would think I had just mooned Ed over the telephone line. Ed is the most devoted horseman I know. He lives, eats, and dreams horses. He can talk about horses for hours, actually for days. He remembers each horse he has trained, every race it ran, even its family tree—going back to many previous generations. He is also the first person in my family whom I told about my dislike for horses.

After the declaration to my brother, there was a brief silence from the other end of the line. Ed then responded, "Eh, … you like horses a little bit don't you?"

Do you now see my point about the delicate situation I have about expressing my aversion to horses? Maybe I should have kept quiet and let sleeping dogs lie, or in this case horses. My brother could not come to grips with the fact that someone in his own family was flat-out stating that he did not like horses. His simple sentence and its intonation was replete with meaning.

As I framed a response to Ed's question, I recognized I couldn't say I did not like horses—an essential and revered animal in the lives of many people in my family. My response was well-meaning, phony, half-hearted, "Oh, Ed … no, actually, I sorta like horses." Uyless Black: A human Switzerland.

After I finished my introduction to this story and as I composed its content, I came to realize that I respect horses. I do "sorta" like them. I am not enamored of horses but I have a high opinion of them. I admire their independence and I appreciate the fact that they (like the cat) have never been fully domesticated. They are high-spirited and proud animals and don't like to take a lot of guff from us humans.

It would have been a privilege to have met and been in the company of Sea Biscuit and I suspect Old Baldy as well. Black Beauty and the beautiful Arabian horse in *The Black Stallion* are okay in my book. The horse in *National Velvet* would have been high in my private poll of admired creatures (but not nearly as high as the horse's rider, Velvet Brown (AKA Elizabeth Taylor).

Nonetheless, Wompus McCue still looms in my mind and while I have come to the conclusion that I (sorta) like horses, I still prefer to keep my distance from them. Pavlov could not have said it better: Conditioning dies hard.

Postscript

Horses have personalities. Like dogs, some are ornery, some are not; some are gentle, some are not. While horses do not kowtow as much as dogs, they surely show trust and affection toward humans; usually if they have been treated kindly. Most are submissive and will follow the lead of their master.

Most people don't pay enough attention to the animals around them and how they use many mechanisms to communicate with us. Some of them are very intelligent.

Most horses will stop on a dime for us, if they trust and like us. But if that trust is broken, stay out of their way.

Like most people, horses need companionship. My brother Tom, a fine horseman, tells me he has seen horses that chew the boards of the pen, simply out of boredom. He has another story about a lonesome horse who welcomed a newcomer to his pen: a goat. And why not? We humans take-in pets to assuage our spirits. Why can't horses as well?

---

[1] *The Lovington Leader*, January 18, 1961.

[2] Of course, like all of us, Ms. Taylor has aged. Perhaps the best defense to growing old is to remember those years of youth.

[3] Quarter Horses are not as tall as Thoroughbreds, because they have been bred to be workhorses. Thus, they are usually bulkier and not as lanky as Thoroughbreds. By the way, a hand is about four inches (in the past it was just over four inches, but the practice now is to round-off the number).

8

THE CARNIVAL

———◆———

Grief can take care of itself; but to get the full force of joy
you must have somebody to divide it with.

—*Mark Twain*

The day was ending for the small prairie town. Rush hour, such as it was, had passed. A receding sun cast a soft glow onto the nearly deserted roads of the community. As the street lights gradually made their presence known to the early evening, a young boy could be seen walking through the quiet town square, using the remaining light of the day to find his way toward the city limits. Just beyond the town's buildings, across a flat horizon, he saw other lights, their colors mixing with the faint residue of the disappearing sunset. As these lights caught the boy's eye, they evoked past memories of pleasant times.

The boy left the town and made his way toward the lights—his neon oasis. During the walk, he experienced a sense of anticipation, one of excitement. For many months, he had waited for this night and another visit to those lights.

Each step down a dirt road brought the glow of the lights into a clearer focus. As he neared his destination, he heard music; the melodies from the calliope were similar to those he had listened-to a year ago. The smells came next. A slight breeze brought forth the scents of dust and manure, the smell of tent canvas, and the fragrance of cotton candy.

The walk from the town square to the lights did not take long, but long enough to test the boy's patience. His excitement peaking, and unable to contain himself, he broke into a run, making the remaining distance to his goal in a few seconds. After sprinting to the oasis entrance, he slowed to a walk, and took it all in.

The lights were now brilliant. Illuminating the surrounding tents, rides, and concession stands, they dispersed any shadowed ambiguity that had lingered in the boy's memory. The music surrendered its identity as it mixed with other noises, the yells and laughter of people, the whine of machinery, and the shouts of barkers. The smells, at first quite pungent to his nose, quickly succumbed to nasal fatigue. The child's senses were overloaded as he marveled at a splendid cacophony of sights, smells, and sounds.

Taking in this glittery dissonance, the boy knew he was in for another adventure. It was finally here. The carnival had come back to town.

The Small Town Carnival

Such were the impressions of an eight-year old boy about the carnival that came to my hometown of Lovington each fall. I suppose if I were to return today to that same spot and that same carnival, my reactions might be different. Perhaps I would not be so impressed, so awed. But who knows? I still like going to a carnival and I am keen on playing the carnival games.

Carnivals were an integral part of the lives of most families who lived on the Llano Estacado and Little Texas. Because external entertainments were few and far between, a carnival was a special happening, especially for the youngsters in the area. In my hometown, the carnival pitched its tents just east of Lovington's city limits. Once up and running, it featured sideshows, games, a Ferris wheel, a merry-go-round, a tilt-a-whirl, and a pony ride for kids. Occasionally, the carnival displayed animals as part of the entertainment. An organ grinder and its monkey were usually present, stationed at the entrance to the carnival to welcome the customers.

I recall one year the carnival featured an elephant. That was it. Other than the ponies and the monkey, no other animals were on display; just the elephant. This show advertised itself as a "Carnival and Circus." I guessed the reason for the addition of the title "Circus" was the presence of the elephant—the monkey and ponies were not glamorous enough to justify the name Circus in the show's title.

The carnival games were the same as they are today. Its customers could be seen shooting darts at balloons, tossing rings around bottles, and pitching coins into saucers. A shooting gallery was part of the carnival, as were cotton candy machines, hot dog stands, and a weight guesser.

Questions lingered in my mind about the carnival and the carnival people. Where did they sleep? How did they bathe? Did they eat hot dogs whenever they wished? Did they have to pay for their cotton candy? Could they take rides free? I had seen children playing around the carnival and sitting in some of the game tents. They were carnival children, or as we natives called them and their parents: *Carnies*. Given the carnival's moving to a different town each week, how did these kids manage to go to school? Did they even attend school?

My questions were almost endless but I had no answers because no one in my hometown knew very much about Carnies.

A Visit with a Boa Constrictor

During the week the carnival was in town, I did my best to attend each day. With an exception here and there, Mom restricted my attendance to a couple visits during the week and one on the weekend. Usually, my older brothers Tom or Jim would accompany me. But they were not taken with the carnival as much as I, so I sometimes went alone. Truth be known, I enjoyed the carnival more when my brothers were along; it was more fun to share a ride than take it alone.

On one of these occasions, Tom and I walked across town to take in the carnival's offerings. It was in the early afternoon.

Arriving ahead of the crowd, we milled about, trying to decide how to spend our money. We were big spenders; each of us had a pocketful of coins. Maybe as much as 25 to 35 cents.

We drifted over to a sideshow featuring: a dwarf; a giant; a combination sword swallower/flame eater; a bearded lady; a fully-tattooed man; a two-headed, dead calf; a one-headed, pickled albino monkey (also dead), and a large, live boa constrictor snake—all under one tent. And for one admission fare. Such a deal!

This show was the main feature of the carnival. It was housed in the biggest tent and occupied a prime spot on the grounds—overall a very impressive sight to an eight-year old child. Notwithstanding the grandiosity of the spectacles, the admission fee of 15 cents was beyond our limited entertainment budget—especially if we wanted to take-in other shows or rides.

For a brief time, we watched the barker, positioned in front of the tent, hawking this show. Without question, he was the most bizarre looking person I had seen in my life. His face was covered with white and gray makeup. On his head was a stove-piped hat, like that of Abraham Lincoln. He sported a beard that fell past his waist. He wore a patch over one eye and a long, dangling earring in one ear. A pale yet friendly ghoul; I shall never forget him.

Tom and I knew the price of admission to the show was too high so we turned away from the barker to continue our search for cheaper thrills. Our leaving the scene left the barker with no one in front of his tent.

Immediately, he called to us, "Boys, what interests you the most?"

Tom responded, "The snake."

Not to lose a remuneration opportunity during a slow day, the barker said, "Tell you what I'll do. For 5 cents each, I'll let you hold the snake, a fine boa constrictor."

What? The barker had the transaction proposal reversed. I would have expected to be paid to handle his serpent.

Snakes. Omnipresent reptiles, ever present in my favorite playing places around our town home and on our ranch. There were very few critters I didn't like. The snake was number one on this list. Tom was of a different opinion. He thought having a boa constrictor wrapped around his body was a fine idea, "Come on, let's take a closer look at that snake."

"Eh, Tom," I wanted to say, "There's a reason the boa constrictor is called a boa *constrictor*. It constricts! That's how it gets along in life." Of course, I didn't make such a clever response because I had not yet been exposed to Clint Eastwood's cool retorts. Plus, I was still learning the English language.

The proposal was okay for Tom because he was pretty big. But I was the size of large monkey; the perfect symmetry for a boa's constricting operations. However, when confronted with a suggestion from my brothers, I was (once again) a human Switzerland, acquiescing to almost anything they proposed. Admittedly, I did not like this proposal but I went along, just for the ride—or in this case, the snake's ride.

Tom agreed to the barker's proposal and after we each forked over a nickel to the man, he took us into the tent. Some of the so-called freaks were inside, waiting for a show to begin. Other than the sword swallower, Tom and I were the only normal looking people present.

Without further talk, the barker took the snake from its cage, brought it to us, and placed it on Tom's shoulders. Age before beauty, I was happy for Tom to go first.

The snake was not a large boa—perhaps four or five feet long, but large enough to intimidate me. My recollections of this specific snake were from the Tarzan movies I watched on Saturday afternoons at the local theater. I had not seen a boa constrictor do anything whatsoever to a human except squeeze the person to death.

As the snake settled on and around my brother's body, Tom broke out into a huge grin. He liked it! Incredible. I stepped back to witness the scene from a safer distance. Of course, nothing happened of dramatic interest. The barker was not about to lose his barking and snake showing licenses for a paltry nickel or two. Anyway, the snake did its snake-like things, slithering and all, and before long, the barker pulled the snake off Tom's body.

My turn had come to earn the loss of my nickel—the logic of the recent financial transaction continued to puzzle me. The barker lifted the snake from Tom and placed it on my shoulders. My first impression, other than fear, was how heavy the boa was. I'm sure it weighed more than I. My reaction to the snake? I stood still as a stone. It was not my intent to provoke the snake and give it an incentive to earn its name.

The boa was curious; it brought its head next to mine and began flicking its tongue on parts of my face. I wanted to scratch or rub the spots it touched because the reptile was actually tickling me, but I moved not a muscle.

Silent words drifted through my cranium. Forbidden words. Four letter words stricken from my Baptist proscribed vocabulary. And a practical question to myself, "What the—am I doing here!?"

My visit with the snake lasted perhaps one or two minutes but this brief time was my idea of eternity. Yet after the ordeal was over, and Tom and I were safely outside the tent, I was proud I had paid the nickel for the snake visit. I think Tom was pleased with me as well. The remainder of the afternoon activities—riding the Ferris wheel, throwing coins in a saucer, and shooting darts at balloons, proved to be anti-climatic.

A Carney comes to my Fifth Grade Class

During my fifth grade year, in the fall of 1949, I was a student in the elementary school class of Ms. Chambers. One morning, in the middle of a semester, a new student came to our class. He was assigned my desk at the front of the class. Other students (and I) were shifted back one row. The teacher had assigned me this front seat so she could keep an eye on me.

Viewed through my fifth grade eyes, the newcomer was a poor looking boy. His clothes were clean but not in the best shape. His hair was combed but long. Overall, he had the countenance of a well-groomed sad sack. He was shy and kept his eyes and head slanted downward, even when Ms. Chambers spoke to him.

The teacher introduced the boy to the class, "Children our new classmate is named Will. He will be with us for only this week. He came into town with the carnival."

What luck! Just in front of me, within touching and talking distance, was an actual carnival person. A Carney! I considered carnival humans to be mysterious, even exotic people. Now, my questions about Carnies could be answered. Even better, if I became acquainted with the boy, I might be able to attend the carnival with him.

I made it a point to take Will into my care—after all, he was going to show me the carnival ropes. During the first recess, I introduced myself and took him to the playgrounds where the fifth graders played.

It was during this recess that I learned about prejudice.

I don't recall knowing about bias and bigotry before I met Will. I'm certain I came across it often. Even though my parents and brothers didn't make comments about cultures, races, or religions—at least in my presence—I must have heard disparaging remarks about blacks and Mexicans by this time in my life.

Lea County was no exception to the fact that humans everywhere showed intolerance toward—well, just about everything. You name it: race, culture, religion, political philosophy, sports team, mammal, bird, insect, language, occupation, sexual preference, sexual position, vehicle choice, author, poet, playwright, coach, etc., and you can find someone who harbors an unfounded, ill-informed, and biased view on the subject. Later in my life, I made up a name of the illness that afflicts these people: *The Ignorant Therefore Prejudiced Syndrome.*

Will and I had not been on the playground for more than a minute when we heard someone shout, "Hey, Carney boy!" Followed by, "Why don't you take a bath?" Followed by, "Get out of town, you ain't welcome here." ... and so on. Several other taunts followed us around the playground, all coming from a group of boys from our class.

Bigotry is ignorance, pure and simple. The fact was, Will did not need a bath. He was not wearing wools and silks, but he was clean and groomed. I would have asked a question, but in a different way, "Where do you take a bath?" My question would have been intellectual, with no harm intended. The bigot's question was hurtful and meant to be so.

Why is it that a person will go out of his or her way to be spiteful—to deliberately hurt someone? I didn't understand when I was a child and I do not understand now. My only conclusion is that something seriously amiss happened to the human brain during its evolutionary development.

Will must have known these taunts were coming. I think he kept his head down for a reason, to avoid as much as possible any interaction with the outside world. After hearing these insults, Will froze for an instant, then kept on walking. He maintained his downward, silent look for the remainder of the recess and the morning's class. He seemed resigned to his fate, almost lethargic.

I was angry and frustrated with the behavior of my classmates. And I was sure of one thing. Will was not going to be subjected to more playground abuse; not on my watch. When the noon bell rang, I gathered Will and left the school grounds. I usually ate lunch at the school cafeteria. Not today. On this day, Will and I were going to my home. Mom did not know she was about to have a guest.

The walk home took a few minutes. Will and I talked about his life (of course). Some of my questions about carnival life were answered and Will seemed pleased that a non-Carney would show an interest in him.

I was nervous about coming home during the noon hour because visits during this time were not permitted. Often, Mom would be absent, working at her job. But on this day, she was home, surprised to see me, and of course, my new friend. I wasted no time telling her about Will's playground reception. Mom listened to my story and after I finished, she said, "If Will's folks approve, you two can come home for the noon hour for the remainder of the week."

Parents can be useful at times, even functional. Mom wrote two notes, one to Ms. Chambers, and one to Will's parents. We ate, returned to school, and prepared ourselves for the next four days of school. Mom's intercession did not solve the recess time on the playgrounds but her lunches kept us away from the playgrounds during the noon hour.

As it turned out, the remainder of the week was pleasant. The playground taunts died down; the taunters likely grew tired of shouting their insults. Will and I continued our friendship and the day after we met, he invited me to come to the carnival, as his guest.

He even gave me free passes for the Ferris wheel ride. My mentorship had worked out just fine. And I had a companion for my carnival visits. Not a big brother, who knew nothing about Carnies, but a Carny himself. As Mr. Twain suggested, I had someone with whom to divide my joy.

The next day, after school was let out, I accompanied Will to the carnival. I met Will's family. He had some siblings, and of course, a mom and dad. His father was in charge of the Ferris wheel. Will told me his dad's job was very important. Who was I to disagree? After all, the Ferris wheel was the most impressive ride at this small carnival.

Will took me behind the scenes. I learned there was a communal tent for eating. I learned they paid for their hot dogs and cotton candy, but not many selected this fare for their regular menu. I learned their admissions to the Ferris wheel and tilt-a-whirl were free but not many used these rides. I learned they could visit the sideshows free of charge but not many took advantage of this privilege.

I thought of asking Will, "What's the advantage of being a carnival person, if you don't take advantage of all these free things?" I suspected he and his comrades grew tired of eating cotton candy and riding a Ferris wheel, so I did not query my friend.

Continuing my investigation, I discovered the carnival workers lived in tents and trailers. Will's mom and dad owned their own trailer. The trailers did not have a full bath, so showers were set up for all the carnival personnel to use.

I was disappointed by my discoveries. The carnival people seemed normal, although some of them didn't look normal. I don't know what I expected—a fantasy had crept into my head about exotic persons. If one looks abnormal, one must be abnormal. I discovered this view was not an accurate observation. Indeed, some normal looking people exhibit very abnormal behavior.

Thanks to Will, brother Tom and I secured a job on the last night the carnival was in town. We helped disassemble the Ferris wheel. I was too little to do much heavy hauling, so Will's dad put me in charge of keeping account of various bolts and nuts. I think he was making up a job for me. As a bigger person, Tom was assigned more demanding chores.

In Later Years

As I entered my teenage years, the annual carnival visit did not hold as much interest. I still attended but my enthusiasm waned. As time passed and I grew older, I spent a few hours at local carnivals in Virginia, my home state, and took my son to some carnivals and theme parks.

While I was thinking about writing this story, it so happened that I was in Las Vegas, staying at the Circus Circus hotel. I took a tour of the hotel's circus/carnival. As I reflected on my fondness for the small carnivals in Lea County, as I thought of my excitement when I learned the carnival was coming to town, I wondered how I would have reacted to the fantastic cavalcade in the Circus Circus hotel? I am not sure I would have known how to contain myself. The variety of rides and sideshow games was almost overwhelming.

But something is missing from this modern carnival. It has none of the lights, smells, and sounds I recall from the old days. It is missing something as earthy as the mixed fragrance of cotton candy and dirt. Cement floors but no turf.

Another conspicuous absence was a sideshow. The ghoulish Abe Lincoln, the bearded lady, the tattooed man, and other freaks were not in attendance. I'm not certain the term "freak" is permitted in our politically correct society. Anyway, the old carnival sideshow freaks are now part of the American landscape. Why bother paying a fee to see them, when they are most likely just ahead of you in the grocery store checkout line?

In today's sterile climate, consider the difficulty of offering a boa constrictor as part of the show, specifically charging a fee to have it draped around a customer; especially an unaccompanied young boy. Imagine the lawsuits that could result if say, a customer fainted, or had a stroke as a result of an encounter with a harmless reptile.

As I walked through the Circus Circus pavilions, my mind went back to Will and his carnival. I wondered how he got along in life? I wondered if he overcame the bigotry he must have experienced time-and-time again? I wondered if he found a friend or two in his visits to other towns? I wondered if he was still being called a Carney?

9

CONFESSIONS OF A SOUTHERN BAPTIST

—————

Worship does not question nor criticize, it obeys.
—Mark Twain

*C*onfession Number One: **I am a Southern Baptist.**
I was baptized in the Baptist Church; as in Southern Baptist; as in evangelical Baptist. The area of the United States where I grew up, southeastern New Mexico, is located in the Bible Belt, a mecca for what is known today as Conservative Christianity or evangelicalism.

Oh yes, about my using the word "mecca." I mean mecca as in "mecca," an important center for a particular activity. Not as in "Mecca," the holy city of Islam. Hmm. In today's intolerant climate, I had better issue a disclaimer: *I do not intend to offend anyone's religion.* By the same token, I believe religions, like other institutions should be examined and critiqued. And I see no harm in poking fun at the pomposity of some religions and their shamans. Our criticisms of religions can only make them better, more receptive to our spiritual and physical needs.

I recognize some folks take the opposite view. They consider their religion to be out of bounds for discussion. At the same time, other religions are fair game for ostracism. Anyway, I trust you will not take offence if I say something critical about your religion. I merely. ... Hey you. Put away that gun!

Confession Number Two: I was a reluctant—and surprised— saved person.

I was baptized—physically immersed in the waters of salvation— when I was ten years old. The First Baptist Church of Lovington, New Mexico served as the venue for my lock on the Pearly Gates. For you readers who need a data-fill, Baptist baptism requires a person to be dunked under water. This ritual symbolizes purification and salvation. The baptized person is accepted into the Christian faith.

What makes my baptism unique was the fact that my mother was my floating mate in the baptismal water tank. That's right, my mother and I were sanctified and freed from sin with joint, successive swoops into the holy water.

On a momentous Sunday morning, the two of us together declared our intentions to be saved. Nonetheless, mother was the supervisor in charge of this part of my life. Toward the end of a Sunday morning service, the standard procedure kicked-in. The choir began singing a haunting hymn as the pastor informed the congregation its members had an opportunity to admit their sins, and to be freed from them—all in the same declaration. Mom and I were sitting together in a pew at the back of the church. Suddenly, she leaned down to me and declared, "U.D. it's time for us to be saved. Let's go."

Whoa Mom! But it was too late for me to offer counter comments such as, *"Hey, I'm only ten years old. I've got time on my side. Maybe you should be saying to yourself, it's time for you to be saved."* Nope. She pulled me up and off we went toward salvation.

Almost attached at the hip (well, my shoulder to her hip) we walked to the pulpit where Reverend Watts awaited our arrival. Many years later, I still recall the look on preacher Watts' face as he saw us approaching his cathedra: He had bagged a prize. I would wager he was saying to himself, *"Mother and son. All in one dipping. What a haul."*

At Reverend Watts' pulpit we confessed our sins and proclaimed we wanted to be saved. The preacher announced our intentions to the congregation, whose members gave Mom and me encouragement with exclamations of, "Amen!" and, "Praise the Lord!"

I will never forget the hymn being sung by the choir as we made our way up the aisle to Reverend Watts: *Softly and tenderly, Jesus is calling. Calling O sinner, come home ... Come home. Come home. Yea who are weary, come home ...* It was (is) a lovely song and very persuasive.

Weary ... come home. ... Although close to noon, it was still morning. I had awakened a short four or five hours ago. I was ten years old. I was not weary. And "home?" If I were to "come home," I would have walked toward the other end of the aisle toward our house on West Avenue D.

Without belaboring the issue, my point is how could a young child understand the metaphors of the song? Not to mention the profound issues surrounding being "saved?" I don't wish to be disrespectful toward religion. After all, many of its aims are to try to curtail the nasty behavior of us humans. But the fact remains that I was not very well informed about salvation.

In fairness, my Sunday school classes furnished a few tutorials on the subject. I absorbed enough data to conclude: Salvation was in and damnation was out. It was pretty simple. I opted for being saved, accompanied with the associated baptismal services.

Confession Number Three: Reverend Watts' sermons scared the hell out of me.

Reverend Watts' sermons scared the hell out of me. In addition to the Sunday school didactics on damnation and guilt, Reverend Watts often informed his congregation how rotten-to-the-core we were and how we were probably headed straight to hell. Especially because we had sinned the Saturday night before this Sunday morning.

I had considerable difficulty in accepting this accusation against me. My childhood sin on Saturday night was asking mother if I could stay up past my bedtime or fantasizing about a new bicycle. It made no difference to Reverend Watts that I was relatively sin free and that I was quite vulnerable to his sermons.

The shibboleths of his exhortations frightened me. I was ten-year old kid who was certain I was headed straight to a fiery, miserable Hades. In my adult years, I became a reluctant church goer until I discovered other denominations had less strident interpretations of religion.

Which might give you a hint as to why I am not a big fan of the "You are damned, hell-fire-and-brimstone" theory. It's too negative for me. I've enough problems in my present life without having to deal with an after-life of fright and misery.

Confession Number Four: My baptismal immersion was not all that spiritual.

The Sunday following our unconventional walk down Reverend Watts' aisle, Mom and I became Christians. Confession number four: I was not ready for this service. I had little understanding of its meaning and significance. But it made no difference to anyone in the church. After all (with my mother's strong encouragement), I chose to rise from my seat the previous week, walk down the aisle to the tune of *Sinner Come Home*, confess my supposed sins, and ask to be saved. Pastor Watts was not a mind reader. He couldn't know what I was thinking.

What *was* I thinking? Standing in the tank with Mom and the Reverend, decked out in a white cotton robe, listening to the music of the choir, hearing the preacher's spiritual prose that I was saved. … Well, I felt saved but I don't recall feeling all that spiritual.

Later, I confessed my baptism tank thoughts to my Sunday school teacher. Her response was a bit vague, something to this effect, *The preferred order is the spirit comes first, leading to the saving. But you've got it half-right. Just stick with it. Things will somehow work out.*

For the actual dunking, Mom preceded me. As she clamped her nose and closed her eyes, the pastor laid her down into the water. My turn was next. And sure enough, I was saved.[1]

Confession Number Five: My favorite church: The Assembly of God.

Our town home was located one block from The Assembly of God church. The pastor was Reverend Vowell, whose family lived next door to us. This church was a GD place of worship for me. I use GD and GU as initials for "geographically desirable" and "geographically undesirable". The Assembly of God was much closer to my house than the other churches in town; thus, it was geographically desirable—GD.

Mom was ahead of her time regarding religions. Maybe she was too liberal in your eyes because she permitted me to attend any church in town. I think she showed wisdom by encouraging me to experience and witness different church ceremonies and their contrasting kinds of worship.

My choice for a Sunday service usually depended on the religions of one of my friends. Because I had a wide variety of friends, I attended a wide variety of churches. Although I sat in on Presbyterian, Methodist, and Church of God homilies, I preferred the churches that had a lot of action and music.

The Assembly of God met both requirements. It was nicknamed the Holy Roller Church because some of the members, excited by the holy supplications from Minister Vowell, supposedly rolled in the aisles. I never saw any aisle rollers, but I watched many enthusiastic worshippers in various poses of standing, kneeling, sitting, dancing, bowing, genuflecting, and prostrating—while singing, chanting, and otherwise praising the Lord.

I found these worshippers to my liking. They were uninhibited and carefree; not worried if they shed the conventional strait laced, religious behavior found in the other churches.

I was a willing participant to the Holy Rollers' celebrations. I was in there with the best of them. Singing, semi-jumping, shouting; having a very good time. That is, until my older brother David accompanied me to a Sunday evening "concert." After watching his little brother cavort about in Christian joy for a half hour or so, he walked out of the church.

Shortly, I returned home to find him telling my family about my "silly, stupid Holy Roller" gesticulations. My older brother was making fun of me, mocking me. But what could one expect from someone currently enrolled in an effete (probably atheistic) Ivy League University? Nonetheless, lacking confidence in myself and my religious beliefs, and practically idolizing my older brother, I stopped attending the Assembly of God's joyful ceremonies and tried to content myself with Reverend Watts' somber, scary incantations.

Confession Number Six: I have been attending Catholic Masses.

Now, in the later years of my life, I occasionally attend Catholic Masses. I'm an aging Southern Baptist, an old dog trying to learn new tricks. Trying to learn about the protocols and rituals of Rome's favorite church; trying to understand purgatory, remedial Latin, and the admission of sin. Given my Southern Baptist background, I have had considerable experience with the latter subject.

But why the Catholic Church? Why not, say, the Methodist or Muslim creeds? Easy answer. My wife is a Catholic. My decision saves on gas.

Confession Number Seven: I found a Catholic ceremony that rivals the Assembly of God Service.

For a while, I considered starting my own church. After reading about the founders of several famous churches, I came to the conclusion my reasons for founding a church could be no weirder than theirs ... and I was certainly no weirder than they. But I decided there were enough churches, enough denominations and quite enough dogmas floating around. Truth is, I had nothing additional to offer to the ongoing inventory of religious faiths.

So, I continue to attend different churches. I watch religious ceremonies on television. I marvel at the tele-evangelists and preachers who have a direct filament to the firmament. I am impressed that they seem to know the answer to everything. But I wish they would not be so dogmatic with their dogma, that they would cut sinners a little slack. Sinners like Jimmy Baker and other tele-evangelists.

I've accompanied my wife to Sunday morning Catholic Masses in numerous parts of the world. One of my favorites is the Mass at the Roman Catholic Church in St. Thomas, Virgin Islands. It's a happy festive, semi-Assembly of God assemblage.

I've a couple other recommendations. Two Roman Catholic churches in Santa Fe, New Mexico. First, the St. Francis Church is one of the oldest churches in the United States. Upon entering this church I thought I was in Europe, because of its classical, beautifully antiquated architecture. Another recommendation is Santa Maria de la Paz. A stunning church, its architecture is a blending of modern and Southwestern styles.

But my main attraction to Santa Maria de la Paz is its music. The hymns are performed with a Mariachi band! I sat in this beautiful church and listened to joyful and happy Mariachi renditions of *What a Friend we Have in Jesus*, and even *There's a Church in the Valley*. For certain, I knew I was not at Reverend Watts' service in Lovington. I also had remembrances of the happy ambiences of the Assembly of God and St. Thomas ceremonies.

Three guitars, a bass, accompanied by Mariachi singers. All that was lacking was the Mexican yell, the Mariachi *grito* of "EEEEE. ... AAAHHH!"

I closed my eyes and thought I had been transported to a cantina in Juarez...a little bit of Heaven. Of course, the words to the music were different from the Mariachi songs. But the spirit was there. And after all, isn't that the purpose of religion?

---

[1] I recall Mom and I standing in the tank as Reverend Watt, also part of the water party, spoke to the congregation about our spiritual passage. I recall looking up to my mother. I smiled and then executed a slight knee bend into the water to wet the bottom of my baptismal frock. Mom was into the spirit of the moment and not into my interpretation of the spirits. She responded with a subtle but pronounced nod and grimace. I took the hint and thereafter took on a religious countenance.

10

WATER LIFE[1]

—·•·—

Unconsciously we all have a standard by which we measure (others),
and if we examine closely we find that this standard is a very simple
one, and it is this: we admire them, we envy them,
for great qualities which we ourselves lack.

—Mark Twain

The dive marked his passage from a world of noise and heat into a sphere of cool translucent silence. The next few seconds—coasting from the dive's momentum, gliding underneath the water's surface, flexing no muscles—left the swimmer with the sensation of an effortless soar though a chilled quiet Ether. The water's mass disavowed flying. It did not matter. His aqueous exploration was more exhilarating than flight.

For those brief moments, the swimmer knew why he swam, why he loved the water. These brief escapes into his underwater world were as fulfilling as anything he had experienced in his young life.

As the water's resistance began to work against the forward thrust of his dive, the swimmer's momentum slowed. He pulled his legs forward, spread them beneath his body and executed a frog kick. With his arms resting at his sides, the leg movement thrust him suddenly through the water—as if he were shot from a water cannon into yet more water. The kick carried him several yards and gave him another gliding respite through his water world.

As he slowed again, he combined his next leg kick with a frog-type arm movement. These actions propelled him to the other side of the swimming pool, where he surfaced—once again hearing the clamor of the public swimming pool and feeling the dry heat of a New Mexico summer day.

Learning to Swim

I learned to swim when I was six years old. In the 1940s, swimming at that age was considered to be a precocious marine event. Today's toddlers, recently wrinkled from their stay in the womb, are now executing Australian Crawls in swimming pools—their new aqueous habitats. It may not be too long before a newborn babe sidestrokes its way through mom's birth canal.

The first day I floated in water was also the first day I swam through it. My brother Tom and I were working and playing in one of the metal water tanks in the Wagon Pasture on Dad's ranch. The pasture was so-named because many years ago, several horse-drawn wagons had been left in the pasture, near the tank. A chuck wagon and several buckboards made up the inventory.

The wagons were falling apart and rotting-away. The staves of the chuck wagon, designed to support a long-gone cover, were now curved belts of rust. The large spoke wheels, yokes, and wagon seats were still intact and in fair shape. The wagons were one of my favorite playgrounds; second only to the nearby aquatic playground.

The water tank sides were about five feet high but on this momentous day, the water level was only two to three feet deep. The water had been drained in order to clear algae from the tank's sides and bottom. Tom and I were removing the green reside and waiting for the remaining water to empty.

Even though I was not yet a swimmer, I was a student of swimming and I had met the perquisites for learning to swim. First, I had watched my older brothers swim. From these observations, I formed a key idea about swimming: stay afloat. Second, I was not afraid to hold my breath under water. Third, for hour after hour, I had watched frogs swim in the tanks and rain puddles that were spread around the ranch.

The half-full tank provided an opportunity to prove if my observations of the frogs had been effective. Without much ado, I lay down in the water and started floating. At the same time, I initiated a rookie frog kick and propelled myself forward a few inches. Not only could I float, I could swim! After this fantastic experience, I surfaced, stood on my feet and shouted to my brother, "I can swim … Can you?"

Sibling competition; I knew Tom couldn't swim. I had bested my brother in an athletic event for the first (and only) time in my life. I recall Tom's surprised look after he witnessed my first aquatic launching. I had succeeded in an endeavor my brother had not yet mastered. Even more, I had accomplished this feat without help from anyone, except some frogs.

Success breeds confidence. It helps build one's ego, especially when facing the everyday accomplishments of five talented, older brothers. On a summer day in 1946, in a water tank located on an obscure ranch in New Mexico, I carved-out a place for my own identity. I forged a tool which helped me build confidence in myself. As I proceeded through life, I held on to that moment and found ways to reinforce it.

I'm now an old man. One could question the significance to my existence of a few minutes in a cattle tank on the arid plains of a southwest cattle ranch. Yet, how our lives unfold is often determined by a single event. A chance encounter with a kind soul; the succoring of a gifted teacher. They can change a person's destiny.

Earlier that morning my father had instructed my brother and me to drain and clean the tank. This one event set the path for much of my life.

My First Role Model

As you may have guessed, frogs were an important part of my life. They acted as swimming role models and I admired them greatly. I admit people have more acceptable role models. Abraham Lincoln, Mother Teresa, and Michael Phelps come to mind. I wasn't looking to frogs for political or divine guidance. I was looking to them for swimming guidance.

Thus, my first stroke was not the dog paddle or a crawl. It was the breaststroke, also known as the frog kick or the frog stroke. By studying the frog, I learned how to execute the breaststroke leg movement as well as anyone I encountered who swam this stroke.

I watched how frogs gained their acceleration through an outward, downward, then backward thrust of their legs, pushing the water away with their webbed feet. It occurred to me that some of their power came not only from their large feet, but also from pushing the water with their inner thighs. For a human, whose feet surface area is relatively small, an added emphasis on pushing and compressing the water with the inner thighs can create a lot of thrust. I practiced this idea until it became an unconscious part of my stroke.

I received no formal swimming lessons for several years. I did what came naturally to frogs and me. I also learned about swimming and the crawl stroke by watching Johnny Wiesmuller in Tarzan movies. For a while, I didn't know the crawl was executed more efficiently with the head in the water. I assumed Tarzan swam with his head up in the air for the practical reason of searching for resident crocodiles. For several years, I swam the Tarzan crawl.

I think the lack of formal training and my observations of frogs and Tarzan allowed me to evolve into a natural swimmer. It might be similar to professional golfers who learn their trade mostly by playing and practicing—without a lot of intervention from anyone. The mechanics of swimming or hitting a golf ball become part of our motor skills. Thinking too much about a breaststroke kick or a putt can be counter-productive.

But Tiger Woods did not become a gifted golfer by himself. He had guidance. As did I with my swimming, recounted shortly.

My Frogman Dreams

In the early 1950s, after I had learned to swim—and it had become my obsession—I experienced another life-shaping event. I attended a WW II movie featuring the Under Water Demolition

Teams (UDT), the forerunners of today's U.S. Navy SEALs. I still recall sitting in the movie theater, watching the frogmen leave the submarine and make their way to a beach to lay waste to the Germans' underwater obstacles. I said to myself, *I can do that! I don't even need flippers. I can swim my frog kick.* I left the movie with one goal in mind: I was going to become a frogman. From that time forward, my swimming efforts were directed toward becoming a member of the UDT.

The movie's swimmers demonstrated the skills I had to possess to be a frogman. First, I would need to develop stamina; the frogmen in the movie swam for miles without rest. Second, I would need to swim underwater most of the time. After all, "underwater" was part of their name. Third, I would need a lot of strength; the UDT swimmers carried heavy gear and explosives. Fourth, I would need to be a quick swimmer, at least on some occasions. Actions such as eluding an enemy or reaching a beach at an allotted time would require a fast swim.

The Entrance of a Mentor

During my junior high school years, I had the good fortune to come under the tutelage of a talented swimming instructor. Her nickname was Tudy; her real name was Dorothy Osburn. Tudy displayed a patch on her black swimsuit that spoke volumes about her status with me—a Red Cross Water Safety Instructor (WSI). In my rankings of admired swimmers, a WSI was just below frogmen, and slightly above frogs.

Tudy taught me to have confidence in my native skills. She gave me confidence in swimming crawls, backstrokes, and sidestrokes. She offered no advice on my breaststroke, declaring it to be satisfactory the way I swam it.[2] Tudy provided the training leading to my becoming a Red Cross certified lifeguard and a WSI. She paved the way for my six summers of life guarding and teaching swimming.

The Red Cross did not teach the butterfly. The stroke had no role in its life saving routines and Tudy did not think it appropriate to explain it. I asked for hints on how to swim the butterfly stroke but she offered no help. So, I never learned it but I wish I had. I think I would have enjoyed swimming the butterfly as much as the breaststroke.

For a boy who loved swimming and who was striving to swim well, I began to view Tudy as my idol. She was a powerful swimmer, with an effortless American Crawl that I envied. And just underneath that flimsy black swimsuit was one lovely hunk of muscle tissue—a 10 in today's rating standards. If I grew weary of listening to her lectures, it was very easy to tune out the air waves and watch her body in motion. Truth is, I looked at her more than I listened to her.

As the summers rolled on, Tudy became my mentor. I think she understood how much swimming meant to me. I was at the pool almost every day and she often gave me extra lessons, free of charge. She was a good sprinter and taught me how to execute a racing dive from the end of the pool.

The Red Cross didn't train swimmers to be sprinters. For the life of me (not to mention the life of a drowning person), I couldn't understand why speed was not emphasized more in the Red Cross manuals. Nonetheless, Tudy required her students to swim sprint after sprint … after sprint. Our arms, legs, and chest drowned in lactic acid.

One day, during one of her luscious lectures, walking before us displaying the WSI patch on her upper thigh … Eh … swim suit, she asked the class, "What's the most important aim during the rescue of a drowning person?" In one form or another, these were our answers:

Student One, "Why. Rescuing the swimmer!"

Tudy, "My question implied the rescue was underway."

Student Two, "Swimming fast to the victim."

Tudy, "A swimming rescue is the last resort. Always use buoys, hooks, boats, or ropes before entering the water. But OK, assuming you must swim to the victim."

Based on my observations of swimming frogs and swimming *Homo sapiens*, I knew I had a lock on the answer, "Swimming in a straight line!"

I knew a lot about geometry. Even in water I knew the shortest distance between two points (the points being the drowner and the drownee) was a straight line.

Tudy, "Yes, but my point is: The aim is *not* to end up with *two* drowning persons; the second person being you." As she proceeded to teach us the defensive skills needed to be an effective lifeguard.

Wisdom. Prudence. Wit. There she was: A swimming sage standing before us, dispensing pearls of intelligence ... all wrapped in a clinging black swimsuit. Anyway, I suspected I was a fast swimmer but my only competition came from July 4th contests at the local pool—in my mind, not much of a challenge. Nonetheless, my training for speed swimming was secondary to my efforts to build strength and stamina.

Easley's Twin Lakes

During my younger days in Lea County, I swam in our ranch tanks and later in a pool at the idyllic Easley's Twin Lakes, a small marine resort about three miles east of Lovington. The owner of the Lakes sold the resort to the Lovington Country Club during my high school days.

I use the word idyllic to describe the Lakes. In my youthful, naïve eyes, they were that and more. I spent as much time as possible at the swimming pool or in one of the lakes at Easley's; often staying all day. While I was there, I rarely left the water.

John Easley was as important to my swimming life as Tudy and frogs, the models for the breaststroke. He was instrumental to my becoming an accomplished swimmer, because he created Easley's Twin Lakes. These lakes were my Disney Land, Sea World, Water Park and Lake Mead, all rolled-up into two tiny bodies of water and a swimming pool.

Easley's lakes would be classified as ponds by most folks. Each measured only about two or three football fields across their widest parts. But to Lea County citizens, having no other significant bodies of water nearby, we were proud to call them lakes. The lakes formed natural pools of water and over many centuries, they evolved to become leak-free reservoirs. Their water evaporated in the county's arid climate, so John kept them full with a frequent infusion of fresh water.

The swimming pool was a large one, measuring about 15 by 40 yards, with a depth of 10 feet in the diving area. John positioned the pool as a peninsula into one of the lakes, as shown in Figure 10-1. I called this lake the ski lake; it was used for boating and skiing. Notice the lake at the top of the photo, surrounding three sides of the pool.

Originally, the pool had no chemical, filtering, or heating system (Later, John added a dangerous, jerry-rigged Chlorine pump to his list of inventions.) We lifeguards kept it fresh with frequent water recharges, straight from the earth through one of John's irrigation pumps. But this system was inadequate and each Monday night we drained the pool, scrubbed it down, and filled it up during the late Monday night and early Tuesday morning. The task made for a tiring day and we rarely finished the draining and cleaning before midnight.

Figure 10-1. The swimming pool.

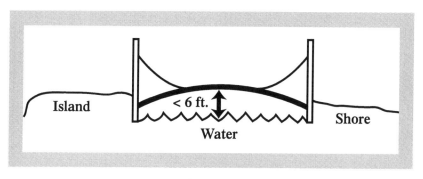

Figure 10-2. The suspension bridge.

For the next two days or so, the pool attracted masochists, the physically comatose, profoundly hung-over drinkers, and people who were unaware of how cold irrigation water was. The water came out of a pipe into the pool at a temperature in the mid-to-high 60 degrees range. My most difficult teaching day was Tuesday and it was not an unusual occurrence when students refused to enter the water (especially the small children). They were not afraid of the water; they were afraid of its temperature.

In addition to the hypothermia-inducing water, another attractive feature of Easley's was a small island placed in the ski lake and an elegant suspension bridge connecting the island to the main shore. The island measured about 100 feet across and was graced by a large Weeping Willow tree. Figure 10-2 does not do justice to this lovely bridge, but my rendition is sufficient to draw your attention to the height of the tallest part of the bridge to the water: about six feet, perhaps less. The restricted clearance meant a skier had to exercise caution and ski directly under the bridge in a stooping position. If the skier were on either side of this center, serious bending-down was an important variable in the avoid-a-concussion equation.

John charged a fee for the use of the lake. A boater would pay the money to an attendant and gain an all-day pass. During the weekends and on holidays, the ski lake was crowded with boats and skiers. It was downright dangerous to be on the lake during the busy times. Keep mind the small size of the lake; take into account that ten to fifteen boats—piloted by beer-drinking helmsmen—would be circling the lake, one behind the other, most of them towing a skier. Accidents were not unusual; I witnessed several serious injuries during my summers at Easley's. The lake sometimes resembled a scene from an aquatic Keystone Cops movie. Here are some examples of accidents occurring in one summer:

- A downed skier was hit by a trailing boat; the boat's blade cut his shoulder into pieces.
- A skier ran into the suspension bridge; he suffered severe head injuries.
- A boat and its skier collided into the island; minor damages to the driver; the skier escaped unscathed.
- A boat collided with another boat, injuries ranged from bruised pride to broken bones.
- A skier collided with another skier; no injuries.
- A boat crashed into the swimming pool area, as explained next.

The latter accident occurred while I was sitting in the lifeguard chair at the end of the pool—the end that jutted into the lake. Imagine my surprise when a high-speed boat crashed through the wooden fence surrounding the pool—BAM!—and landed on the pool's deck, about four feet from my chair.

After the flying pieces of the fence had settled, I looked over to the boat. Three passengers slowly raised their heads and peeked a view. They saw surprised swimmers and hundreds of pieces of wood, floating in the pool or resting on the pool deck. The driver was the last to emerge. His grin disappeared when he discovered several gaping holes in his boat's bow.

To further enhance the recreational risks at Easley's, John installed a water slide on the north side of the swimming pool, at an oblique angle to the pool's side. Figure 10-1 shows the bottom of the slide on the left side of the picture, as well as a typical Sunday afternoon crowd. The baby pool is at the bottom of the picture. The life guard chair where I watched the boat crash through the fence is at the upper right in the picture. Yours truly is the boy standing at the baby pool looking out over the big pool. A fellow life guard is

to my right, kibitzing with me, but not watching the baby pool, which was his duty.

This slide was not like those you see today in amusement parks. It was a playground slide—no sides, no protective awning—nothing to prevent a person from falling off the slide onto the cement deck of the pool. The sliding area was kept wet with a rubber hose, extended to the top of the slide, about 18 feet high. The water ran down into the pool, keeping the sliding area wet and slick.

Several of the swimmers at Easley's became accomplished slide "jumpers." We would stand at the top of the slide and leap down toward the water, with our knees bent to receive the slide. A good jump carried us almost to the end of the slide. The resulting acceleration catapulted us into the middle of the pool. Because I hung-out at the pool for many hours, I had a lot of time to practice these jumps and I became an adroit slide performer.

Serious injuries occurred on the slide. I am surprised no one was killed. Several times, we lifeguards had to administer to people who had fallen off the slide onto the pool deck, "U.D., break-out the Iodine. Bobby fell off the slide ... left most of his skin on the concrete."

"U.D., Get on your clothes. Jimmy broke his arm on the slide. Take him to the doctor."

As your chronicler of Lea County stories, I am not exaggerating these injuries. Serious accidents also occurred on the high diving board. We kids used it as a surrogate trampoline, bouncing on it four to six times until we were suspended three to five feet above the ten foot diving platform (none of that meter stuff in Lea County). Then, executing varying numbers of somersaults, we entered into the pool's ten foot depth. I also favored the dives in which I faced the board, a maneuver we called a cut-away jack knife or a cut-away one-and-a-half.

The same Bobby described in the water slide scene broke his ankle by missing a jump on the board. After several springs, Bobby came down a bit crooked. Losing his balance and falling backwards, his body hit a hand rail positioned on the side of the board. He rebounded off this railing, allowing gravity to fulfill its job description, to land partially in the water and partially on the side of the pool. Sitting on the lifeguard stand, I was a witness to Bobby's aerial maneuvers and his crash landing—a messy scene.

In spite of our injuries, and without the supposed wisdom that comes with adulthood, we kids kept performing our daredevil jumps from the water slide and our trampoline jumps from a non-trampoline. To this day, I carry marks on my knees that were the result of my hundreds of water slide jumps.

The Baby Pool

The baby pool is shown at the bottom of Figure 10-1. Notice the happy little children cavorting about in the pool. A cheerful aquatic ambience. Small *Homo sapiens*, rekindling their primordial H_2O dispositions toward liquid environments. Not to mention emptying their bowels and kidneys in accordance with Mother Nature's dictates.

On more than one occasion, my duties required I scoop-up the toilet deposits of one of the small children, who had exited the baby pool, dropped his or her pants, and made his or her contributions to the food-chain cycle on the pool deck.

However, as strange as it might sound, my pool-side pickup was better than making a retrieval in the pool water itself—a task requiring the closing of the pool, draining the water, and refilling it with a fresh supply of John's almost icy water. On two occasions, nocturnal miscreants sneaked over the pool fence and made offal offerings to the water. Yours truly had the job of cleaning it up. Who said the job of a life guard was glamorous?

Fourth of July Festivities at Easley's

Many Lea County citizens spent the July 4th holiday at the Lakes. They arrived early in the morning to reserve choice spots and stake their claims around the lakes. The goal was to secure a prime spot for viewing the evening's fireworks display. By mid-morning, the lakes' shores, the swimming pool, and all picnic tables were packed with people.

The pool managers organized swimming contests and passed-out medals to those who won a race. Ribbons were also awarded to second and third place finishers. A lifeguard colleague was named H. P. Harris. He was a short boy with undersized legs, but his shoulders, chest, and arms were huge. H.P. swam with no lower body movement whatsoever, as if his legs were trailing, useless pieces of string. I instructed him on how to use a flutter kick but he responded that a foot kick slowed him down. He demonstrated, and sure enough, he swam faster without the use of his legs—faster than anyone I had met.

H.P.'s style and strength almost propelled him out of the water. Watching him sprint across the pool reminded me of a Saturday afternoon movie cartoon, in which the character boosts himself onto the water's surface with his arm actions. I never know what his initials meant but I called my friend Horse Power Harris, because of the phenomenal strength of his crawl stroke. I admired that man's uncanny swimming ability almost as much as I admired Tudy's swim suit.

On one 4th of July, H.P. won the freestyle race and I won the breaststroke contest. With two other lifeguards hired for the day, we also won medals in the relay races. Our opponents complained to a pool manager that the lifeguards should not have been allowed to compete in the holiday contests, but to no avail.

As the July 4th day came to an end, we would close the pool and head for a place to watch the fireworks. I usually drifted over to the island or to a location populated with some of the girls who had just left the pool.

John shot-off the fireworks in such a way that they would ignite and explode over the middle of the ski lake. The scene was right out of Norman Rockwell: Cars parked around the lakes, folks sitting on blankets next to the water, some still munching on chicken, others drinking soda and beer—gasping, shouting, and laughing at each incendiary display. It was a happy, tranquil, and yes, idyllic time in my life and the lives of those celebrating the 4th at Easley's.

Hazards but no lawsuits

In today's culture, Easley's pools and lakes could not exist. They would have been closed down by OSHA-type agencies or forced to shut their operations due to exorbitant insurance fees. No question, skiing, swimming, diving, and boating could be risky ventures, but the customers accepted the risks. I know of no injury-related lawsuits brought against John and his tiny resort.

Comparing the Jobs of Roustabout and Life Guard

One summer, I asked the pool manager for a week-off from my swimming pool job. I wanted to work in the oil fields. Even now, I wonder what possessed me to seek such a diversion. I worked for two days with a seismograph crew and for the remainder of the week, I toiled away as a roustabout, the lowest position in the oilfield social register. The roustabout was a jack-of-all-trades position and the work was dirty and exhausting. The job consisted of digging ditches, assembling or disassembling pumps and tanks, and cleaning sludge from the bottom of the oil tanks. After the week was over, I happily returned to my job at the pool, and continued my so-called "work" as a lifeguard.

Words cannot describe adequately the differences between the jobs of a roustabout and a lifeguard. But I will try. The table on facing page provides a summary of why I stayed away from the oil fields as much as possible and why I stayed in the lifeguard business for as long as possible.

---

[1] This chapter, with minor changes, is also in my book *Frogman*.

[2] I invented two strokes during that time in my life. If you wish to sign-up for lessons, just let me know.

Job Attribute	Roustabout	Lifeguard
Danger to life and limb	Above the national average.	Very little, as long as I stayed out of the water.
Sanitary conditions	Far below the national average, but above that of garbage collection.	Excellent, given all that Chlorine.
Calories burned per hour	Far above the national average for menial work.	Perhaps a few hundred, just to keep my eyes open, and lungs and heart pumping.
Ambience of work place	Below the jobs of garbage collectors and dog catchers.	What can I say? It was a country club swimming pool.
Chances of encountering the opposite sex	Very high, if one was not too concerned about the species encountered in a pasture.	What can I say? It was a country club swimming pool.
Chances of doing any good once the opposite sex (of the same species) was encountered.	Non-existent.	What can I say? It was a country club swimming pool.
Remuneration	About the same as dog catchers.	Who cares? It was a country club swimming pool. Anyway, for swimming lessons: obscene rates of return.
Status of job	Between that of dog catchers and garbage collectors	Higher than Enron officers— admittedly, a low bar for comparison.

11

LITTLE TEXAS MUSIC 101

The power of music, that magician of magicians;
who lifts his wand and says his mysterious word
and all things real pass away and the phantoms of your mind
walk before you clothed in flesh.

—*Mark Twain*

The community youth centers in Little Texas towns were a magnet for teenagers. They presented an opportunity for the young people to mingle without the towns' preachers and teachers looking over their shoulders. Along with the Bull Barn dances, it was at the Center where I honed my dancing skills and where I am certain I was part of the group who created many of the modern dirty dancing movements. We didn't call our style dirty dancing. Later in life I nicknamed it the "Lea County Two-Step."

Patrick Swayze had nothing on us. Oh, perhaps he executed few more dips and spins in this repertoire. However, we teenagers could have developed an equally exciting and dirty routine had it not been for the Center's chaperone, Lucille Daley. She kept a close eye on the dance couples' hip movements and body contacts.

Spotting an unacceptable dance routine, Ms. Daley left her post at the entrance door of the Center, walked onto the dance floor, and placed her arms between the bodies of the offending couple. She then spread her arms apart—separating the thwarted dirty dancers as if they were two clinched boxers, now unable to land a telling blow on each other.

Later in life, friends and dance partners asked where on earth I had learned to do the dirty dance. They didn't believe my reply, "The Youth Center in my hometown in New Mexico." They suspected I had enrolled secretly in the Fred Astaire School for Dirty Dancing.

Ha! Can you picture Fred Astaire and Ginger Rogers doing the dirty dance? *"There they go folks. With demure steps, and lighter than air prances, Mr. Astaire and his dance partner now execute a pelvis grind, followed by two groin jerks."* Maybe John Travolta and Debra Winger, but not Fred and Ginger.

The State Line Bars

Dancing was also a popular past time with the adults. So was drinking. But with a few exceptions, teenagers and children did not drink alcohol. Booze and beer were too difficult to obtain in a small town. Behind a saloon's bar counter stood a parent, a parent of a friend, or a neighbor—all forearmed to force the under-aged person to forego a Coors beer (the favored drink in those days).

But for the adult drinkers, Lea County had a distinct advantage over the neighboring counties across the state line in Texas: Lea County was wet. The Texas counties were dry. Booze flowed in abundance in Lea County and thirsty Texans flocked across the state line to consume their spirits. It was a win-win situation for all. The Texans' consciences were clean and their counties were free of sin. The Little Texans' consciences were not quite as clean, but their coffers were filled with Texans' money. Let's put it this way: Lea Country put economics before ecumenics.

The Texans didn't travel all the way into Lea County's towns to imbibe. If nothing else, capitalism is efficient. Bars were built near the state line, but within Lea County. The wet, sinful saloons—miniature replications of Sodom and Gomorrah—were just a short haul from Texas' dry Elysian fields.

The bars were aptly named. One bar was called the Half Way Bar. Another bar was named the State Line Bar. The Half Way Bar did not have a dance floor. But the State Line bar did, and this feature made it the favored place to go if a citizen wanted to drink *and* dance. The decision of going from one bar to the other was not done with a flip of a coin. Half Way and the State Line were about 20 miles apart.

During my summer breaks from college, I can still recall pulling into the parking lot of the State Line Bar on a Saturday night. Cars and pickups were askew, parked here and there, depending on when they arrived. From the front, the bar looked tiny, but the small facade belied its size; the building was built as a deep rectangle. Assorted neon signs proclaimed the name of the bar and some of its products, usually Coors, Hamm's, and Pabst Blue Ribbon.

Walking from the vehicle toward the bar entrance, and taking in the dry, silent prairie air, I looked forward to the smoke, noise, beer, and the presence of females. Especially young ladies who enjoyed the Texas Two-Step and my variation, the Lea County Two-Step. A beer or two. Who knew what the night might bring?

For a while, during the early evening, the people usually mixed well. No fights just yet. And of course, no men with men; no women with women. Didn't happen in those days. New Mexico and Texas may have had their differences, but sexual preferences were not among them. The citizens were straight as arrows or very well closeted.

As the evening wore on and the alcohol loosened inhibitions, the State Line patrons became either friendlier or more belligerent. I gravitated toward the former crowd, thinking myself as a (prospective) lover and not a fighter. But one never knew if asking a seemingly single lass to dance would be inviting the ill-feelings of a nearby cowboy. But such were the risks of the Texas Two-Step on a Saturday night in Little Texas.

More often than not, my nights of dancing at the State Line Bar were trouble-free. A bit of irony: I met some of the finest Texas Two-Steppers I have ever known at a country bar situated a just few feet *away* from Texas.

The Lucky Lager Dance Hour

Country music was not all we teenagers listened to. Like most kids in America, we were slowly turning on to Rock and Roll. But the voyage to this new music had a few stops along the way. They involved swing bands and the smooth voiced crooners. Little did anyone know in the 1950s that Tommy Dorsey would be replaced by Fats Domino and later, the Doors; that Eddie Fisher would be replaced by Eddie Cochran and later, Joe Cocker.

During my Freshman year in high school, radio station KOB in Albuquerque broadcasted the "Lucky Lager Dance Hour." It was beamed to remote Lovington, about 250 miles by the way the crow flies.

I recall Dad and I listening to "Oh! My Papa," sung by Eddie Fisher. While it played, he moved not a muscle, sitting next to me in my bedroom. After the song was over, Dad turned to me, patted me on the head, and said he enjoyed listening to the song. I think he was complimented that I invited him to listen to the music— especially one about the greatness of fathers.

I was tempted to push the parent/child civility envelope by putting Bill Haley's "Rock around the Clock" record on my player, just to test the generation gap waters. But better judgment clouded my teenage reasoning, and I let sleeping dogs (and Bill's Comets) lie.

Another Dance Hour favorite that came along in 1955 was "Love is a Many Splendored Thing," sung by The Four Aces. Later, this record became the sweetheart song between Beverly and me (the heroine in my story "Idle Minds"), and we would not dance with anyone else to the tune. If she were asked for a whirl around the floor at the Youth Center while this song was playing, she refused. And of course, I never asked anyone else for a dance to the song. When "Splendored" played on the juke box, if Beverly and I were in each other's immediate vicinity at the Center or at a party, we interrupted our on-going social activities, looked for each other, simultaneously met at the dance floor, and performed our teenage ritual—all with Lea County's prototype dirty-dance style.

Here Comes Rock and Roll!

In the mid-1950s, rock and roll was just getting started. Few hit songs came from the big bands; they were receding from the scene. Pop quartets and soloists were the "in thing." The disk jockey at KOB was an old guard, conditioned to the old ways. He could not understand the new songs and their suggestiveness. A prime example was "Dance with me Henry" (The Wallflowers). He complained every time he played the tune to his audience. The song was a harmless tale of two kids wanting to dance. But the DJ had other interpretations. I recall his tirades about the sad state of the world of music. And during his lamentations, rock and roll was slowly but surely exterminating "The Rock and Roll Waltz."

One of my friends brought back my recollections that some of the music was indeed suggestive. As examples, the "Annie" songs of "Dance with Me Annie " "Work with Me Annie," and "Annie Had a Baby" were highly volatile lyrics for the conservative 1950s.

Listed below is a random sample of the popular songs dominating KOB's musical missives. If you remember any of them, I wager you don't like rap music.

- "This Ole House" (Rosemary Clooney): A funky song, regaling an old house, and at the same time, thinking the old house is pretty neat, but not sufficiently neat to warrant fixing-up.

- "Hold My Hand" (Don Cornell): Crooner Cornell confused sexual fusion with the solitary act of holding the hand of one's potential lover. He made the claim that he and his lover would be immortal because of their holding hands. Maybe it worked; later the Beatles picked up on the idea with their, "I Wanna Hold Your Hand."

- "Papa Loves Mambo" (Perry Combo): My Dad would have gone through the ceiling if he had heard this song. Thinking Mambo was a person (Dad danced only the Texas Two-Step) he would have woven sexual triangulations into the verse: "Papa loves mambo; Mama loves mambo."

- "Misty" (Erroll Garner): A song on the Hit Parade in 1954. As ageless then as it is now.

- "Hearts of Stone" (The Fontaine Sisters): I offer no parody for this song. How can I? It resonates with a continual "doole-woop-doole-woop-a-do."

If you can find any of this old music, play the songs. I did and found them pleasant, but staid, even boring. I suspect we kids in the 1950s felt the same way, because anarchy was in the air—as well as the airwaves. Trouble was brewing and my parents' generation had trouble accepting the changes. Truth is, they never accepted them, but who could blame them? The new rock music was distasteful to the ears of parents and other adults. They had grown accustomed to listening to Glenn Miller and Tommy Dorsey.

Based on these explanations of my musical tastes, I suspect you are wondering if I like all music? No, I could never fathom Pat Boone's attempt to sing rock music. If your musical pain threshold is high, put on one of his renditions of Elvis. And Mr. Boone's rendition of Little Richard's "Tutti Fruiti" is surreal.

Anyway, the changing musical landscape was not just about rock. Music was undergoing a fusion; black gospel was merging with white country rockabilly. By 1955, Bill Haley and the Comets had cut "Rock Around the Clock." Bo Diddley was becoming a force, impressing many people at the Apollo Theatre in New York. So was Buddy Holly and the Crickets—singers from Lubbock, Texas a town on the Llano Estacado. Little Richard was mesmerizing teenagers and offending teenagers' parents.

The arch nemesis of all grown humans, Elvis Presley, appeared on the scene in the mid-1950s. Elvis threw salt on parents' melodic wounds, expanding their audio aversion of him to another of the senses, the visual. At this time, his gyrations were largely unknown in Lovington; TV was still a rare appliance in our homes. But word of mouth sometimes rivals the speed of a radio wave. We teenagers knew of his stage charisma before we saw him (charisma to us; anathema to our parents). And Lea County's citizens lived near places where Elvis performed in his early days, such as Lubbock, Texas and Clovis, New Mexico. One of my high school friends saw Elvis perform in Lubbock and relayed to most of the teenagers in town that Elvis was a sure-fire replacement for Bing Crosby.

Joy, Anarchy, Energy ... and no Bing Crosby

What did the music of my generation in the 1950s and 1960s have that the older generation did not possess? Joy, melodic anarchy, energy, and the absence of Big Crosby. Just listen to Little Richard. If you aren't energized by his music, you are in serious need of an attitude facelift. His joy, his fun, his enthusiasm leaps out of the speakers. The same goes for Jerry Lee Lewis, as well as two of my all-time favorites, Chuck Berry and Fats Domino. Eddie Cochran as well. His "Summertime Blues" were not blue to us teenagers. We were too busy dancing to this song to be blue.

Time marched on; so did my stroll through young adult years and middle age. The popular music of the 1970s and 80s built-on the legacy of the 50s and 60s. The Doors, Creedence Clearwater Revival, The Moody Blues, Bread, The Guess Who, Jim Croce, Leonard Cohen, The Beatles, and Cat Stephens. All showed talent, originality, energy and joy. Joy? Well, exceptions come to mind. Leonard Cohen and the Doors were not fountains of bliss, but they were not boring.

I'm amazed at the number of good songs some of the artists recorded. Two bands come to mind in this regard: the Beatles and Creedence Clearwater Revival. This latter group, with John Fogerty as the lead composer, created a phenomenal track record on the music tracks. I listen to them frequently. I bet you can hear in your mind ... "Suzie Q," ... "I Heard it Through the Grapevine," ... "Proud Mary," ... "Who'll Stop the Rain," ... "Hey Tonight," ... and on and on.

Preparing to Lift-off to Another Planet

I began to lose touch with popular music in the 1980s and 1990s but not because of my age. I allocated my time to other activities, principally research about computer networks and the emerging

Internet. While I did my writing, I would often put on a tape or CD, usually preferring, say, The Modern Jazz Quartet to David Bowie. This pattern, one of playing my standbys and ignoring new offerings, eventually relegated me to pop music illiteracy. It placed me out of the loop with many of the goings-on in our society.

Figure 11-1. Two Jewels.

For example, I thought Jewel was, literally, a gem—until son Tommy sent me a picture of the two of them at a concert where both their bands performed. They are shown in Figure 11-1. After examining the photo, I kept my opinion: She is indeed a gem. And I watched one of her performances on TV recently, discovering I liked her music as well. Jewel, and my son's involvement in music, re-awakened my interest in pop music and encouraged me to see what was happening in front of my nose (and ears).

Tommy became quite good at his craft. Of course, a parent would say a son is a great musician, even if the lad couldn't strum a one-string guitar. But I speak with authority, buttressed by a review of his band's record, "Heroes and Villains," by the *Rolling Stone* magazine.

Successful Arrival at Another Planet

The *Rolling Stone* article sealed my fate to a life on another musical and cultural planet. Tommy told me over the phone the recent issue of the magazine had a review on page 90 of his band's new record, "Heroes and Villains." He said the cover had a picture of "M and M" on it. I didn't say anything because I don't follow current popular music and my hearing impairment often dissuades me from asking for a repeat of something that is not vital to my survival or integral to my happiness. I assumed I had the ability to ferret-out the *Rolling Stone* on a magazine rack.

Excited by Tommy's news, I went to the local drug store to buy the latest issue of *Rolling Stone*. I couldn't locate it on the magazine rack, so I approached a teenage clerk and explained I was looking for *Rolling Stone*. I gave her an incentive to assist in my search by saying my good looking son was shown with his hot new band on page 90, and I had to have a copy.

Whether she was empathetic toward me because of my parental enthusiasm, curious about Tommy, or just doing her job, she walked me back to the magazine rack, immediately found *Rolling Stone*, and handed it to me.

I glanced at the cover and I said, "This is the wrong issue. Tommy said the cover features M and M, whoever they are."

She responded, "It does sir. 'They' is a 'he.' There he is on this cover, Eminem." Pause....

"You've never heard of Eminem?"

Yes, I had heard of the name Eminem, immediately dismissing it/him/her/them from my mind (and memory) as an insignificant encumbrance to my gray matter. So, I replied, "Yes, but I am not into rap."

"Oh, Eminem is much more than rap. You should hear his music."

"Good idea. I'll buy an album. Thanks for your help."

I have never felt more like an out-to-lunch old man than those few seconds in that drug store. Two youngsters were looking through the magazines and had listened-in on our conversation. I glanced up at them as I was thumbing though the magazine, working my way to page 90. They were smiling at me with that all-knowing look of youth toward older people, most likely thinking, *How do these old folks manage to transport themselves to another world mentally and manage to stay attached to earth physically?*

Ah, dear young children: Little do you realize you are only one generation removed from the same metaphysical transport. Good luck kids, enjoy your current time, for your future will come all too soon.

Anyway, I read about Tommy and later turned to the cover story article about Eminem. The reporter's take on the man was that he appealed to crabby white teenagers. I wager a reporter in the 1950s said the same thing about Elvis.

What I wouldn't Give for the State Line Bar

The world of those kids in the drug store is far removed from the world I knew in my youth at the State Line Bar. I sometimes wish I had a time machine. I wish I could ask a fair young lady to accompany me on a few circles around the dance floor at the State Line Bar. A Texas Two-Step would be a fine dance for our adventure. A waltz or "Put Your Little Foot" would be just as pleasurable. It's difficult to imagine our dancing to a rap song, especially in a country bar in Little Texas. Nonetheless, as I remember those times and the fair damsels, I think I would have danced to almost any tune just to be able to take us around the dance floor.

Back to reality, and taking the clerk's advice, I bought an Enimem CD. I listened. Hmm. I guess my mind is still on another planet, but then I am not "a crabby white teenager."

12

THE CHRISTMAS CANTATA

We often feel sad in the presence of music without words;
and often more than that in the presence of music without music.
                                                    —*Mark Twain*

During the Christmas season, I put away my Credence albums, along with my favorite rappers, and break out the Christmas CDs. It pains me to part with Eminem, the idol of crabby kids, but it is important to attempt to be well-rounded.

During these holidays, Handel's *Messiah* is my first selection, followed by Joan Baez's *Noel* album. Pleasantly sedated by these yuletide carols, I then play lighter fare. But I continue to return to the *Messiah* and Joan's songs. My reason for replaying this music is because, for a brief time in my life, I was exposed to some "serious" Christmas music; songs beyond "Jingle Bell Rock" and "Rudolph the Red Nosed Reindeer." Early in my life, I developed a love for Handel and the songs in Joan's album.

Origins of My Love for Christmas Music

When I entered school in Lovington in the 1940s, the student population was small. One music teacher was sufficient to handle grades one through twelve at Lovington's schools. As I made my way from the first grade to grade twelve, and as the population of Lovington's schools increased, my first grade music teacher remained my teacher until the end of my high school years. Florence Anderson, several of my classmates, and I made our way together through all twelve grades.

With the gift of hindsight, I have come to understand that Florence was an extraordinary teacher. Consider this: By the third grade her students were familiar with *Peter and the Wolf*. Is that not an awesome accomplishment? Perhaps, but I have also come to understand that *Peter and the Wolf* is no great shakes for third graders. My friends tell me their children learn it before they are in kindergarten.

Fine then, forget *Peter and the Wolf*. Consider this: In junior high, Florence's music class students knew each score to Greig's *Peer Gynt*, and some of the symphonies of Beethoven. She had us listen to the music. She watched us as we listened. She made sure if we weren't listening, we were executing a convincing emulation. She interspersed comments to have us focus on what was happening with the music at that time.

I recall we students gave *Peer Gynt* mixed reviews but most of us were fond of Beethoven. But who could not like his music? He was the precursor to our modern fixation on repetitive scores. I wager some of Beethoven's critics accused him of being a modern day's rap artist...That was a hard sentence to write, even in parody.

Anyway, during our later grade school years, Mrs. Anderson had us reading and writing musical scores, including the nuances of flats, sharps, the treble and bass clefs.

EGBDF and FACE became part of our musical repertoire. I can still hear her, "EGBDF! ... FACE! ... EGBDF! ... FACE!" At times I thought of the typing class cadence, "FDSA space! ... JKL semi-colon space!" Nonetheless, repetition instills learning. There is rarely a short-cut to competence. Florence was a master of repetition and she molded many of us into fine singers.

The Christmas Cantata

Florence became a Lovington celebrity because of her creation, direction, and production of the annual Christmas Cantata. The performance was a big event in our community and the evening performance for the public was highly attended by Lovington's citizens.

Mrs. Anderson recruited her concert choir from her music classes and the high school athletes. Unlike some schools, the Lovington High School culture did not consider it wimpy to sing in a chorale, and singing athletes became a fixture of the Cantata. In fact, some of the best athletes in our school were members of Florence's tenor and bass sections.

Based on my vast musical experience (Hank Williams, Jimmie Rogers, as examples), I thought the Cantata performance to be an impressive feat by a bunch of high school kids. After the audience was seated, about 150 singers marched into the west-side bleachers of the high school gymnasium. Wearing choral robes and singing Christmas songs, we gradually filled-up the middle bleachers, from the top row on down to the bottom.

Considering the location of the performance—the backwaters of rural New Mexico—I thought our procession into the gym was pretty impressive. For us hicks, it was replete with pageantry. Festooned in frocks, and to the tune of "Angels We Have Heard on High", we executed a grand march into the gym.

As a Southern Baptist, I was pageantry-impaired. Truth is, I was probably a repressed Catholic. Thus, the robes and scary music made a big impression on me.

Figure 12-1 shows our grand chorale after the entry and during our performance. I copied this picture from our school album. I could not locate myself in the photo and then I remembered I had been banned from performing in the Cantata. Mrs. Anderson threw me out of the music class. For the remainder of the year, I spent this time in Study Hall. It was a sad ending to a ten year relationship with Florence, but she finally got fed up with my buffoonery.

I didn't care, I was tired of singing. But I did care about the stop before my first stop at the Study Hall. It was the principal's office, where I received a whipping from Mr. Crouse. Then, to the Study Hall ... where I never studied, but put together some extraordinary tic-tac-toe victory strings against myself.

Figure 12-1. The Christmas Cantata Choir.

In spite of my absence, the choir assembled and sang a fine variety of Christmas music, including several songs from Handel's *Messiah*. Florence interspersed serious pieces, such as, "What Child is This?" with trendy, current songs. One of the popular pieces was, "Twas the Night Before Christmas."

Mormon Tabernacle Choir? Stand Aside!

Modesty aside, we sounded like the Mormon Tabernacle Choir. (Who can debate my claim? I know of no recordings made of our Cantata). We knew our notes and we knew how to stay in harmony with them. See any sheet music in the hands of the singers in Figure 12-1? Mrs. Anderson had drilled verse, tune, and cadence into our heads and vocal cords for several weeks. What is more, she kept a large group of unruly teenagers in line, while at the same time, she taught us music.

At times, Mrs. Anderson reminded me of a good-looking, talented, female musical drill sergeant. And she had the best looking set of legs I have ever had the pleasure to see ... maybe with the exception of Juliet Prouse. Truth is, I probably kept enrolling in her music class because of her legs. I've never been one for music classes, but I am a student of female legs.

Florence was also a shrewd showman. If a student possessed an exceptional voice, she made sure this boy or girl was given opportunities to perform solos, sometimes singing an entire song for the Cantata. For several years, two classmates, Linda Earnest and Wayne Pruitt, sang solos at the Christmas Cantata. Wayne sang "I Wonder as I Wander" and Linda sang the lead to "Oh Holy Night."

Linda and Wayne possessed astonishing voices. Their interpretations of these songs were of such beauty, of such clarity, they became Florence's showstoppers. To this day, well over five decades after my last Christmas Cantata performance, I can still hear the voices of Linda and Wayne—as if they were singing now.

To give you an idea of the crystalline beauty of Linda's voice, think Joan Baez. Linda was that good. A few moments ago, I listened to Joan sing "Oh Holy Night." It could have been Linda singing the song and I would not have noticed much difference.[1]

Wandering and Wondering ... eh, Wondering and Wandering

I recall one rehearsal where Wayne was admonished by Florence. She claimed he was singing, "I wander as I wonder" when he should have been singing "I wonder as I wander." Mrs. Anderson was a stickler for diction and pronunciation—a significant challenge for students who spoke Southern New Mexican. Of course, Wayne's interpretation put a different spin on the meaning of the song. Anyway, with Wayne's Southwestern drawl, no one (*except* Mrs. Anderson) had any clue whatsoever whether Wayne was singing "I wander as I wonder", "I wonder as I wander", "I wonder as I wonder", or "I wander as I wander." I suspect interesting verses could have been composed for any of these four song titles.

Wayne's "I Wonder as I Wander" was sung without choir support or musical instruments. Just Wayne. There he stood, all 5 feet 8 inches of him, singing this simple song with beautiful vocal harmony to the notes. I recall one of the afternoon concerts of our

Cantata—performed for schoolmates before the big revue in front of Lovington's citizens. After Wayne had finished his solo, a moment of complete silence pervaded the gym. Not a silence of, "What's next?" A silence of, "Oh my God, what a voice."

If you know the lyrics to this song, you will remember their messages are a bit of a downer. They speak about we humans being "poor ornery people" and so on. Whatever our opinions may be about the song, Wayne's beautiful voice never failed to leave the audience spellbound.

Singing Jocks

About the jocks in the chorus, I am still amazed how Mrs. Anderson was able to corral Lovington High School's male athletes for about four weeks during the lunch hour, place them in a choral setting, and persuade them to learn at least fifteen complex Christmas songs—all without Hank's guitar or Jimmie's yodel. On the night of the performance we boys knew (and knew well) the verse and tunes to "And the Glory", "O Thou that Tellest Good Tidings from Zion", "For Unto Us a Child is Born", "Glory to God", and of course, "Hallelujah."

We also sang other Christmas songs, such as "Adeste Fidelis", "The First Noel", and acted as the backup chorus to Linda's solo of "Oh Holly Night."

Part of Florence's success came from her toughness. The noon-time rehearsal was not an easy affair for Mrs. Anderson. We males often kidded around and made wise cracks, sometimes disrupting the rehearsal—but only to a point. If matters started to get out-of-hand, our music teacher would walk to the offending party, pull him up from his chair by his shirt collar, and banish him from the rehearsal. The banishment was not the end of the punishment because the boy was sent to the principal's office to deal with Mr. Crouse and the possibility of a butt whipping with a very big paddle.

In today's coddled culture, paddling, however soft, will likely earn the paddler an exit visa out of the teaching profession. I'll wager Ms.

Anderson's pulling up a student from his chair by his shirt collar would land her in hot water in today's environment.

Another Study Hall

I was the benefactor of two paddlings in high school. My science teacher, Mr. Wagoman tossed me out of 4th period Science Class (with a resulting F) for mixing-up a sulfur type substance and setting it ablaze during the class. This ban was an unsettling experience, because:

(a) I was the Parliamentarian of the Science Club, but no longer a scientist. And I had yet to grasp what a Parliamentarian did at the Science Club meetings, because the Science Club never had a meeting.

(b) Flunking Science and failure to get a credit put me on the cusp of not having enough classes to graduate from high school. But the school administrators found a way to get me out our their lives. They did not want me around for another year.

After forfeiting my Science Class visa, I visited Mr. Crouse for another caining, then spent the remainder of the 4th period in Study Hall. Thus, a fair amount of my school time was spent in a studious location, but not spent in studying. During these times, with the Study Hall monitor checking me as if I were a felon, I brought to a high art the illusion of studying. I could look at a page of text, seemingly taking in its arcane facts, but actually absorbed in a vast cornucopia of teenage fantasies.

Celebrating each Performance

The truth is, Mrs. Anderson captivated me. In hindsight, I came to love the woman. She cared and was competent. She was confident and positive about her work. She had a commanding yet supportive way of teaching. Part of her success was because of her love for her profession. Whatever her secret was, the results she obtained from her students made a lasting impression on me. She was a fine role model.

Another aspect of Florence's job stuck with me during my career. Time and again, I watched her go through the same repertoire, a recurring inventory of motions and actions. During those days, I was often bored stiff, and I wondered (as my mind wandered) how on earth anyone could be a teacher, with the job description of running the same pedagogical gamut day after day, week after week, year after year. Yet, she never wavered. As far as I could tell, she was never bored or exhausted

Many years later, I listened to a television interview of a famous opera singer, who talked about her "burn-out," of singing the same arias night after night. She addressed her problem with what can only be described as an attitude adjustment. She told us (and I paraphrase), "For me, the evening was one of many. For my listeners, it was one of one. After thinking about this idea for a while, I decided to walk onto every stage with this thought, 'Each performance is a personal celebration.' "

I'll bet Florence did this unconsciously. All of us should take this quote to heart. For myself—getting on in years—the idea is, "Each day I wake up and see the sun ... which is cause-enough for a personal celebration."

A Lapse into Choirdom

On several occasions, I have watched the Mormon Tabernacle Choir perform the *Messiah* on television. Of course, the group sings several songs that we kids sang during our Christmas Cantata so many years ago. I still remember the words to these songs, as well as the musical score. During the program, I fire-up my brittle vocal cords and try to sing along with the Choir. It is pathetic, but my wife doesn't complain, the neighbors remain quiet, and our dog mutes any howl of protest. All in all, a successful return to Choirdom.

During the holiday season, I often think about Florence Anderson and the Christmas Cantata. I reflect about our teacher's gift of teaching. And as I grow older, I reflect on perhaps her greatest gift of all to her students: fond, even joyful memories of past times in a public school.

I thank the Florence Andersons of the world. I thank the teachers of the world. In closing this chapter, I would like—for the first time in my life—to also thank my high school teachers and my principal who found a way to let me get on to the next phase of my life.

---

[1] You want a few thrills this Christmas, and some accompanying chills down your back? Play track 10 on *Noel*, Joan's interpretation of "Ave Maria."

13

IDLE MINDS

━━━━◆━◆━◆━━━━

In my experience, boys are the same in all ages.
They don't respect anything, they don't care for anything or anybody.

—*Mark Twain*

My high school days in the mid 1950s were spent in the same way young people spend them today. Okay, with a few exceptions: Armed security guards did not patrol the school buildings. Metal detectors were unnecessary. Lockers were occasionally searched for cigarettes but not for weapons and drugs. Booze was not allowed and sex was confined to after-school hours. Teachers could criticize our hair styles and how we dressed. Spankings (read whippings or canings) were allowed (I was an experienced recipient). We were not concerned that one of our classmates might annihilate half our class with a semi-automatic assault weapon.

Other differences dealt with the matter of food. For example, our school didn't display Burger King ads on the walls. McDonald's hamburger kiosks were absent. Nor did we have access to Coca-Cola machines. We loved Cokes; the more sugar, the better. Yet our consumption of soda was considerably less the current rate in the USA, which is about fifty-six gallons per person annually—some six hundred twelve-ounce cans of sweetened water.[1] Our consumption of milk exceeded our consumption of Pepsi because milk was the only non-water liquid served at the school.

Bland and Safe

My high school in those times reminds me of Singapore's culture today—bland and safe—although LHS was more permissive than Singapore. For instance, we were allowed to chew gum. Until recently, the deprived Singapore citizens had to sneak-in chewing gum as contraband and imbibe in secret. We had no TV in school. During my visits to Singapore, I found the television shows to be so bland that I was not certain I was watching a TV program.

I am not singling out Singapore for criticism, just making light of some of Singapore's customs. The culture at LHS was a healthy one, so is Singapore's. Perhaps we're learning in these violent and truculent times that boring might have something going for it.

Nor do I mean to suggest my classmates and I were without fault, or for that matter, without sin. We had ample capacity for both and often took opportunities to demonstrate our failings. Several such occasions are the subjects of this story.

Idle Minds—even before TV

Someone once said, "An idle mind is the devil's workshop." I would amplify this adage with, "Especially if the mind is housed in the body of a teenager." In the 1950s, TV was a rarity in Lea County and was not yet readily available to encourage our somewhat idle minds to become even idler. Rupert Murdoch was living in Australia and TV programming for the socially deprived and depraved was far into the future.

A few privileged families owned a TV set but the reception was poor. Some folks resorted to watching the picture after it was reflected from a mirror. It seemed to work; the fuzzy images, not to mention the snow, looked better when viewed through the mirror.

These TV viewers presented a weird sight to an outside observer. One night I visited a friend whose family had the distinction of owning the town's second television set. I found my friend and his family in their living room, sitting in their chairs, facing away from the TV, holding mirrors up to their eyes watching TV. They appeared to be participating in a strange séance.

Scrap Iron Men

To fill-in our idle time, some of the teenage boys in Lea County resorted to theft. Not grand larceny, just small stuff. A favorite pilfering item was scrap iron, an abundant commodity around the oil fields of the county. My practice was to make early morning excursions into the oil fields, before daylight, prior to reporting for my lifeguard job.

Scrap iron pieces were easy pickings and the items lifted from the fields were indeed scrap. I looked upon the venture as doing the oil companies a favor—providing a hauling service free of charge. We sold the metal to a local scrap iron dealer with no questions asked. The oil field administrators turned their heads if they spotted us in their fields.

My Dad owned a large Dodge pickup, although it was more on the order of a truck. Outfitted with a manual transmission, a four-wheel drive, a wench, and a long, strong cable, I could retrieve large, heavy objects with ease. With my set of scrap metal wheels, and thanks to Dodge, I was an adolescent scourge of Lea County's oil fields.

The live-and-let-live approach between the oil field managers and the scrap iron hunters contained an accepted, silent protocol: We were not to remove metal from a functioning oil rig, tank, or pump—any operating system. Judgment was sometimes called for as to what constituted useless metal. But as a general practice, we abided by the protocol and passed-up any iron that might have been useful metal for the oil workers.

A scrap metal friend drifted away from this protocol. Truth is, he became lazy. He was once an energetic scrap iron hound but decided to break the unstated code of behavior. Bob began to raid operational systems. He looked for an easy load of metal, which led to his demise.

One of his targets was an automobile dealer, who also operated a garage for repairing vehicles. Several engine blocks were stored in an alley at the back of the dealer's garage and Bob decided the metal in these fully-functioning motors was scrap.

On an early morning, Bob came by my house to ask for assistance in his raid on the garage. Tap, tap, tap. Bob's gentle rapping on my bedroom window awoke me.

"Hey U.D., I found a large bunch of scrap iron and need some help getting it onto my truck. Give me a hand."

"No thanks. I made a haul last night and need some sleep. Wayne will help; he needs some money for tires."

"OK," and off Bob went—first, to pick up Wayne; second, to pick up engine blocks; third, to be picked up for theft.

He was nabbed the day after he had pinched an engine block and sold it to the scrap metal dealer. The garage manager reported the theft to the police, who paid a visit to the metal dealer. The trail led straight to Bob.

Lucky for Bob, his father was a member of Lovington's police force. It sometimes pays to live in a small town and Bob got off with a slap on the wrist. As a loyal friend, he didn't tell the law that Wayne was his accomplice. However, Bob was forbidden to engage in any further scrap iron adventures. He was exiled from the scrap iron hunting herd—a minor dishonor, but one that put a crimp in Bob's wallet.

Watermelon Men

Watermelons were a prime target of our criminal activity. Unlike scrap iron, filching this fruit was stealing, pure and simple. Lea County was populated with many farms, and with the use of irrigation water techniques, the raising of fruits and vegetables became a profitable endeavor. As such, a farmer considered his crops to be a cache of potential cash. Naturally, the farmer protected his crops from marauding animals, including teenage boys.

My friends and I considered the farmer's watermelons to be community property. We thought we were as entitled to these fruits as the farmer. Don't ask me to explain or justify this warped sense of logic. I don't know where it came from. We had not yet been subjected to, and conditioned by entitlement programs.

Occasionally, a few of us would get together and raid a farmer's watermelon crops. The operation took place as follows:

- With the headlights turned-off we would drive our pickup to a watermelon patch. (Or pickups, if we were staffed for a big raid.)

- Silently, we would leave the pick up and crawl into the patch.

- There, we would pick the watermelons and crawl back to the pick up, with the fruit under our arms.

- After placing the melons in the back of the pickup, we would quietly disengage and head for town.

A farmer did not take kindly to watermelon thieves. On one occasion, an irate farmer fired on us, scattering buckshot across the watermelon patch. He was firing from far away; the buckshot was harmless—as we stayed low to the ground.

Shortly, this farmer walked off his patch and sprayed a few shots over our heads. I could hear the buckshot hitting the foliage and ground around me—an event encouraging me to consider purchasing watermelons at the local market.

But we suffered no casualties. And in our defense, the number of melons we took from an individual farmer was a drop in the bucket in comparison to what he had on the vine. Easy for me to say because I was not growing the fruit.

Distributing the Melons

After eluding the irate farmer, we returned to town to dispose of dozens of watermelons. As strange as it may seem, we did not eat many of the melons, nor try to sell them. A few were consumed on the night of the raid and some were saved for a later feast.

Many of the melons were tossed onto the yards of people who, at that moment, were out of favor with us. Alternately, a sizeable part of our plunder was placed gently on the front porch of people who had passed our muster as acceptable human beings.

The out-of-favor population changed from one melon deposit to the next. With the passing whims of those passing the watermelons, a bunch of melons might end up on a porch or on the front yard. If an unfortunate soul was the recipient of tossed melons, and if our harvest from the farmer's patch had been abundant, the resulting raid on a yard left a mass of broken fruit—a red and green carpet of sweet-smelling produce. Perhaps a future watermelon patch.

One memorable night, with the watermelon men commanding two full pickup loads of watermelons, a high school classmate was selected for a yard deposit. In previous visits, we had left whole melons on her porch. But she was out of favor on this specific evening. The reason? I was out of favor with her. She and I had recently become an "ex-item" at our school.

One spurned suitor might have let her off the hook but there was another lad in the group that night who also had been left hanging-out in her winds of romance. It is said by some that "revenge is sweet." In this situation, it was indeed.

We were experienced watermelon throwers. Like a raiding army, we knew time was short to make the assault—about five to ten seconds. The bursting watermelons made enough noise to awake a light sleeper. The idea was to coast up to the target (lights off, of course), where each of us would throw several melons as quickly as possible, then take off into the safety of the night. Until this evening, I was batting 1.000 as having never been identified and caught. After this night, my average dropped a bit—which contributed to my last appearance in a watermelon patch.

The father of the girl, Mr. Freeman, was not asleep. He informed us of this fact the next day. He fooled us; all lights in the house were out. Later, in our post-raid analysis, we came to the conclusion that the man was either saving on electricity or had very fine hearing. We were at the Freeman residence for no more than a few seconds, throwing watermelons at a frantic pace, when he suddenly opened the front door, turned on the porch light, stepped onto this porch, and drew a pistol on us!

A pistol is not a shotgun—in my eyes, a pistol is more deadly—and the arms bearer was not several hundred yards away, as were the watermelon farmers. He was about twenty feet from us, at least at the instant we saw him emerge from his house. A few seconds later, we were many paces removed from his gun. Each boy immediately disappeared—seemingly evaporated—from the Freeman yard. My classmates had never displayed such motivation to leave a place.

Because of my panic, I didn't return to the pickups. I darted out of the yard and ran to my home, about a half-mile away. Silently, I entered the house and went to bed, panting like a runner who had just finished a marathon. As I fell asleep, I was not aware Mr. Freeman had identified several of the melon attackers, including one of the ex-sweethearts of his daughter.

The next morning, as my family and I were having breakfast, my Dad received a telephone call from Mr. Freeman. Dad's conversation with Mr. Freeman unfolded before us.

"Hello ... yes, this is Jim Black. Hello Mr. Freeman."

I knew I was in trouble.

Silence permeated our kitchen for a moment or so, as Dad listened to bad news (for me).

"You don't say," Dad said.

Silence once again, as Dad listened to more bad news (again, for me). "Your yard is red? ... Yes, I can see why."

Silence one more time ... then Dad responded to Mr. Freeman, "It was U.D.? ... You're sure? ... OK, fine. Thank you for the call. I'll take care of it."

Dad had never whipped me—never came close. But as I listened to this depressing telephone conversation, I was certain another record, besides my recent less-than-perfect watermelon raid performance, was about to be broken.

The conversation with Mr. Freeman came to an end. Dad put down the phone and sat staring at me for what seemed like an eternity. His staring was accompanied with a frown. That was it: A long, hard, frowning stare.

You can imagine my surprise and relief when Dad only said, "Get on down to the Freeman's. You and your friends have some cleaning up to do and some apologies to make."

I was out the kitchen door in a nanosecond. I was at the Freeman's in a millisecond.

There, I found my buddies cleaning up Mr. Freeman's yard. He was standing on the porch, inspecting the scene. I was embarrassed to be there. Mr. Freeman and I had become friends during the time I dated his daughter. I felt guilty, as if I had betrayed a comrade.

Beverly Freeman, my ex-sweetheart, was also an observer. She stood inside the house, next to the screen door, surveying our clean up. As we were rolling up the watermelon carpet, I stole an occasional glance her way. She returned my glances—with a slight smile on her lips. Her demeanor was a seminal experience for me regarding the opposite sex. Her bearing was not one of anger. Her smile was gentle, even pleasant. Perhaps it was a smile saying to me, "At least you were thinking of me." Or: "It's OK U.D., I understand the futility associated with rejected love—therein your frustration, resulting in your watermelon demonstration." The metaphysical concepts of teenage love.

I didn't understand her behavior toward me because her countenance was probably built into the female genome. Whatever the source, I was completely impressed and it melted my heart down to the I-want-to-grovel state. God, I loved that girl.

A couple years or so after the melon battering of the Freeman's yard, I passed by the house, just for old times sake. I noticed several large, luscious-looking watermelons growing next to the front porch.

Years after this incident, my brother Tom informed me that after I sprinted from our kitchen to head for the Freeman's, Dad burst out laughing. His frown was an artful put-on, a nifty bit of play-acting. Dad never mentioned the incident and I was savvy enough to let sleeping dogs lie.

Dynamite and Doodle Bugging

As recounted earlier, during the 1950s, Lovington was a booming oil town, as were the other towns in Lea County. The famous Permian Basin was a large and rich reservoir of oil, and for several years, Lea County was a prolific source of crude oil for America. Oil prospecting was an important part of the oil industry and prospecting crews were a common sight in the countryside. These teams were called doodle bugging crews.

One of the prospecting tools was seismograph technology. The crew's task was to drill holes into the ground, lower dynamite into the holes, set off the explosives, and record the resulting vibrations. These activities helped find pools of oil beneath the earth.

Dynamite Men. On another summer night in Lovington, several idle male teenagers were looking for something to do (including me). The girls in town were locked in for the night, which reduced our options. It was too early to go to bed, which opened up our options, say like blowing something up with dynamite. Why not? After all, our minds were idle.

As we sat around a house of one of our classmates whose parents were out of town, another classmate informed us he had stored a cache of dynamite in a nearby pasture. Paul worked as a doodle bugger, and taking the notion that one must save dynamite for a rainy day, he had secretly lifted a few pounds of the explosive from a seismograph truck.

Who knows? The dynamite might be needed for some future emergency. The Soviets were rattling a lot of sabers in those days. Texas politicians were still talking about annexing Lea County. Our fair state was stolen from Mexico; perhaps the Mexicans might want their property back. It pays to be prepared.

Our reaction to Paul's revelation about the dynamite was a natural response of, "Let's put it to good use." After all, give a child a hammer and he looks for something to pound. Give a teenage boy dynamite and he looks for something to blow up. What could be more logical?

Our minds were no longer idle. But what could we destroy? Blowing-up Mr. Freeman's house was not the same as tossing watermelons in his yard. Although, in hindsight, it would have been interesting to counter his pistol waving with some dynamite waving: Ten teenage boys holding dynamite canisters in his front yard would likely have diminished his zeal. Anyway, we had to do some exploring, to ferret out a target.

Attacking the Target

To the west of town, a few miles outside the city limits, we found our target: a windmill—a tall structure, complete with four legs and a sucker rod in the middle. The windmill was an enticing object; big and lofty; worthy of our attention; worthy of destruction. An example of this type of windmill is shown in Figure 13-1.[2]

At this juncture of my story, I must make a rare diversion into the world of solemnity and seriousness. I ask for your forbearance, if only for a few moments. I don't think any of us boys would have considered destroying a tool as important as an *operational* windmill—a vital instrument to ranchers and farmers. Unless the ranchers or

Figure 13-1. Example of our target.

farmers had gone to the expense of installing mechanized engines and pumps, their ability to pull water from the earth was dependent entirely on the windmill.

Granted, some of our classmates damaged our football stadium later in the year with graffiti painting, but even this act of vandalism did not threaten the livelihood of the victims (the public in this case). The windmill we selected was located next to an abandoned house (with a "No Trespassing" sign in clear view), and it was not in operating condition.

My conscience is clean. We can leave the world of social psychology and return to the matter at hand. Our windmill destruction unfolded as follows:

- Dynamite was tied to one of the legs of the windmill.
- Wire from the dynamite was run to one of our cars.
- The wire was inserted into the cigarette lighter.
- BOOM!
- The leg of the windmill disintegrated.
- We awaited the climax of our act: The collapse of the windmill.
- The windmill stayed erect, sustained by the other three legs and the sucker rod.
- We had failed *Blowing-Up Windmills 101*.

The sound of the boom was just that, a loud resounding BOOM. Some of us had heard dynamite explosions from the deep recesses of a doodle bugging hole in the earth, where its noise was muted. The volume of this explosion startled us and we knew it was also heard in town. We realized the local constabulary was probably headed our way. But we knew the territory, so we took a back road on the return to town.

The explosion left us at the same time exhilarated and disappointed. The power of the explosion, the disappearance of one leg of the windmill, was an impressive experience. But the emergence of a standing windmill also left us with a sense of failure. Clearly, the windmill had to go, but now was not the time for remedial action. As I said, we left the scene as soon as possible.

"Mysterious Blasts Puzzle Lovington"

The next edition of the local paper (Figure 13-2) carried an article about the dynamiting of the windmill, as well as earlier explosions we had crafted. The police chief was interviewed about the case. He stated his men were hot on the trail of several suspects.

A round table discussion among the "suspects" did not leave us with a feeling that the law was breathing down our collars. In fact, none of us had been questioned about the incident. Well, at least

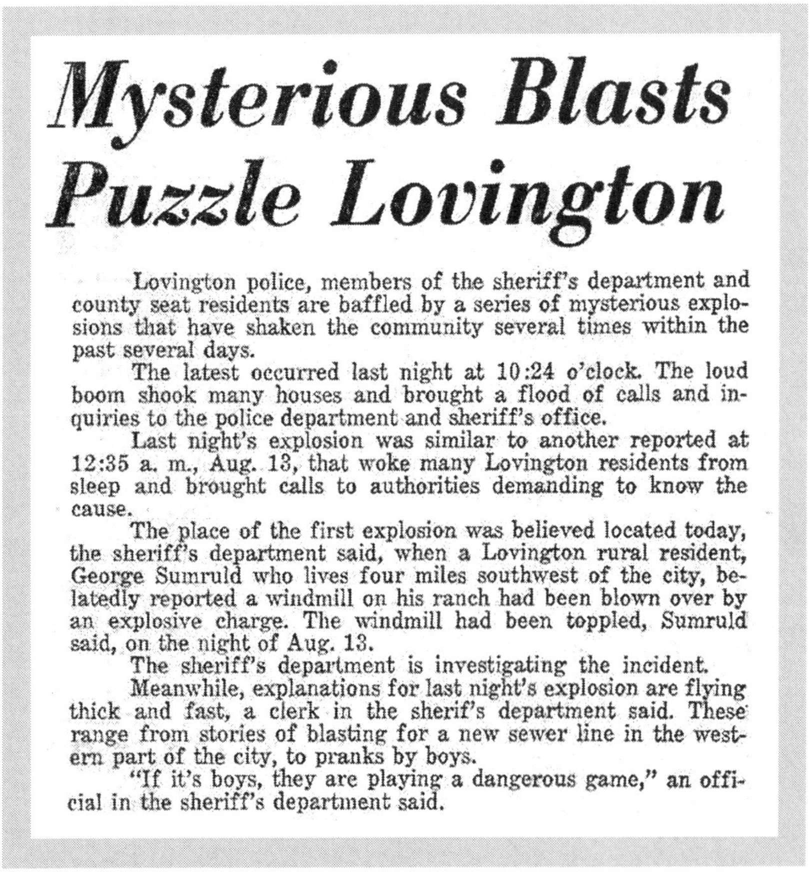

Mysterious Blasts Puzzle Lovington

Lovington police, members of the sheriff's department and county seat residents are baffled by a series of mysterious explosions that have shaken the community several times within the past several days.

The latest occurred last night at 10:24 o'clock. The loud boom shook many houses and brought a flood of calls and inquiries to the police department and sheriff's office.

Last night's explosion was similar to another reported at 12:35 a. m., Aug. 13, that woke many Lovington residents from sleep and brought calls to authorities demanding to know the cause.

The place of the first explosion was believed located today, the sheriff's department said, when a Lovington rural resident, George Sumruld who lives four miles southwest of the city, belatedly reported a windmill on his ranch had been blown over by an explosive charge. The windmill had been toppled, Sumruld said, on the night of Aug. 13.

The sheriff's department is investigating the incident.

Meanwhile, explanations for last night's explosion are flying thick and fast, a clerk in the sherif's department said. These range from stories of blasting for a new sewer line in the western part of the city, to pranks by boys.

"If it's boys, they are playing a dangerous game," an official in the sheriff's department said.

Figure 13-2. Persistence is the mother of delinquency.

not by the police. After reading the article, Dad posed a question to me, "You wouldn't know anything about these explosions would you?" My old man knew me well.

I could not say yes. To do so would have exposed … well, not just myself—a person very high on my list of people who did not want to be exposed—but also my classmates. We could face charges of stealing explosives, trespassing on posted property, and destroying private property. But I had never lied to my Dad when he confronted me with a direct question (my childhood years of the ages of 0-10 do not count in my statistic).

Even though I was an indolent student, I had picked up on parts of a teacher's lecture about a citizen's right not to incriminate himself. I was in a very sticky situation but had to say something. I replied, "Dad, I'm sorry, but I can't answer your question."

My father was a perceptive man. Additionally, as an ex-law officer, I think he knew what I meant and what I was trying to convey to him. His approach to the problem was indirect, but effective, "I see. Well, if I knew anyone who was involved in the destruction of private property, I would offer some advice to that person. Don't do anything like that again. And if that windmill had been in an operating condition, I would have to turn that person in."

Case closed. Lesson learned. The final destruction of the windmill, which indeed took place, had one less conspirator involved. My co-conspirators carried the idleness torch to another level—leveling the windmill and a few other assorted targets. Again, Figure 13-2 shows an article taken from the local paper about my buddies' determination. Dad was on my trail; I was no longer part of this conspiracy.

What Happened to these Thieves and Bombers?

This story might leave you with the impression my classmates and I were unsavory kids. In defense, most of our antics were harmless. But I'm sure some of our tricks, if enacted today in a larger community, would have landed us in jail, or at least subjected us to some form of juvenile penalty. To a great extent, I think we were protected by our community, by its smallness, by the familiarity and trust of its inhabitants.

As far as I know, none of us resorted to crime in our later lives. I don't think any of us landed in jail. We matured, and found more productive jobs than scrap iron and watermelon theft, but not nearly as much fun as a country club lifeguard.

Interestingly, our dynamite specialist became a successful scientist, working in (wouldn't you know), ordnance systems for the U.S. Navy. Currently, he is president of a museum dealing with armaments. Perhaps his Lea County experience is included in his resume.

The boy who hosted the initial meeting of the demolition conspirators became a coach and teacher. The driver of one of the getaway cars joined the Marines. One of the other conspirators became president of a bank. Another became a librarian. Another became a computer network consultant and wrote books about the Internet. Still another became a medical school professor, specializing in psychiatry.

Overall, I think we turned out OK.

---

[1] Schlosser, Eric, *Fast Food Nation*, HarperCollins Publishers, Inc., 2002, page 53.

[2] My thanks to Lynn Mauldin for a picture of this windmill. I wanted to use a photo of the actual windmill in this story, but of course, it was scattered by our dynamite and later, the Southwestern winds. See Mauldin, Lynn C., *Lea County New Mexico: A Pictorial History*, The Downing Company Publishers, Virginia Beach VA, 23462, 1997.

14

THE DOG CATCHER

If you pick up a starving dog and make him prosperous,
he will not bite you. This is the principal difference
between a man and a dog.

—*Mark Twain*

As seasoned dog catchers like to say, let's cut to the chase. First, being a dog catcher has its drawbacks. If you are an average, non-sadist person, catching and perhaps killing man's best friend is not a lot of fun. Second, telling people you are a dog catcher is not an effective way to win friends and influence people.

For example, let's assume I meet someone at a get-together. This someone says to me, "Hi there. Nice party. I'm Doctor Jones. I'm a brain surgeon."

"Yes, it's a nice party. I'm Uyless Black. I'm a dog catcher. Would you like to talk shop?"

Third, a dog catcher is not rated very high on the list of coveted jobs. Just consider the well known quote, "He couldn't get a job as a dog catcher." In contrast, you never hear anyone say, "He couldn't get a job as a brain surgeon."

Nonetheless, for a few weeks, I was a dog catcher for the city of Lovington, New Mexico. But not just a dog catcher. The job description for Lovington's dog catcher was quite varied. I was also designated to maintain all stop and yield signs within the city limits, all parks (two small, almost barren plots of earth), the "No Parking" curbs, and the parking stripes surrounding the county court house. In addition, if I were not busy, I was to join the local street repair crew and give them a hand in laying or repairing asphalt. Stray cats were also my responsibility.

Securing the Job

I became a dog catcher because of the same reasons other people become dog catchers: I was unemployed and marginally competent to work gainfully at another occupation. Lucky for me, my brother's father-in-law, Police Chief James Robinson was in charge of several city government departments in Lovington. Vagrant people *and* vagrant dogs came under his jurisdiction.

The dog catcher's position had been vacant for several weeks, leading to a couple of situations affecting my new job: (a) a considerable number of dogs were on the loose, and (b) as the Chief informed me, a number of "pending" dogs were in the local dog pound. Initially, I thought the term pending meant the dogs had not found a home with a human.

I liked Chief Robinson. But I was naïve about certain duties of the job and the Chief did not explain all the details about Lovington's Dog Catcher until after I was sworn in. (The following conversations are paraphrased, but convey the spirit of the dialogue. Italics represent the author's license to tell tales):

Chief Robinson, *Do you swear you will faithfully uphold the dog catcher's creed? Will you discharge your duties faithfully to the citizens of Lovington?*

Me, *I do and I will.*

I take a lot of leave with his charge to me. I think the Chief said something closer to, "U.D., we have a serious dog problem in the city. But we can't find anyone to take on the job of dog catcher and our pound is full of pending dogs. (*But for some weird reason, you accepted!*) So, here are the keys to the dog pound and to your pickup. Go to it."

New dog catcher, *Chief, I like dogs a lot. Some of my best friends are dogs. I'm sure I can take care of the problem. No big deal. And I can't think of a time a dog has shied away from me. I'll deliver those dogs to the pound in no time and we'll find a home for them—and the other 'pendings' at the pound.*

Look up "gullibility" in the dictionary. There it is: a picture of me.

Chief Robinson replied, "Hmm. Well, I didn't mean pending as in awaiting ownerships. You see, our police have rounded-up several stray dogs over the past few weeks. No one has claimed them. A couple of the dogs are sick and some of them are mean as hell. You have to get rid of them."

Get rid of the dogs? What, export them to Texas? I said, "OK, where do I take them?"

He hesitated for a moment, and replied, "Sorry, U.D., you don't 'take' them anywhere. You have to dispose of them. We can't deal with any more dogs. The pound is full of them. There's a concrete pit next to the pound. You're to place the dogs in this pit, put the cover on it, run an attached hose to your pickup tail pipe. The disposed bodies are to be taken to the city dump."

Sweet Mother Mary. It then sunk into my dull witted mind: "Pending," as in "awaiting" their Big Chill.

I was dumbfounded. I felt disconnected to the conversation. I was being asked to kill adored animals—not jackrabbits. I was not above shooting wild critters, some of them damaged my Dad's crops and grazing grass. But not dogs. Dogs were to me what horses were to most Lea County citizens: revered creatures.

At the risk of diverting into tear jerking mush, it will be helpful to explain that I am a *perro afficianado*. For the readers of this story who are not bilingual, its translation into English is: I love dogs.

But I was between a rock and a hard place. I had just accepted a job and had been given an order from my boss about this job. My brother and his father-in-law had gone out of their way to grant me this exalted position. Reneging was not an option; it didn't run in my genes.

The First and Last Time

The ride to the dog pound was one of the longest I remember taking. I started to turn back at each intersection but I made excuses to myself. Sick and mean dogs; they were going to be killed by someone anyway. I rationalized all the way to the dog pound.

I won't explain my disposal of the dogs. I will say that with my first task completed in my new job, I was saddled with guilt and regret. I then headed off to paint No Parking curbs and to mow the few blades of grass in my parks. But in the back of my mind, I made a decision, "Never again."

Other Duties as Assigned

Because my job had been vacant for a while, a wide variety of tasks needed my attention. One job was repainting the parking stripes around the four sides of the county courthouse. To the chagrin of the politicians from the city of Hobbs, Lovington was the county seat of Lea County. As the custodians of the county seat, Chief Robinson and the city fathers (it was too early in the feminist movement for city mothers to be elected) wanted Lovington to take proper care of its responsibilities. For example, one of the tasks was keeping the white parking stripes around the court house looking clean and fresh.

Another chore was washing the streets surrounding the court house. Using a rigged-up pickup with a water tank in the pickup bed, the city employees made certain its citizens did not drag any street residue onto the county court house floors, whose sheen was like a mirror. I recall seeing images of myself as I walked down a court house corridor. Actually, I could only see the reflections of the bottoms of my shoes, but those reflections reflected the care and concern of the citizens for their court house and surrounding streets.

I was not in charge of street cleaning or the hall ways of the court house. The former task was delegated to the Lovington Water Department, consisting of one person who had almost has many jobs as I. My government colleague took as much pride in his street cleaning as the person doing the court house hallways. You could almost eat a meal on those court house streets.

Shortly after my initiation into the dog catcher profession, Chief Robinson informed me the stripes around the courthouse needed repainting and that I had to perform this job early in the morning, prior to rush hour—such as it was.

For this part of my job, I had to coordinate my department's schedule with that of the Water Department. Over a cup of coffee we worked out the arrangements. The next day, he washed down the streets around the courthouse—the day before I painted the stripes.

From Lifeguard to Dog Catcher

It bears mentioning that in my previous summers in Lovington, going back to my high school days, I was the head lifeguard at the local swimming pool (okay, so there was only one other lifeguard. Still, I was in charge of him). I had started the summer occupying this high-status position but I fell-out with the pool managers and quit my job.

Walking away from this job was a big mistake. Not only had I vacated the prestigious position of Head Life Guard of the Lovington Country Club, I had given up a high paying job. I was the only person in Lovington who was certified as a Red Cross Water Safety Instructor. As such, I had organized a successful and lucrative swimming lesson program at the Country Club. I still encounter some of my former swimming students on my visits to Lea County. I even taught the (future) Lt. Governor of New Mexico to swim. But not in political waters, as he did not last very long in New Mexico politics.

How could I have come to this place in life? The week before I was a high-roller. Now I was consigned to a paltry fixed income. Just as distressing was my demotion from the City Life Guard to the City

Dog Catcher. A humbling and humiliating dissent down through the ranks of Lovington's social register.

In reading the last paragraph, you may be thinking I am offending the profession of dog catching. You are absolutely correct. But I cast no aspersions whatsoever on the profession known today by names such as of Canine Control Engineer, Dog Parenthood Planner, Animal Boarding Specialist, and Pet Transportation Technologist. In fact, I am making references to a defunct occupation. I ask you to find anyone who calls himself a dog catcher nowadays.

Esoteric questions about job titles aside, as I reflect on those times, I realize I learned a lot about humility. I had become too full of myself with my seeming importance at the swimming pool. I began to refuse to take orders and when forced to do so, I quit. Not too bright, even for a teenager.

But in the long run, the job change was a positive experience for me. It wised me up and ignited some nascent maturity cells in my makeup. As well, the "humble" job of dog catcher (as well as others I had in later years) gave me a respect and perspective for those who labor in unglamorous positions.

None of us start as the CEO, the Senator, or the esteemed teacher. Most of us begin our trek through the work world as clerks, waiters, ditch diggers, even dog catchers. Movie stars did not begin their profession as movie stars. They started in more humble jobs. Same goes for bank presidents, even America's Presidents. I gauge the worth of a person as to how he or she handles success, not the success itself.

The Art and Science of Dog Catching

Dog catching was not as easy as I had thought it would be. *Hello Skip. Good boy. Looks like you could use a pat, a scratch around your neck. That's it. Here we go. Now that wasn't so bad was it? What do you think of the cage?*

The free dogs of Lovington were free for a very good reason: They knew the ropes, so to speak. They were crafty animals, rightly suspicious of people. Occasionally I encountered a gullible pup, one who was looking for some food and affection—my two main baits. They were easy snares. But the older dogs were wary. Like Pavlov's dogs, these critters had been conditioned to their surroundings.

One of my dog catcher tools was a lasso (called a rope in New Mexico). Perhaps you have seen this tool on a wild life television show. The noose of the rope is tossed around the neck of the animal. The animal (the ropee) is kept at bay with a long stick attached to the rope, held by the person doing the roping (the roper).

My rope was a prototype to the TV rope. I call it "Rope, Version 0." The TV lasso was at least "Rope, Version 1" in that it was equipped with one tool that my Version 0 did not have: the stick. My dog catcher rope was just that, a rope; no stick.

A rope was an integral part of the lives of New Mexico ranchers. My Dad and brothers used it often in their work on our cattle ranch and I was a fair roper myself. However, I discovered there was a big difference between roping a calf and roping a dog. The lassoed calf continued to try to avoid the roper; it pulled away from the direction of the roper. Not so for the lassoed dog, at least the dog in this story.

I was called to a neighborhood by concerned parents. A stray dog was hanging around their children and the parents were afraid the dog would injure their kids. My job was to rid the neighborhood of this "dangerous menace".

As I approached the dog, I tried my standard dog protocol of, "Hey Skip. Ha'ya doing fella?" But my greetings fell on deaf ears. This dog was not user-friendly. It was growling and snapping; its teeth were bared; its ears were folded down on its head.

After executing a number of canine thrusts and parries, I succeeded in roping the dog. Great, but in my focus to capture the animal, I didn't plan what I would do after it was captured. I assumed it would take the stance of a calf and pull away from me, trying to release itself from the rope. Nope. Unlike a lassoed calf, this dog reacted with very un-bovine and very canine characteristics: It attacked the roper.

Even if you don't like dog catchers, I ask you to consider my situation. A lowly civil servant had been asked to rid the neighborhood of a mettlesome dog. *Don't worry folks, I've got everything under control.* With the flick of a lasso, I found myself surrounded by children, adults, and one very pissed-off dog.

As to the action of the dog catcher? Running like a bat out of hell, trying to avoid the teeth of an unhappy dog who was snapping at his heels and ass. I was supposed to save the neighborhood and I myself was being taken hostage.

My ass and I were saved when the rope, trailing the pursuing dog, became entangled in a bush in one of the yards of a house. I heard the dog let out a yelp. Only then did I turn my head to see the captured creature biting and clawing at the rope.

Make no mistake, this animal had not read the book *Dogs, Man's Best Friends*. But in the dog's defense, I don't know of anyone or anything that takes kindly to having a rope put around its neck. Anyway, social issues aside, I was in a quandary; I couldn't approach the dog. The dog was in quandary; it couldn't attack me.

Thanks to my ranching experience, I came up with a solution. Thinking about the team roping events in rodeos, I would use another lasso and secure the dog's legs. But I had no more ropes, so I called the police department and asked for supplies. Within a few minutes, a policeman arrived—one of Chief Robinson's stalwarts.

This part of the story is another unpleasant aspect of the tale. He ordered me and the other folks on the scene to stand back. He then drew his pistol from his holster, walked toward the dog, and stopping just short of his jaws, shot the creature in the head.

I discovered this practice was commonplace, not just in Lovington, but in many towns in and around Lea County. I'm speaking of events and a culture of some 60 years ago. No PETA, dog lobbies, or animal rights activists. Instead of sedating the animal, which would be done today, the dog was shot.

Make no mistake, the dog was a menace. Trying to capture it with more ropes would have placed the police officer and me at risk. Today, the hostile dog would be captured with a lasso/stick and "put to sleep" with an injection at the pound. Given the circumstances, the bullet to the head was no less inhumane.

The policeman informed me I should have used my .22 pistol (kept in my pickup) for a situation in which I encountered a difficult dog. I contritely agreed. But I couldn't grasp how I was first to rope a deranged dog, then pull out my pistol, draw an accurate bead on the charging animal, and bring it down—before it bought me down. I posed my question to the officer.

He advised me not to use a rope on a dog that was acting strangely. The strategy was to chase the dog to an area where there were few or no people, then shoot it. He polished off my humiliation, "If you want to rope a mad dog, you deserve an ass bite."

Free at Last

Toward the end of my short dog catcher career, as I was preparing to resign and depart for college, a police officer drove by the dog pound and conveyed his observation to the Chief that apparently, I had not dispatched any more dogs to the canine pearly gates. I had held the job for several weeks and I had captured about ten or so dogs, but not one of them had walked the final mile. They were alive and well in the dog pound.

The Chief asked me why there were so many dogs in the pound? Implicit in the question, was why there were not more of them in the city dump? I answered I was going to tend to the matter before I left for college. I outright lied because I had no such intention. Never again.

My last act as the town dog catcher was one of atonement. The night before I left town to return to college, I took a drive out to the dog pound, where with an exception or two, I was greeted as if I were the best thing they had encountered since their last wet bone. I had consigned these dogs to a death chamber but they weren't aware of their fate and took me in as their friend. The cliché, "Man's best friend" came to my mind on that evening.

I don't like maudlin prose. But the simple, incontrovertible fact remains that we humans, over many centuries, have conditioned the dog to our wants, to make it trust us, and to accept us as its protector. I can understand prisons for humans. For a limited population of depraved humans, I can understand a death sentence. And dog pounds are needed to keep urban streets relatively safe and clean.

But death sentences for those whom we have subjugated and trained to satisfy our wants and needs? To abuse and maybe even kill animals who have been conditioned to do nothing more than obey us and make us think we are grand? It's instructive to think about this idea: *If we were only as great as our dogs think we are.* I sometimes wonder who is higher up on the food chain, dogs or humans.

Atonement, of Sorts

Have you witnessed scenes in your life of unbridled joy, of uncontained happiness? Your answer is probably yes. For example, your first marriage. As another example, your second divorce. I witnessed one of those scenes as I opened the gate to the pound and set the dogs free.

I not only witnessed this joyful scene, I was part of it, for I was the jail-breaker. As the dogs ran away from their prison, as they disappeared into the night and the Lovington suburbs (such as they were), I felt relieved. My guilt vanished, as if it were a passenger on the backs of the disappearing critters.

In closing this story about my short tenure as a dog catcher, I recognize the dog jail break violated my dog catcher creed. It has taken a long time in coming, but I now offer my apologies to the city council of Lovington, to the Chief, to Lovington's lawns, shrubs, and fire hydrants, and to any unwary citizens who were subsequently bit by these dogs.

In case some of my escaped canine prisoners made their way to a nearby state, I make no such apologies to the fire hydrants and citizens of Texas.

15

Buzz Off!

—————◦•◦•◦—————

The thing which has made labor great
and powerful is labor-saving machinery.

—Mark Twain

Several buzzards are in-flight, headed for warm areas and seeking prey. These birds like to fly when the air surrounding their wings and bodies is warm. They can be seen leaving an area as the weather cools or landing after the warm thermals have cooled-down. Eventually, they look for a place to stop and rest for a while.

What could be more enticing to a bird than a cluster of trees? One of the buzzards, designated as the look-out for such trees (we call her Roxelle), spots a place on the ground covered by several acres of trees. Roxelle informs her fellow buzzards, "Hey, down there to the left; a bunch of trees."

Horace, the head buzzard, takes a look and makes the decision to stop for the night, "OK, it's time for a rest. Let's circle-around for a while, like they show in the movies, and settle in the middle of that tree orchard."

It so happens some of these buzzards decided to make one of their regular stops in a pecan orchard belonging to my brother, Ross. This story is about the buzzards and their assault on his orchard.

As a sidebar, the term buzzard is used incorrectly to identify two North American vultures: the turkey vulture and the black vulture, two scavenger birds who dine on carrion. The term is used correctly by the British to identify the European broad winged hawk. For this story, we will continue to use the term buzzard for the turkey vulture. Let's now see how these buzzards invaded Ross' pecan orchard and how Ross countered their assault.

Pecans and Lea County

"Dad, Uncle Ross has built a buzzard pit stop." This statement was the conclusion of my son, Tommy, after he and I had spent a few hours at Ross' pecan orchard. The two of us were visiting Ross, who lives in Lovington, my hometown I have spoke-of often in this book. A retired school superintendent of the Lovington schools, Ross decided several years ago to grow and harvest pecans. He thought the business would be a source of income and a welcome addition to his retirement stipend. He had some extra land (34 acres) surrounding his home. Why not put it to use?

Even though the land in Lea County is hostile to plant life (I have mentioned several times that the area is semi-arid), sagebrush and flowers somehow thrive. These plants survive with very little water. Many remain dormant and invisible to the human eye most of the time, and show themselves after the occurrence of a rare rain shower—the annual rainfall in Lea County ranges from 8 to 12 inches. After a heavy rain, the flowers and sage bloom profusely, but after a few days, they retreat beneath the hard soil, to await another infrequent soaking.

So little rain comes to Lea County the indigenous plants and trees do not look kindly on interlopers. Pecan trees fit into the category of intruders, as they are not native to the region and they need a lot of water to grow and bear fruit. If the indigenous plant life could talk, they might say to the pecan trees, "You are welcome but bring your own water. And while you are at it, bring some for us."

Ross solved the problem. An inventive man, he installed an underground watering system. A small submersible pump sent water to the trees in the orchard. Because the water flowed though underground pipes, the precious liquid was protected from evaporation. This system saved 80% of the water in relation to a conventional sprinkler system.

The Buzzard Pit Stop

For several years, Ross's pecan orchard did not attract one solitary buzzard. When they appeared later, their numbers were modest. Initially, a few score of them would come in on the thermals, stay for the night, and leave the next morning. But this limited population soon expanded to hundreds of buzzards. It was as if Ross had posted a giant "Vacancy" sign in the orchard. Within three years of the first buzzard landing, the orchard became a frequently-used buzzard motel.

Large clusters of trees in southeast New Mexico are as rare as a mountain in Florida. If there are tree groves in Lea County, they have been planted and nurtured by people, just as the mountains in Florida are there, courtesy of Disney World. Consequently, tree pit stops are few and far-between in this part of the world. Unfortunately for Ross, hundreds of birds decided to light-down for the night in his orchard. If orchards had been plentiful in Lea County, perhaps the buzzards would have spread themselves among them. But such was not the case; for they had chosen Ross' orchard.

The visit occurred each day around sunset. Taking advantage of the last thermals of the afternoon, the buzzards could be seen circling-around above the orchard. Gradually, they descended down to the pecan tree foliage and lost themselves in the trees.

Buzzards do not have a good reputation among humans—our images of these birds are not complimentary. But if we can ignore their penchant for eating dead, rotten meat and think about their size and flying ability, their soaring skills can be a pleasure to watch.

They are capable of riding thermals for five or six minutes, and with their large wingspan, they appear to be majestic artisans of the air.

Nonetheless, their habits on the ground are not very majestic. Excuse my language, but there is no delicate way to put it. While they perch on the trees, they shit a lot. That was the crux of the problem. The buzzards' waste matter was slowly killing the trees because their defecation was poison to the leaves. They were so numerous that parts of the tree became white from the buzzards' bowel movements. Later, the tree turned brown as it died.

Like all birds, buzzard feces contains germs. Not only was the buzzard presence in Ross' orchard affecting Ross' livelihood, it had the potential of creating a health problem. Additionally, the aesthetics of the situation was not insignificant. After all, who wants to live in the middle of a buzzard colony, surrounded by buzzard shit? I'm making light of the situation but Ross had a serious problem on his hands.

What comes to your mind when you think of walking through an orchard? For myself, this walk brings to mind a pleasant pastoral jaunt. I think of bucolic images when strolling this green habitat. In contrast, picture a stroll through a buzzard-infested orchard: ugly birds, their droppings, dying trees, possible disease—not exactly the image we have in mind when thinking about orchards.

I mentioned earlier the buzzards descended down into the orchard and lost themselves in the trees. This perspective depended from where one viewed the pecan trees. The birds were quite visible to a person walking through the orchard. The end result of the landing was astounding. In the early hours of morning, before the buzzards took flight, parts of the trees in the orchard were almost hidden by the festooning birds. Interestingly, they did not land on all the trees. Rather, each evening they selected specific trees and used them for their roost.

The left photo in Figure 15-1 shows several of the buzzards flying over one of Ross' trees. The leaves reflect the damage the birds had done to this tree. It was one of their favorites. The black and white photo prevents a view of the browning leaves. They were still somewhat green, but unless Ross could get rid of the buzzards, they too would end-up brown.

Figure 15-1. Scenes from the orchard.

Taking a walk one day, I experienced an eerie sensation as I slowly made my way through the orchard. Some trees seemed to have more birds than pecans; many of the branches were bent-over from the birds' weight. Buzzards are known to show no fear of people. In some parts of the world they perch or walk serenely amongst crowds of humans. During my walk through their motel, they were almost oblivious to my presence, periodically casting a condescending glance down my way.

You may be asking, why not just shoot the birds? After all, Ross would be protecting his family's assets and health. The answer to the question is due to the Buzzard Lobby: The buzzard is a protected bird. It can't be killed unless one has a buzzard killing permit, issued by the Society for the Preservation of Buzzards, otherwise known as the government. Indeed, Ross has a permit for buzzard self-defense but he is allowed to send only 25 buzzards a year to buzzard heaven. Consequently, Ross' buzzard self defense procedures were confined to somehow convincing Horace, Roxelle, and the other birds to find another pit stop.

Tackling the Problem

As I mentioned, Ross is an inventive man. Using his mechanical skills, he rigged-up a gun and placed it in the middle of the orchard and set it to fire every few minutes. This labor-saving device allowed my brother turn to other chores besides shooting guns. The explosions of the shells were not lethal to the birds. The sounds were meant to frighten and discourage them from landing. Unfortunately, the noise distracted the buzzards *and* a few of Ross' neighbors as well. Eventually, the buzzards got wise to this ploy and landed anyway.

Uncle Sam is Everywhere

We need to add another character to our buzzard story, the government. In so doing, permit me to make a few comments about Uncle Sam. Modern government increasingly addresses our every problem and seems to have its finger in just about every facet of our lives. I challenge you to go through one day of your normal activity without coming into contact with a government program. In relation to this buzzard problem, a responsible response would be, "Too bad about your trees, but grow something else, or buy some hawks. It's your responsibility to fix your problem. If the birds are endangering your health, take necessary actions to protect your family."

More often, the response is, "It is the government's responsibility to fix all your problems. We will get rid of those pesky buzzards by sending them somewhere else. That way, we can keep our job by moving them to yet another orchard, then another. By the way, we're also increasing your taxes in order to expand our more-enveloping cocoon around your sheltered, managed life." Thomas Jefferson must be turning over in his grave.

In fairness to Ross, he is not a government groupie; he is a self sufficient individual. However, for this story, New Mexico and Lea County participate in a government program that deals with game control. Through this program and the local animal control officer, Ross learned about a buzzard control program in Florida.

The program was designed to rid orchards and other areas of buzzards. After preliminary discussions between Ross and the program administrators, a Florida government agent came across the country to help Ross with his buzzard problem. *Your tax dollars in action!*

I called this man the "Frank Buck of Buzzards," named after the famous safari explorer and hunter. Tommy and I were visiting Ross during the time Frank Buck was there and I listened to Frank explain the central idea behind the anti-buzzard program.

"Mr. Black, the solution to your buzzard problem is straight-forward. Erect a very tall pole, one that is higher than the pecan trees. Place this pole in the middle of the orchard. On the top of this pole, hang a dead buzzard. Then, no more buzzards in your orchard!"

I couldn't believe what I was hearing. In so many words, he suggested that Ross erect a dead buzzard effigy. The dead birds would supposedly frighten away Horace and his band of defecating marauders. With multiple poles, strategically located in various parts of the orchard, Frank claimed the orchard would soon be buzzard-free.

The trees under assault were not mine, so I said nothing. I awaited the response from Ross, who looked at Frank Buck for a long moment. I thought my brother might have been thinking that his main problem was how to get rid of Frank, not the buzzards. After the pause, Ross expressed skepticism but said he would defer to the buzzard expert's experience and would do as he recommended. Ross was gracious in his response, "You came all the way from Florida to help. I'll do my part."

The program in Florida focused on preventing buzzards from roosting on microwave radio towers and other communications facilities. After much experimentation, the game control officials discovered the buzzards would not land in an area near their deceased cousins. (Who says only humans have respect for the dead?) The agent told Ross he and his program administrators did not know why the idea worked. They only knew that it did indeed work.

A Buzzard Effigy

The day after his talk with the buzzard man, Ross constructed the towers; one is shown in the right photo in Figure 15-1. He planted them in several locations on the 34 acres. Next, he attached a rope to the legs of the buzzards, then pulled them up to the top of each pole. The pulley system resembled those used on a flag pole. Ross devised this arrangement to permit him to lower a decomposed bird and replace it with another, without having to upend the tower.

Actually, the towers resembled a gallows more than a flag pole. Ross welded a bar to the top of the pole to allow the bird to hang away from the pole itself. After the buzzard was pulled-up to the top of the tower, it did appear as if it had been hung—perhaps for the capital offense of defecating on a pecan tree.

The Buzzards Go Away

The upshot of this story is: The dead buzzard effigy worked. Another example of the power of inventiveness; not to mention that it saved Ross a lot of hours re-loading his gun. The buzzards went away, probably downwind to pillage someone else's trees. Where ever they ended-up, gradually, fewer buzzards came by and landed for the night. Within a few days, the orchard was completely free of buzzards.

Perhaps our anthropomorphic scenario unfolded something like this. Roxelle, acting as the tree locator, informs her boss Horace, "Say Horace, we're coming toward that set of trees we like so much. It's been a hard day, scavenging for dead meat and all. Let's land there for the night."

Horace takes a closer look at the orchard and lo-and-behold, spots the dead buzzard effigies, "Whoa, look at that! Roxelle, isn't that your Uncle Jerry hanging head-down on that pole? And look over there, a bit to the right. It looks like Billie Jean is suspended on that other pole! This spot doesn't look all that inviting any more. What say we use the last thermals and glide on over to another spot. Besides, I hate sleeping in cemeteries."

Needless to say, the discovery of these buzzard effigies created a lot of concern among the buzzards that were flying along with Roxelle and Horace. Buzzards are not known as the most intelligent creatures on the planet (after all, they are called buzzards) but even the most obtuse buzzard could take a hint. So, off they went, on to greener pastures and trees, and they hoped, ones with fewer dead relatives hanging upside down.

Nothing in life is simple. The buzzards had to go somewhere and it is likely that some unwary orchard growers in Lea County experienced a sudden influx of buzzards. On the other hand, Ross was now buzzard-free. Like the Ancient Mariner, he lifted a dead bird off his neck, and his unwelcome visitors relocated to a more hospitable pit stop.

Ross and I exchanged theories about the reasons the dead buzzard poles were effective in warding-off the buzzards. He discounted my idea (actually it was Horace's idea) about buzzards not liking to sleep in cemeteries. His theory made sense:

By hanging the bird by its legs, the buzzard looked as if it were plunging toward the ground. Its large wings acted as weights and gravity had the effect of spreading the wings open, away from the body. It appeared as if the buzzard was flying into the earth. This image could have been a deterrent to other buzzards, perhaps instinctively fearing a deadly downward thermal wind was nearby.

A plausible theory. But Horace and Roxelle did not share their reasons with us. They were too busy decorating another orchard. So we could only surmise about how and why the buzzard effigy had done the trick.

16

Duds for Dad[12]

It is a wise child that knows its own father,
and an unusual one that unreservedly approves of him.

—Mark Twain

"Morning Dad, how are you?"

"What's good about it?"

"I didn't say 'Good morning.' I said 'Morning.' Anyway, how are you?"

"Without."

"Without?"

"The pickings are slim."

"Pickings! What do you expect? You're an 85 year old widower living in a retirement home full of other old people."

"As we say in here, 'We're old, but not dead.' Anyway son, I told you yesterday I don't need any clothes."

"Sure you do. Your shirts are scruffy. Your Stetson hat is older than I am."

"I haven't worn a Stetson in years."

"I guess I've lost track of the fashions out here in New Mexico. By the way, what do you wear now-a-days?"

"My hat's a Davis. Anyway, I told you I don't need any clothes. Looking for them's a waste of time."

"I looked inside your closet yesterday. I didn't see a single good-looking shirt ... well, to attract someone. And your boots have seen their better days."

"I don't need to attract no one anymore."

"Oh? Maybe that's one reason for your response to my question. Old man, you're not going to do much good with scruffy shirts. You need some new plumage to help you along."

"Ha! Like those ostriches they've brought into the county. That's pretty good. Well, I do need to go to the bank today and I'd like to pay a visit to Herb Love. Haven't seen him in a long time."

"Herb Love of Love's Boot Store. Dad, you're as transparent as a Lea Country rainstorm. Let's hit the trail. You're going to come back to the Good Samaritan Home looking better than Roy Rogers."

"Don't compare me to that goddamn dandy. I'd rather look like Trigger."

"You almost do Dad; you're not a cowboy model."

"Son, sometimes you talk another language. Anyway, let's get moving."

* * *

"Where'd you find this car?"

"Hertz car rental in Lubbock. Picked it up after I landed at the airport."

"Good looking. Good leg room. My old leg doesn't bend much anymore; have trouble getting into and out of cars."

"I noticed. The leg's not getting any better?"

"Nope."

"I recall your leg kept you out of World War I."

"Yep. A horse bucked me off. Broke my leg in two places. I was banged up for months. By the time I healed the war was over. Your uncles came back from Europe—all in one piece. I guess in the long run, we were all lucky. Hell, I got more injuries over here than they did over there."

"Yep. And I suspect you no longer walk into town from the Good Sam Home. You must have given it up a long time ago."

"I gave it up last year. I liked to get out of Good Sam. Too many old people. And I enjoyed going down to the Smoke House, having a beer, playing some shuffleboard. But the place is closed now. Can't find a shuffleboard anywhere in town. Don't know hardly anyone anymore. Thelma Smith still works at Cecil's bar. But Cecil's has no shuffleboard. At my age, a bar's not worth much without a shuffleboard."

"Maybe, but a bar's still got beer … Here's the bank, Dad. You mean to tell me you were walking over a mile each way into and out of town; with one leg and a crutch; when you were 84 years old?"

"Yep. The Good Sam folks didn't care. I signed-out and signed-in. Just as long as I didn't stay out overnight."

"Overnight! *Where* would you stay overnight? You sold your house several years ago. And not just 'Where' but *why* would you stay overnight?"

"I don't stay out overnight anymore. Last time I did was a trip I took up the Texas Panhandle to see an old friend."

"When was this?"

"A few years ago after your step mom died. I got lonesome and took the Greyhound bus from City Drug. Right pleasant trip. Stayed two days, then took the bus back."

"Who was the old friend? Anyone I know?"

"Nope. A lady I met in my younger days. I heard her husband was dead, so I gave her a call. Took the bus to a place near Amarillo. We had a good time. She's a good cook."

"Cook. Sure. Dad, did you ever hear the saying the way to a man's heart is through his stomach? Do you believe that?"

"Sure, but with a side trip here and there."

* * *

"OK Dad. Banking done. Where's the best place in town to buy a Western suit? I know where to go for the boots; Love's."

"A suit? When am I going to wear a suit? I haven't had one on in years."

"You never know when a fine Western suit, with all those fancy pockets, will come in handy. Maybe you'll be admitted to the Lea County Cowboy Hall of Fame. Can't have you accepting an award dressed in Levis."

"Won't work. I've had fights with over half the members."

"You know Dad, that's something I've never understood about you. Always up for a fight. Always hitting somebody"

"I never laid a hand on you."

"No, not me. But you did some major damage to several Smoke House patrons."

"I've told you many times son, don't do as I do, do as I say."

"Anyway, you and Mom were pioneers in this part of the country. And you took my stepmother's run-down spread and turned it into one of the best ranches in Lea County. You were one of the best Quarter Horse breeders around and I heard from several folks that you were the best farrier in this part of New Mexico. I'd say these accomplishments are fine credentials for a Hall of Fame candidate."

"There you go again—fancy words. I shoed horses."

"Dad, a farrier shoes horses. That's the name of his occupation."

"Not in Lea County. Anyway, I got into too much trouble with the law. Your brother had to bail me out of jail more than once. Why even Ross' father-in-law, the Chief of Police, and I had more than one ruckus. I'll never be in the Hall of Fame."

"Maybe not Dad. But you are a sure-fire candidate for a movie or book. By the way, you're pretty well-known in other parts of the state. When I was in Albuquerque at the University of New Mexico, one of my fraternity brothers knew about you. In fact, he told me a story that I had not heard at the time. ... Dad did you really bring your horse into the Smoke House to shoot shuffleboard? That's the story my fraternity bother told me. Seems impossible."

"Sure did. But it wasn't the Smoke House. It was Al's Bar, near the courthouse square. And my horse didn't shoot shuffleboard but I did bring her in from the trailer into the bar. I had been to Carlsbad for a roping match, and stopped by Al's on my way home. I started playing shuffleboard with a big blowhard who talked a good game and liked to bet a lot of money, but couldn't play shuffleboard worth a damn.

"After a while, I got fed up with his talk and bet him I had a horse that could shoot better shuffleboard than him. He was so dumb he accepted the bet. I couldn't believe it. How could any man with any pride at all agree to shoot shuffleboard with a goddamn roping horse? And for money! Beats the hell out of me what some folks do when they're drinking and gambling. Anyway, I went outside to my trailer, put a halter on my little mare, Freckles; backed her out of the trailer and led her into the rear door of the bar."

"That's what my fraternity brother told me. Come'on Dad! The noise and people in Al's would have spooked Freckles. She would have torn-up the place."

"Nope. Freckles was never spooked by noise. She was the calmest horse I ever owned. So, all I had to do was put some blinders on her and lead her into the bar."

"Blinders! How could she play shuffleboard with blinders?"

"Goddamn son, you're dumber than that drunk shuffleboard player! She couldn't play shuffleboard—blinders or no blinders. Anyway, I walked Freckles into the bar; she was cool as a cucumber; just stood there swishing her tail now and then. Everyone was getting a big kick out of my joke—except for the man playing shuffleboard against me. He didn't think it was funny."

"Just joking Dad. Amazing. I heard the same story my college friend. What did your opponent do?"

"Opponent? That crazy asshole did nothing. He got up and left. I led Freckles back to the trailer, went back to the bar for a couple beers, and headed for the ranch."

* * *

"Son, Tead's Department Store is down Main street about six or seven more blocks. Make a right at Washington Street. About your job. Still at the bank?"

"Nope. I left the Fed. I'm working with my own company. Working with communications networks, mostly software-based protocols."

"Don't know what you're talking about. Any work involved?"

"Work? Yes sir. I write code—programs. And I consult and teach others to do the same."

"Let me see your hands son. ... Like I said, what do you do for work?"

"OK, I don't toil-away like you did. I don't shear sheep, breed mares, castrate calves, or dig postholes. And I never walked half-way around the globe to the school house."

"Toil-away. There you go again. Anyway, are you making any money?"

"Yep."

"Okay."

* * *

"Dad, here we are at Tead's."

"Let's get it over with."

"Hello Jim Black! Who's that good-looking man with you?"

"Hello Millie. This is my youngest boy, U.D."

"U.D.! I remember you. Oh my word. You've grown up. I remember you as ... small, real small."

"I got a late start Millie. And I remember you too. You used to work over at Yarbrow's."

"I did. Yarbrow's went out of business—oh, ten years ago or so. After the Yarbrows closed up their store, I went over to Tatum's Women's Apparel. After they closed up, it was Tipp's Men's Store. But Mr. Tipp nearly went broke; he went down along with the oil industry. So, he left town and started another store somewhere around Midland. Anyway, we don't get much business here at Tead's. Most of the town folks go over to Hobbs to shop at the Walmart."

"Walmart Millie?"

"Yep. Walmart was the nail in the coffin for quite a few businesses in Lea County."

"Too bad. Same thing's happening all over. Anyway, we're here to outfit Dad with some duds."

"Jim, you want a complete outfit?"

"That's U.D.'s idea."

"Millie, look at the man! He resembles Gabby Hayes."

"I sure as hell do not! I remember Gabby Hayes; I don't grow a beard. And clothes or no clothes, doesn't make a hill of beans to me. Millie, U.D. got me out of Good Sam to take me to my bank and to see Herb Love."

"And also to do … what Dad? Remember? Upgrade your plumage in order to …"

"Eh, let's get on with it."

"I don't know what you boys are talking about. Anyway, let's start with the suit. Follow me."

* * *

"There you go Dad. That wasn't so bad was it?"

"No, not too bad."

"Let's head for Love's … Say Dad, I've been wanting to ask you a question about your staying at Good Sam. I recall you didn't have to live there; you had your place in town; you moved into the Home when my step mom Gayle was sent there. Why did you go in the first place? Why didn't you leave—go back home—after she died?"

"She needed company and I guess I did, too. By the time Gayle passed away, I had grown used to the place. And as it turned out, I grew to like Good Sam."

"And you found someone to fill Gayle's absence?"

"On occasion son. You know, young people try to put old people into an early grave. Well, I'm not dead and while I'm alive, I plan on living!"

"I agree. Our society's problem with the aged is we stereotype them. We …"

"We do what? Stereowhat?"

"We try to fit them into convenient cubbyholes."

"We sure do. Why didn't you say so in the first place?"

"Next time I will. Speaking of old people and old folks homes, have you heard this one? At a retirement home the nurses knew hanky panky went on. They overlooked it; thought it was a good idea; healthy. Anyway, this man, Frank, had a girlfriend named Mary. Every night Mary would pay a visit to Frank's room, get in bed with him, place her hand of his private parts, and the two of them would lie with each other, watching television."

"That's it? She didn't do anything else. He didn't do anything else?"

"Nope, they just lay there. So, one night Mary was entering Frank's room and found Betty occupying her place in Frank's bed. She was startled by this sudden change in her job description and backed out of the doorway to return to her room. The next morning she confronted Frank at breakfast. She asked him, 'What has Betty got that I don't have?' Frank replied, 'Parkinson's.'"

"Ha! That's good one son … Hmm, I don't think I could tell this joke around Good Sam's. Might hit too close to home."

"Dad, you can't tell that joke anywhere. It's not politically correct. Anything that might touch or hurt anyone's feelings, funny or not, can't be uttered. Humor often comes at someone's expense. We're becoming a sterile, touchy-feely society. We …"

"I get your point son."

"Well, anyway, let's get you some boots over at Love's … Say, I've heard another story about you that I have never brought up. Brother Ed told me about the time when you were a young man. You were out in the pasture tending to some chores. You got bucked off your horse onto a barbed wire fence. The way I heard it was that your crotch hit the wire first and it tore your testicles up pretty bad. Ed told me you were so tangled up with the barbed wire that you had to cutoff part of your scrotum to disentangle yourself from the fence."

"I had to do a bit of carving that day. Lost part of one of my balls."

"Did you know I had a loss like that during my Navy training?"

"I remember. Sorry."

"Me, too. Anyway, like father like son. The acorn does not fall far from the tree. Or in this case, the testicle!"

"Ha!"

"Say Dad, after that accident, I guess you had a bit more empathy for those calves you castrated each spring during the brandings?

"Eastern talk again. If you mean did I felt sorry for them. Yep, a little bit. But it was a job that had to be done. Besides, I like mountain oysters."

"Here we are at Love's. The sky's the limit Dad. Pick out anything you want."

"Don't need much. Seems to me you need boots more than I do."

"Don't like my penny loafers?"

"Don't think much of them. Couldn't do a lick of work wearing those sissy shoes. Anybody wear boots in Virginia?"

"Not many. Boots in Virginia are like penny loafers in New Mexico. Different cultures you know."

"Talk English son."

"OK Dad. Lost my head for a moment. ... Still, some of your sayings would sound funny out East. By the way, do you know that some of the people who live in Virginia don't know what 'I'm afoot' means?"

"No! Everyone knows that."

"No sir. Let me tell you a story of what happened to me my very first day on the East Coast. I had driven from the West to report to my Navy job in Washington, DC. When I was nearing DC, my car stopped running, so I hoofed-it to a pay phone up the road. I called what I thought was a local towing service. A man answered the phone with a thick foreign accent, something like, "Joe's Tow Service.

"I said, 'Look, can you give me a hand, I'm afoot.'"

"He said, 'You're a what?'"

"I said, 'I'm afoot.'"

"He said, 'What are you talking about?'"

"I had no idea he had no idea of what my slang meant. I said, 'Look can't you hear? I said I need a hand. I'm afoot.'"

"He said, 'Mister, you're not a foot. You're an ass!' And he hung-up the phone."

"Ha! I'll bet you could have really confused him if you had said, 'I'm afoot, and need a tow!'"

"Yeow! Wish I had thought of that."

* * *

"Here we are; back at Good Sam's. Let me help you move that leg out of the car."

"Thanks son. Damn; it's hell getting old. Can't do much of anything anymore."

"Seems to me you still have quite a lot left on your plate. Anyway, let's see what the Good Sam folks think about your new duds."

* * *

"Jim Black, where in the world are you off to? I'll say! You're looking real good."

"Where you been Jim? A wedding or something?"

"Where're you going Jim? To your own funeral? Ha!"

"I'll swear Mr. Black; you are sure turned out! That's a good looking hat."

"Mighty fine looking suit Jim. Mighty fine looking. Mighty fine."

---

[1] This story was written before Mom became a resident at the Good Samaritan Rest Home. After my stepmother Gayle passed away at the Home, Dad continued to live there. He didn't have to; he just liked the place; you'll learn why in this story.

[2] Abridged conversations, taken from recordings.

17

LOST IN LEA COUNTY[12]

The compass in my head has been out of order from my birth ...
—Mark Twain

*O*lee oh le he he he. I le oh le he ho. I le oh le ee he, oh le ee he,
ee de ee oh le he

*A dee oh le he he he. A dee oh le he he ho. I le oh le ee he, oh le ee he,
ee de ee oh le heeee.[3]*

Brother Ed, "U.D., who is the yodler?"

U.D., "It's Jimmie Rodgers. Ed, as a former yodler, I thought you would recognize him. I selected this music for our trip—put it in the car's CD player yesterday, so it would 'fire up' as soon as we took off to find the horse."

"I thought it might be him. I haven't heard Jimmie Rodgers in years."

"Me either, but yodeling is not a big scene on MTV nowadays. Anyway, we're headed for a ranch between the cities of Lovington and Hobbs, right? To see a horse? The papa of your colt? Am I on track so far?"

"Yep."

"And you want to see this horse to check out his body, his physique, for possible future breedings. Right?"

"Yep."

"And if I'm still on track; you don't know the name of the ranch? You don't know the location of the ranch? You don't know the name of the horse's owner? And you don't know the name of the horse?"

Oh de le de oh, le ee eh, le eeee I de de oh de le de ... I de de oh de le de ... oh de le de ... oh de le de ... oh de le de hoooooo.[4]

"Yep ... Damn! That Jimmie Rodgers is one fine yodler! I wish I could still yodel."

"Yeah, I know what you mean. I recall you used to yodel a lot around the house. Damn near drove everyone crazy! Anyway, let's get this horse search narrowed down to one specific area on planet Earth. Maybe we can narrow it down to this part of New Mexico. Do you. ..."

"Funny. And I do know the approximate location of the ranch. Yesterday, two men in the grocery store told me the ranch where the stud lives is on Knowles Road, located near Hobbs. The road intersects the Lovington-Hobbs highway. Not only that, there is a fire station near the ranch. They're pretty good directions, so I think we can find the horse with those mappings. U.D., it's real important that I get a look at that horse and I know he is in this part of Lea County."

"A fire station. On Knowles Road. OK! Let's hit the road for Knowles Road!"

T for Texas, T for Tennessee.
T for Texas, T for Tennessee.
T for Thelma, that gal that made a wreck out of meee.
Oh de le de oh, le ee eh, le eeee.[5]

"I recall that last song—one of my favorites. By the way, U.D., I'm sorry I'm making you slow down at each intersection on this highway. But the road signs are too small to read at the speed we are going."

"85 mph … sorry Ed. I was caught up in Jimmie's lyrics to the song playing now. They remind me of an old joke. Here, let me rewind the CD back to …"

I am dreaming tonight of an old southern town
and the best friend I ever had.
For I've grown so weary of roaming around,
I'm going back home to my dad.
Your hair has tuned to silver.
I know you're fading, too.
Daddy, dear ole daddy, I'm coming back to you.
Oh de le he ee oeh de oh le of le he …[6]

"OK, what's the joke?"

"Well, it's not so much a joke as it is a ditty. It goes something like this. Let me sing it for you."

Darling, we are growing older.
Silver threads among the gold.
For the hair around my jewels has turned to silver,
and the hair around your jewels has turned to gold.
Darling, let's be sweethearts ever …
Silver threads among the gold![7]

"I suppose it's funny."

"Funny! Can't you just picture Jimmie Rodgers singing it, along with a yodel or two? Especially after the last lines:"

Darling, let's be sweethearts ever …
Silver threads among the gold!
Oh de le de oh, le ee eh, le eeee a de de oh de le deeee!

"Not too funny, eh? OK, let's try to find Knowles Road. But I'm not optimistic. There's the Hobbs city limits sign. We've traveled twenty miles from Lovington already. We've looked at every intersection between Lovington and Hobbs. No Knowles Road. No fire station. No papa horse."

"OK U.D., let's go through Hobbs, and then head back toward Lovington, but on the Denver City highway. Maybe those men meant the Knowles Road intersected the Denver City highway, and not the Hobbs highway."

"OK, Ed ... off we go!'

I'm a pistol packing papa.
And when I walk down the street.
You can hear those mamas shouting.
Don't turn your gun on me.
Now girls, I'm just a good guy.
And I'm going to have my fun.
And if you don't want to smell my smoke,
Don't monkey with my gun.
Oh de le de de oh, de le de oh, de le deee.[8]

"Ed, we've gone quite a distance on the Denver City highway. Ten miles or so. What's next? By the way, what do you think of Jimmie's *Pistol Packin' Papa*? Freudian connotations, right? George Carlin would have a hoot with this one!"

"You think he's talking about other kinds of pistols? Ha! That's what we thought when we listened to it as kids. Anyway, make a right here, and let's stop at that ranch house. I'll ask them if they know about the horse."

"Yeah, everyone thinks his song is a metaphor for a penis. Knowing Carlin's humor, I'll bet he would get off on the verse of 'smelling smoke and monkeying with my gun.' Eh, Ed, those dogs don't look friendly."

"Right, let's go to the next ranch ... down the road ..."

My good gal's trying to make a fool out of me.
Lord, my gal's trying to make a fool out of me.
Trying to make me believe I ain't got that ol' TB.
I've got the Teeeee ... Beeeee blues.
When it rained down sorrow, it rained all over me.
When it rained down sorrow, it rained all over me.
Because my body rattles like a train on that old ST.
I've got the TeeEEE ... BeeEEE blues.[9]

"Man, what a song. I'm convinced there's a country song lamenting *every* misery on earth. Tuberculosis. Far out. Say Ed, did you notice that we just crossed the state line? We're now looking for Knowles Road in the state of Texas."

A dee oh le he he he. A dee oh le he he ho. I le oh le ee he, oh le ee he, ee de ee oh le heeee.[10]

"Yeah, I saw the sign, and the roads are better—a dead giveaway we're in Texas. OK, let's turn around and head back to New Mexico. And let's stop at the ranch we passed just before the state line. Maybe they'll have some information on the firehouse or Knowles Road."

Weeeueee, Weeeueeee …
All around the water tanks, waiting for a train.
A thousand miles away from home, sleeping in the rain.
I walked up to a brakeman, to give him a line of talk.
He said if you got money, I'll see that you don't walk.
I haven't got a nickel, not a penny can I steal.
Get off, get off, you railroad bum; he slammed the box car doo(r).
Oh de le he, de le he, de le he.[11]

"U.D., let's cut across this road, and visit a couple of those ranches to the west. I've given up on the Hobbs and Denver City highways taking us to Knowles Road. Say, just listen to how Jimmie sounds like one of those old train whistles."

Weeeueee, Weeeueeee …
Weeeueee, Weeeueeee …[12]

"Yep. Remarkable resemblance. You know, we've stopped at several ranches to ask about the stud. Not one place has any people on it. Not one of your knocks has been answered. Kind of eerie; reminds me of that movie, *On the Beach*."

"Oh? What happened in the movie?"

"Well, everyone in a town in Australia had taken a suicide pill because a nuclear cloud was headed their way from the North. The U.S. and the Soviet Union had nuked each other. A crew from a navy submarine visited a town and it was completely deserted. Not even any carcasses or skeletons ... just like this part of Lea County. No inhabitants whatsoever. It was as if everyone had left town for a permanent sleep over."

Sleep baby, sleep.
Angels watching you.
Listen to your mother dear,
While she sings to you.
Yee do ol de lo de leeee,
Oh de ol le dde a le ee eee.[13]

"Another non-answer to your knocks, Ed. What do you think? Should we be looking for graves out back?"

"Ah! I forgot. It's Sunday morning. The people have gone to church! No wonder we can't find anyone."

"Well, we're running out of time. We're supposed to meet our cousin June at that Hobbs motel at noon. It's 11:30 now. Should we head back? By the way Ed, do you think it's a good idea to walk into people's barns and corrals uninvited? Who knows, there could be a non-church goer lurking about in those corrals. Most of these ranch houses have NRA decals on the windows."

"Get serious; you've been living away from Lea County too long."

"OK ... just hope we don't run into any of those pistol packing papas."

And if you don't want to smell my smoke,
Don't monkey with my gun.
Oh de le de de oh, de le de oh, de le deee.[14]

"Look U.D., there's Knowles Road ... and down the way ... there's a fire station! We're close. Let's check out some more ranches. Maybe our luck has turned. Damn! Those men gave me the wrong directions. Knowles Road doesn't *intersect* the Hobbs highway; it *parallels* it. No wonder we couldn't find it."

"Yep, I thought we were lost in Lea County for a while— wandering and roaming, just like Jimmie's songs. OK, let's check out some more ranches. Don't get down Ed, we're making some progress."

I'm lonely and blue,
I'm downhearted too.
No body but you can hear me.
You left me alone.
You wandered from home
Oh why do you roam my dear one …
Oh de le de de oh, de le de oh, de le deee.
Oh de le de de oh, de le de oh, de le deee.
Oh de le de de oh, de le de oh, de le dee.

* * *

Oh de le de de oh, de le de oh, de le deee.
Oh de le de de oh, de le de oh, de le deee.
Oh de le de de oh, de le de oh, de le deee.[15]

"Well, we tried more ranches … still no luck … U.D., I'm sorry. I've taken you on a wild goose chase. I was sure those men in the grocery store knew what they were talking about. I thought we could find Knowles Road; we would drive to the fire station; I would ask around, and we would find the horse. I've just wasted your time."

"Ed, I have never spent a finer morning in East New Mexico and West Texas; with my brother; listening to Jimmie Rodgers to boot. And you're right. You got bum directions. I think we could find the horse if we had more time and it wasn't Sunday morning. Well, we did lose an hour going into Texas on our search, but we regained it on the way back. Yeah, we need to head for June's hotel. You know, we've played Jimmie's CD over and over. How about some Slim Whitman? Talk about a yodler!"

"You've got Slim Whitman, too! Do you have *Cattle Call*?"

"You bet, and his version is much better than Eddy Arnold's. I think Whitman had one of the purest tenor, falsetto voices ever recorded, including opera."

"Eh … U.D … opera music has yodlers?"

"Hmm. Maybe not. But while listening to opera, I have heard some very high tenors singing yodel type songs."

Hoooooooooooo, HoOOOoo, Hoooo, Hooo, HoOOOoo, Hooo, Hoooooo,
hooooo, Hoooo, do, loooop, de … ohhhhh …
When the cattle are prowling,
the coyotes are howling,
out where the doggies bawl.
When spurs are a jingling, the cowboy is singing,
The lonesome cattle call.
Hoooooooooooo, HoOOOoo, Hoooo, Hooo, HoOOOoo, Hooo, Hoooooo,
hooooo, Hoooo, do, loooop, de … ohhhhh …[16]

"Ed, I tell you, Slim Whitman's yodel is chilling … listen to that high pitch. … Oops, that's a steel guitar. Wow, hard to tell the difference between the two. OK, we're headed for Hobbs. Don't be too disappointed bro. After all, we gave it our best shot. By the way, what is the name of the motel where June is staying?"

"I don't remember."

"What street is it on?"

"I can't recall."

"Hmm … Did you get directions to the motel from those guys in the grocery store? Is this trek another secret?"

"Don't get funny U.D. I know how to get there."

Keep it a secret, whatever you do.
Why should you tell me and break my poor heart?
Then foolish pride would just drive us apart.[17]

"There's the motel U.D. I told you I knew where it was."

"Damn straight Ed. And we are batting .500 for the day. Missed the horse, found the motel. Actually, for me, much better than .500. This is the first time in years you and I have had more than a few minutes together. I know you wanted to see that horse. For your sake, I also wanted to find it. But, what the hell; we had a good visit; we listened to Jimmie and Slim; and we found cousin June."

… There is so much to say, as I walk away
But I'll thank you for … something beautiful to remember.[18]

[1] The song verses in this story are from (a) The *Essential Jimmie Rodgers*, RCA Records; (b) *Slim Whitman, Greatest Hits*, CURB Records. The ditty is from my friend Paddy Fitzpatrick, a fine Irishman, who wouldn't know a yodel from a noodle, but knows some fine Irish jigs.

[2] Abridged conversations, taken from recordings.

[3] *Away Out On The Mountain*, Jimmie Rodgers.

[4] Ibid.

[5] *Blue Yodel No. 1 (T for Texas)*, Jimmie Rodgers.

[6] *Daddy and Home*, Jimmie Rodgers.

[7] From that famous balladeer, Pat Fitzpatrick.

[8] *Pistol Packin' Papa*, Jimmie Rodgers.

[9] *T. B. Blues*, Jimmie Rodgers.

[10] Ibid.

[11] *Waiting for a Train*, Jimmie Rodgers.

[12] Ibid.

[13] *Sleep Baby, Sleep*, Jimmie Rodgers.

[14] Ibid.

[15] *I'm Lonely and Blue*, Jimmie Rodgers.

[16] *The Cattle Call*, Slim Whitman.

[17] *Keep it a Secret*, Slim Whitman.

[18] *Something Beautiful to Remember*, Slim Whitman.

18

THE REAL HEROES

Our heroes are (those) who do things which we recognize,
with regret, and sometimes a secret shame, that we cannot do.

—Mark Twain

Many years passed between my stint as a dog catcher and my old age. Somehow, I made my way though adulthood and headed into my later years. During this all too brief interlude between youth and senior citizenry, I spent most of my time working with computer networks in Virginia, Europe and the Far East. I was far removed from the horses, ranches, and cattle of Little Texas. On occasion, I would return to Lea County to visit my parents and the school chums who had remained in our home town to make their living.

My Mom and Dad lived long lives; both saw their nineties. They resided all their adult years in Lea County. When they became too old to care for themselves, we had the good fortune to have a fine old folks' facility in our town. Mom and Dad's children moved Ruby and Jim to the Good Samaritan Rest Home.

Each week at "Good Sam" an aide takes anyone (who so wishes and is able) on an ice cream run. This short journey is to a local fast food restaurant for a vanilla ice cream cone, followed by a short jaunt around the town where the rest home is located.

A short time after Dad died, I accompanied my mother, who lived at Good Sam at that time, on one of these trips. There were 16 passengers (at, 60, I was the youngest of the group; Mom was 91). The aide and driver Tracy made for a total of 17 in the tour group.

We left Good Sam and drove directly to one of the few fast food places in Lovington, New Mexico, MacDonald's. Tracy pulled the van up to the drive in window and ordered 17 vanilla ice cream cones. Good Sam treated me to my ice cream. To earn my keep, I helped distribute the treats.

After everyone had their cones firmly in their hands and into their mouths, we set out for the next hour or so to explore Lovington's surroundings. As I rode along, it became obvious Tracy had made this outing many times, as had most of the riders in the van.

My hometown is hardly a tourist mecca. There's not a lot to see in this part of America. I've mentioned in earlier chapters that the terrain of Llano Estacado is flat and dry. In this part of the Llano, it also smells of the fumes escaping from the gas and oil wells that dominate the landscape. If you drive through most of Lea County, you will see almost endless networks of oil rigs, pumps, and tanks. They dwarf the nearby mesquite and sage bushes, offering a modern profile to a southwestern sunset. Many of these behemoths are no longer in operation. Some have been abandoned—waiting for better times, for oil prices and energy demands to resurrect the local industry.

Lovington reminds me of the town in *The Last Picture Show*. Some businesses are boarded up, as are some of the homes. The town saw its peak during the 1940s and 1950s, when oil was pumping out of the ground in Lea County at a pace per pump equal to most other oil producing regions of the nation. The oil industry has faded away and with the exception of a few cottage industries, farming and ranching are the principal industries.

I bring up these aspects of Lovington to make the point that tourism and sightseeing in this part of New Mexico are not considered growth industries. But this fact made no difference to the Good Sam people, or to Tracy. The point of the ice cream and sightseeing trip was to get the van riders out of the Home, and to offer different venues in their lives. I suspect the idea of the Good Sam caretakers was to give the ice cream sojourners something different to do. I bear witness that the idea worked.

The Peach Tree Visit

Based on some suggestions from the tour group, Tracy developed an agenda. One visit—let's call it a tour stop—took us about five or six miles out of town, down a couple of country roads. During the drive to this place, she talked about the peach orchard we were to visit. Several members of our group offered their views about whether the trees would be in bloom, perhaps in fruit. A couple of skeptics claimed the orchard would be dead.

There was no consensus on what the state of the peach orchard might be, but Tracy's chatter had the effect of starting a conversation about the fate of these trees, and what we might expect to see when we arrived at the orchard. Granted, the conversation was limited, interspersed with periods of silence. Truth is, most members of the tour group seemed to be sleeping.

The peach "orchard" contained one solitary miserable looking peach tree, trying to survive in front of an abandoned home, several miles into the country, away from the metropolis of Lovington. Except for the flat semiarid prairie, there was not much else around the home; not even oil well equipment. But somehow the Good Sam explorers had found the tree, perhaps months or years ago, and they had obviously paid it a visit on their previous ice cream outings.

It seemed they were looking for a surprise, hoping to find luscious peach trees, laden with fruit. And why not? Most people look forward to surprises in our lives. I look forward to a situation that is framed in my mind from a past experience and wonder if the situation has changed the next time around. For example, I am eager to see the changes that have taken place in the forest surrounding my home in the Shenandoah Valley from one spring season to the next.

But is one friendless peach tree really significant and worthy of a trip to see it? I suspect it depends on one's perspective. On that day, the scrubby tree was a worthy sight from the perspective of my companions. When we arrived and parked next to the tree, the bus occupants seemed to wake up. They chatted about the condition of the tree; how its leaves were holding up in the hot summer sun; about its growth.

Tracy sat in the driver's seat, silently smiling. The short jaunt had worked. Her minions were engaged and animated. I swear, if I had known that lady better, I'd have left my seat, walked to the front of the bus, and planted a kiss on her.

The Ostrich Visit

Our next episode was a visit to a small farm on the way back to town. The main attraction at this farm was ostriches. For some reason (which I have not yet had a chance to research), a lot of ostriches have been moved into the Lovington area since my departure in the late 1950s. For this trip, we stopped and visited with several birds that were housed in a corral at this farm.

Ostriches are inquisitive creatures. They came toward the van as we approached them. Tracy pulled the vehicle next to the fence of their corral. Apparently, a gentleman sitting in the front of the bus was equally eager to see the ostriches. As the vehicle stopped, he left his seat and (almost) made it to the door, which Tracy had opened for ventilation.

Tracy caught the wondering, wandering man just as he was about to exit the van and enter into what would likely have been a short lived monologue with the ostriches—creatures known for their strength and dislike of outsiders. She wasn't concerned, but the brief situation gave me a start. I wasn't used to the idea of taking care of old people. They require a lot of attention. (To my son Tommy, prepare yourself.)

After the bird stop, Tracy fired up the van, took off for the next stop and kept up the chatter. She dared us to suggest venues and asked us to offer thoughts about them, "Who has seen this before?"

... "Bill, what do you remember about this tree the last time we were here?" ... "Mary, do you still think that ostrich over there is small?"

Lovington International Airport

After we checked out the peach tree and the ostriches, we visited the Lovington Airport. Lovington has had an airport since my childhood. We teenagers called it the Lovington *International* Airport because a noted citizen occasionally made a run in his Piper Cub to Juarez, Mexico ... a story more fitting for another book.

I suspected none of the ice cream caravan expected a lot of air activity during our visit. This situation was the case for this visit; the airport was dead still. Not one solitary plane was in view. Four tin sided sheds comprised the airport's hangers but their closed doors hid Lovington's air fleet.

This part of the ride seemed to disappoint the tour group. Without success, Tracy wound her way around several of the sheds, in hopes of spotting an airplane. As we left, Tracy said, "Well, last week, we saw an airplane. Maybe next week we'll see another one." I looked around at my fellow explorers; there was not a lot of response. A couple of the men nodded their heads in the affirmative but as a whole, most seemed under whelmed.

The Golf Course

I was the newcomer to the group but after Tracy asked if anyone could put forward another place to visit, I suggested we drive to the Lovington Country Club golf course. I knew some funny goings on could be seen there. Having started playing golf the summer of the ice cream tour, I believed I was an authority on the amusing aspects of the game.

The golf course stop was the highlight of the trip. Tracy later told me the ice cream tour had never made a stop at the golf course. Plus, this stop was enhanced because a foursome was teeing off just as we arrived.

Each player had something different to offer to the spectators. For example, one golfer missed hitting the ball on her swing. She was the favorite of our ice cream tour group and her miss was the only time on the tour when most of the folks laughed.

I had visited Good Sam frequently during the past few years. I had talked with Mom's friends at Good Sam and other residents whom I met as I was walking through the halls. I had become somewhat familiar with the mental deficiencies that accrue with age and I had begun to experience some of those deficiencies in my own behavior.

I mention this aspect of my life because I was tempted to ask our ice cream tour group to vote for their favorite golf player of the foursome. However, by the time we had cast votes on the fourth player, I knew some of the group would have forgotten the player who had missed the ball, or would have confused this player with one of the other players.

As they say, capture the moment. The vote wasn't important and it was just a passing thought in my mind. What counted was the momentary joy of watching the players and the laughter they provoked from our side of the fence.

End of the Line

The golf course was the last stop on the tour. We had been on the town for over an hour and I suspected Tracy had exhausted her tour site repertoire. For one fanciful moment, I considered suggesting we visit a nearby pasture south of Lovington. At this momentous meadow, we high school teenagers parked and experimented with the mysterious world of sex. But I kept this parochial interest to myself, concluding that it would be of marginal interest to the tour group.

We didn't visit my pasture of Eden but returned to the Home. Everyone made it off the van unaided, except Mom. She had little strength left. With the help of the Good Sam nurses, I placed her in a wheel chair for the trip back to her room.

The Real Heroes in our Society

After leaving Mom and driving to Lubbock, Texas for a flight to my home in Virginia, I reminisced about the ice cream trip. I remembered how Tracy engaged the old folks. Persistent to the point of many repetitions, she tried her best to stimulate them. She never wavered in her quest. I thought about her job and her day-after-day chore of invigorating people whose invigoration threshold was very high. I recalled the residents of Good Sam; some with Alzheimer's; some incapable of relieving themselves; some unable to get in or out of bed.

Capture the moment. There are only so many of them left.

I also thought about the other employees at Good Sam. I thought about their mindful attention to the needs of their dependents and their loving care of my parents. I reflected on the day and concluded I could not do what they do. I walked the corridors of Good Sam and beheld semi-skeletons in wheelchairs, some barely able to remain upright. I sat in the dining room and watched semi-comatose diners try to eat their bland food, some had to be spoon fed. I'm ashamed to admit it, but the atmosphere left me with a sense of dread—knowing a place like this is likely on my itinerary later in life.

But the Tracys of that world were up to their tasks. These caretakers took on their job with an air of goodwill and attention that I know I could not duplicate. If I could cast ballots on who might gain entry to the Pearly Gates, the Good Sam attendants will be first in the queue.

During the airplane ride, I read an article in the sports page about the *heroics* of a professional basketball player in scoring 50 points against *stiff competition*. Stiff competition? Nothing like the competition the Tracys of the world face. Heroics? Hardly. The word fits Tracy, not a slam dunk artist.

Mom is gone now. The ice cream trip is a pleasant memory. If I return to Lovington, I'm going to Good Sam for another ice cream trip. This time, I'm treating and I hope one of the tour stops is the peach tree. If not, I'll settle for another ostrich.

19

Thus Far, It's been a Good Life and I'm Hoping for Better

Remember all thou canst—seem to remember all else.

—Mark Twain

*Nothing remains the same; when the man goes back to look at
the house of his childhood, it has always shrunk; there is no instance of
such a house being as big as the picture in memory and imagination call
for. Shrunk how? Why, to its correct dimensions: the house hasn't
altered; this is the first time it has been in focus.*

—Mark Twain

We are nearing the end of our journey to past times in southeastern New Mexico and Lea County—Little Texas. Earlier, I mentioned my parents were born in Texas, but grew old in Lea County. Eventually they moved into the Lovington Good Samaritan Home and they are now gone, resting in our family plot at the Lovington Cemetery. Figure 19-1 shows my parents on their wedding day and in their later years at Good Sam.

Figure 19-1. My parents in their younger and older years.

Many of my friends of those years have moved to other places. For some unfathomable reason, Texas seems to be their favored repository. Other friends have died and my ties to that part of the world are fading away.

I say ties in the context of loved-ones, friends, and acquaintances—those who have bound me to Lea County and the Southwest—are slowly dying. But if I speak of ties in the context of memories, the bonds to my home shall remain with me as long as I live. For older people the memories of our past keep the present alive.

Yet with each passing year, I find it more difficult to recall accurately the past times of my childhood and youth. Frances Mayes wrote, "Nothing is harder to hold than the reality of the past."[1] I agree. I also think there is nothing sad with an occasional substitution in our memories, at least for those memories that become harder to recall. I believe we exchange bits of reality of our past for more pleasant, less traumatic episodes. These mental surrogates become our new truths.

Nonetheless, whatever form reality takes as I move into old age, I hope my stories in this book have reflected the reality (and not my imagination) of an epoch in which I have lived. This idea is important to me because I have written these stories with the intent of passing them to my son—before I too am no longer able to hold on to the realities of the past and my recollections become hopelessly confused.

I have probably benefited from writing this book more than you have in reading it. I started the project both enthusiastic and hesitant. I was enthusiastic because I was eager to pass these stories to son Tommy and I looked forward to the task of putting them on paper. I was hesitant because I was not certain I would enjoy the process of exposing the adventures and capers of my past. Some were silly; others foolish. Yet why bother writing about my past for my son if I had nothing of interest to tell? I also came to believe these stories might be of interest to others. You are reading the last chapter, so I can assume I was correct.

I should have known better about my initial hesitation in writing this book. For over thirty years I have derived immense satisfaction in writing. Frances Mayes also describes her feelings, and mine, about taking up the pen (well, the computer keyboard), "What comes from my own labor and creativity, regardless of what anyone else thinks of it, stays close to the natural joy we all were born with and carry always."[2]

Roots

After returning from Navy duty in Asia, I lived in Virginia most of my adult life but I have never felt this state to be my home. I have come to realize even though Virginia is a bountiful, beautiful land, and most of my current friends are Virginians, I have not taken root there. My heart tells me my home is the Southwest, New Mexico, Lea County, and the town of Lovington. The family cemetery plot, containing my parents, my grandparents, as well as assorted aunts, uncles, and cousins, attest to my origins and roots.

Visits to this cemetery, one of the few places in Little Texas that is green and verdant, leave me with a feeling of pride and a sense of celebration for the Black family, my parents, my brothers, my relatives, Tommy, and myself. There is no question that my mind, which is relatively immune to symbols, is vulnerable to the symbols of the tombstone and our family plot.

I gained yet more appreciation of my ties to New Mexico when I witnessed Tommy's first visit to the family plot in the cemetery. As he walked with me through the rows of graves, I explained to him my admiration for Uncle Joe, my childhood crush on cousin JoLetha, my love and respect for my stepmother, Gayle; my fondness for many citizens buried in other plots in the cemetery. With the visible graves and tombstones, Tommy's heritage was on display. I think he was deeply moved.

My deceased brothers David and Jim chose cremation for the disposal and dispersal of their bodies. I wish they had not. I wish they were buried with my parents and other loved ones in our family plot in Lovington. I would like to pay a call on them. But direct visitation is not possible because their ashes are strewn across Northern New Mexico, where Jim had a ranch, and the outskirts of Santa Fe, where David lived—places too spacious for a proper visit with my brothers.

Where am I to be laid to rest? For a while I thought of Arlington National Cemetery but I learned restrictions are in place to limit ex-servicemen and war veterans taking up space at this hallowed ground. It doesn't matter, because I no longer have the desire to lie in the Arlington cemetery. My final stop is Lea County. Yes, Little Texas. And my wife has chosen to be with me—a great sacrifice for my Southern California beauty whose family plot is on lovely Santa Catalina Island.

A Return to Lea County

To help in writing this final chapter, I paid a visit to New Mexico recently, timing my trip with the Lea County Fair and Rodeo. I entered Lovington's city limits, greeted by a billboard sign (shown in Figure 19-2) declaring the city to be the hometown of Brian Urlacher, the famous Chicago Bear linebacker, and a generous soul who has donated considerable equipment and clothing to Lovington's athletic teams. This billboard had been erected on only one of the four highways coming into town: the Hobbs highway. I suspect it was another example of one-ups-manship contests between Lovington and Hobbs.

Figure 19-2. Lovington's (recent) claim to fame.

Walking down Main Street in Lovington placed me in a time warp; I could picture the drug stores, the pool hall, the variety store, and the other places on the street as if they had been resurrected from the past. I was reminded of the adage, *What went before, returned once more.*

Ole Jax was still there, serving hamburgers and milkshakes. But Jack was gone. The fare had also changed. A Poncho Burger and similar Tex-Mex delights reflected the changing tastes and population in that part of America. Some of the old eateries were still thriving. Indeed, they had outlasted a globalized franchise, Burger King, which sat empty on Main Street, proclaiming its past with a faded sign and boarded windows. On the other hand, McDonald's and Pizza Hut were doing well. Perhaps Big Macs help assuage Lea County's economic downturn and the capping of dry oil wells.

Jake's Fountain and Peck's City Drugs were gone, so were Jake and Peck. But the buildings where they did business remained. As I walked by Jake's I recalled the blue and white booths, the colors of our high school teams. I could taste the Wildcat Sundae and the

Wozzie Dog. As I walked by Peck's, the memories of my childhood curiosity about the beautiful female models in the photography magazines were still vivid. Plummer's, my fantasyland variety store, was still stocked with fantasyland wares; the current store sold party favors and decorations. Next door, my birthplace, the Lovington General Hospital, was boarded-up.

The Lakes. The trip to Easley's Twin Lakes revealed a golf course covering the (former) lakes. The only remaining water was represented by hazards placed around a few holes. The lakes were gone, so were the swimming pool, the island, and the suspension bridge. The loss of my childhood water wonderland was alleviated somewhat by the fact I was taking up the game of golf and learning to mimic a golf player.

Originally, the golf course was a modest nine holes with rock-hard fairways, as it struggled to survive New Mexico's dry climate. Fortunately, an abundant water table compensated for the lack of rain and a fine watering system was installed a few years after the course was built. With the addition of another nine holes, built over Easley's ski lake, the course was a welcome relief to the arid plains of southern New Mexico.

Walking the course was a study in visual incongruities: I took-in its lovely greens, then cast a glance to the surrounding countryside of dry, almost barren pastures, riddled with abandoned oil field equipment.

The Museums. One of my favorite places to visit was the Lea County Cowboy Hall of Fame and Western Heritage Center. My friend LaJean Burnett, the Director of the Museum, helped me learn some important facts for this book, notably the middle name of my namesake, Uyless Devoe Sawyer. It took the investigation of the head of a museum to unearth this name, so I now understand why my parents didn't know it. Anyway, if you are in the Southwest, take a trip to Lovington, and visit this museum. Its exhibits are first-rate, beautifully-rendered, and full of old treasures.

While you are in the area, visit the Lea County Museum, housed in an old, lovely hotel, and ask for Jim Harris, the Director. Jim will show you around and answer your questions. This museum displays many beautiful artifacts and houses several original buildings of times-past. Touring the exhibits at this museum, I came across a commemoration to Dessie Sawyer, the wife of my namesake, Uyless. Dessie was a bigwig in the New Mexico Democratic Party and was famous for her fund raising parties and her fantastic dresses. One dress was covered with dimes—she used it during the March of Dimes fund drives as a gimmick to draw attention to the charity. Dessie was not a large person and I often wondered where she summoned the strength to lug-around hundreds of dimes. Anything for the cause.

As I walked though part of the Museum, I came upon a set of old cribs for newly-born babies. The cribs were taken from the Lovington General Hospital, the place where I was born. There it was, my first bed! Where I slept for the first few days of my life … during which I was misnamed three times.

Old Places. I drove past the Youth Center. The original, authentic birthplace of the dirty dance revealed a building for the Lea County Electrical Coop; a new Center (for youths and old people) had been constructed across town. My First Baptist Church was now a parking lot and a new church was housed nearby. The Saddle and Smoke House bars were only memories. The buildings in which the saloons did business were still standing. The Saddle Bar was a real estate agency but the Smoke House was boarded-up.

Amazingly, the Lea Theater was still in operation, even sporting the same neon sign at the front of the building that it had when it opened in the early 1950s. For my visit, Arnold was sporting his fiercest looks for *Terminator 3*. The pool hall was history, as were the drive-in theatres and the Katty Korner Kafe.

I drove by the location of the old filling station whose men's room contained the only condom machine in town. The building had been torn-down and replaced with an empty lot. I visited a nearby station to fill my car with gas before returning to Lubbock, Texas for my flight home. I discovered a new-generation condom machine in the men's room. It advertised its wares with this come-on: "Light up your life with glow-in-the-dark condoms. Only 75 cents." A new approach to setting the romantic lighting for an intimate evening.

The dances at the Barn Dance were history; the Bull Barn had been torn-down, and replaced by a more efficient, modern structure, *but without* a dance floor—an inexplicable omission in my eyes.

The Good Samaritan Home was still thriving. I paid a visit to see some of Mom and Dad's friends, but I had not been at the Home for two years. Thus, the residents did not remember me. But they were able to hold onto some of their memories of the past and we spent a few moments recollecting older times in New Mexico.

As I was leaving the home, I spotted a new resident sitting in the front of the dining room. He gained my attention with his size and his white, pristine cowboy hat—worn while he was eating. He had been looking at me while I visited with his fellow residents, so I walked to his table, sat down, and began a conversation. It turns out this handsome man was a rancher in the Fort Sumner area, and knew many eastern New Mexico pioneers. I asked him if by chance he knew Uyless Sawyer. He replied, "U.D.? Yes, I knew him for many years." He then proceeded to tell me several stories about my namesake. I was tempted to ask this man if he knew the middle name of U.D., but I suspected it would be an unfair question and decided to bid my farewell to Good Sam and the old cowboy.

Dad's and step mom Mary's ranch was still standing. The place is owned by Billie Fort, the wife of Troy Fort, a former world champion roper and the owner of the famous horse, Old Baldy. She was a gracious hostess and let me wander around the place at my leisure. The barns and corrals were much the same as they were over fifty years ago. The tank where I learned to swim was gone, so was the bunkhouse for our hired hands. The chuck wagon, old when I was a child, had dissolved into the Wagon Pasture dirt. The corral where I came close to leaving life early was standing; its occupant, the mean stud, Wompus, was long dead. The ranch house, the barns, the corrals, all seemed smaller to me. But when I was roaming around them in the 1950s, I was still a small boy and most things appeared big.

The Fair and Rodeo

The fair and rodeo were (and are) the biggest events in Lea County each year. They had changed very little since my childhood days. Fair prizes were still awarded for the best pigs, chickens, goats, cattle, horses, jams, jellies, melons, quilts, pottery, painting, and scores of other human toils. The number of categories to evaluate was so numerous I wondered if all county citizens had been recruited to act as judges for the events.

Figure 19-3. Peanuts and Billy the Kid.

A memorable event of the rodeo was the performance of a cowboy and a small, young cowgirl, only eight years of age—and two critters. As shown in Figure 19-3, the humans came into the arena on their respective mounts: a Brahma bull and a Shetland pony, named Billy the Kid and Peanuts respectively. During the rodeo, all four animals entertained their audience with a wonderful set of acts, all to the delight of the crowd.

A couple of rodeo events had survived our politically correct, PETA-oriented, protect-the-child-at-all-costs culture. Mutton busting was still a popular event, one in which small children, protected with helmets and pads, rode a sheep out of a chute, usually for about one millisecond. While watching this part of the rodeo, I was reminded of my riding the milk pen calves on our ranch.

I was surprised the second event had not been shelved due to pressure from the animal rights and children's rights groups. For this event, children ranging in ages from around six to twelve years of age were invited into the rodeo arena (and several tots of younger years slipped past their parents and participated as well). Next, three calves were required to make a mandatory appearance at one end of the small stadium. There they waited for the announcer to line-up the kids—a difficult task, because a couple of the younger ones had begun to create sand boxes in the arena turf. Next, with a, "Go!" fifty or so frenzied children attacked three bewildered calves. The goal was to gain a hold of the animal, just long enough to bring it to a halt.

Melee! Chaos! Running children and calves! Fun! Happy children! Unhappy calves! Falling children! Several kids were knocked down by the fleeing calves; some fell on their own, tripped-up by the thick, moist turf. A couple of unfortunate pursuers were knocked a short distance into the air by a butt from a calf. Landing on the soft turf, they showed their mild pain and extreme displeasure with wails and tears. How on earth this event had escaped the *Society for the Prevention of Fun and Mild Abuse to Bovines* remained a mystery to me.

The Fair and Rodeo Parade. The Fair and Rodeo parade was held during the middle of the week. While it was not exactly on the scale of the parades seen on TV, it was by far the most popular event. The parade was led by mounted cowboys and cowgirls; not much different from my descriptions of the parades a half century ago. Next, the audience was treated to: A couple of floats; two or three bands; Cub Scout, Brownie, Boy Scout, and Girl Scout troops; county and city officials decked out in new cars. As well as: fire trucks, oil well equipment trucks, dump trucks, and garbage trucks. In addition: Small tractors, large tractors, huge tractors, and gigantic tractors.

Perhaps the parade assemblies seem boring as you read about them, but I watched the crowd take-in the show and I am certain no one was unhappy while they watched a phalanx of machines, interspersed with a few horses and humans, pass by them. My favorite parade participant was a very small girl, riding a very large horse. I called to her from the side of the road and snapped the photo you see in Figure 19-4, just as she turned her head in my direction.

Figure 19-4. A small rider in the parade.

Thomas Wolfe and Mark Twain

During my return to Lea County ... Little Texas, I walked and rode through Lovington and its countryside. I visited my elementary school and childhood playgrounds. I recalled the experiences with my frogs, my dogs, and those fanciful carnivals. For those few moments, I was a small boy again. I visited my high school, Jake's Fountain, the county courthouse, and my favorite parking place where I learned the art and science of necking. For a while, I was a youngster again. The brief visit to my home town brought forth years of memories. I was reliving, if only briefly, the treasured days of my life in Lea County.

Thomas Wolfe wrote, *You can't go home again*. Yes you can Mr. Wolfe, if you allow your memories to take you back in time.

One last quote from Mark Twain, the only one in this book with which I disagree, "We are so strangely made; the memories that could make us happy pass away, it is the memories that break our hearts that abide."

Not for me Mr. Twain. I'm holding on to the memories that make me happy. The others, those that might break my heart, are nothing but, as you once said, "blank cartridges."

---

[1] Mayes, Frances, *Bella Tuscany*, Broadway Books, New York, 1999, p. 92.

[2] Ibid., p. 100.

CREDITS

The Mark Twain quotes at the beginning or ending of each chapter are sourced from *Mark Twain: His Words, Wit, and Wisdom*, R. Kent Rasmussen, Editor, Gramercy Books, New York, NY, 1997. These works of Mr. Twain can also be found in:

Chapter 1: Rasmussen, p. 189, and from Twain: *Mark Twain in Eruption: Hitherto Unpublished Pages About Men and Events*, ed. Bernard DeVoto, 1st ed., New York, Harper & Brothers, 1940, p. 108.

Chapter 2: Rasmussen, p. 34, and from Twain: *Mark Twain's Notebook*, ed. Albert Bigelow Paine, 1st ed., Harper & Brothers, New York, 1900, p. 345.

Chapter 3: Rasmussen, p. 90, and from Twain: *Mark Twain's Speeches*, ed. Albert Bigelow Paine, Harper & Brothers, New York, 1923, p. 353.

Chapter 4: Rasmussen, p. 151, and from Twain: *Mark Twain's Letters*, ed. Victor Fischer, Michael B. Frank, and Lin Salamo. 1st ed., University of California Press, Berkeley, 1995, p. 240.

Chapter 5: Rasmussen, p. 73, and from Twain: *Early Tales and Sketches, vol 2, 1864-1865*, ed. Edgar Marquess Branch and Robert H. Hirst, University of California Press, Berkeley, 1981, p. 286.

Chapter 6: Rasmussen, p. 107, and from Twain: *Mark Twain's Notebook*, ed. Albert Bigelow Paine, Harper & Brothers, New York, 1935, p. 344.

Chapter 7: Rasmussen, p. 131, and from Twain: *Mark Twain Speaking*, ed. Paul Fatout, University of Iowa Press, Iowa City, 1876, p. 351.

Chapter 8: Rasmussen, p. 151, and from Twain: *Following the Equator; A Journey Around the World*, 1st ed., American Publishing Co., Hartford, 1897, p. 447.

Chapter 9: Rasmussen, p. 302, and from Twain: *What is Man? and Other Philosophical Writings*, ed. Paul Baender, 1st. ed., University of California Press, Berkeley, 1973, p. 354.

Chapter 10: Rasmussen, p. 126, and from Twain: *Mark Twain's Autobiography*, ed. Albert Bigelow Paine, Harper & Brothers, New York, 1924, p. 264.

Chapter 11: Rasmussen, pp. 188, and from Twain: *Personal Reflections of Joan of Arc*, 1st ed., Harper & Brothers, New York, 1896, p. 282-283.

Chapter 12: Rasmussen, pp. 188, and from Twain: *More Maxims of Mark*, privately published, 1927, p. 14.

Chapter 13: Rasmussen, p. 32, and from Twain: *A Connecticut Yankee in King Arthur's Court*, ed. Bernard Stein, University of California Press, Mark Twain Library, Berkeley, 1983, p. 96.

Chapter 14: Rasmussen, p. 81, and from Twain: *Pudd'nhead Wilson and Those Extraordinary Twins*, 1st ed., American Publishing Co., Harford, 1894, p. 214.

Chapter 15: Rasmussen, p. 146, and from Twain: *Mark Twain-Howells Letters: The Correspondence of Samual L. Clemens and William D. Howells*, ed. Henry Nash Smith and William M. Gibson, 1st ed. 2 vols., Harvard University Press, Cambridge, 1960, 2:597.

Chapter 16: Rasmussen, p. 46, and from Twain: *More Maxims of Mark*, ed. Merle Johnson, privately published, 1927, p. 9.

Chapter 17: Rasmussen, p. 79, and from Twain: *Following the Equator; A Journey Around the World*, 1st ed., American Publishing Co., Hartford, 1897, p. 567.

Chapter 18: Rasmussen, p. 126, and from Twain: *Mark Twain's Autobiography*, ed. Albert Bigelow Paine, Harper & Brothers, New York, 1924, p. 264.

Chapter 19, first quote: Rasmussen, p. 175, and from Twain: *Prince and the Pauper: A Tale for Young People of All Ages*, University of California Press, Mark Twain Library, Berkeley, 1983, p. 42.

Chapter 19, second quote: Rasmussen, p. 176, and from Twain: *Mark Twain-Howells Letters: The Correspondence of Samual L. Clemens and William D. Howells*, ed. Henry Nash Smith and William M. Gibson, 1st ed. 2 vols., Harvard University Press, Cambridge, 1960, 2:595-596.

Chapter 19, third quote at the end of chapter, " We are so strangely made...": Rasmussen, p. 176, and from Twain: *Personal Reflections of Joan of Arc*, 1st ed., Harper & Brothers, New York, 1896, p. 439.

Chapter 19, fourth quote at the end of chapter, "...blank cartridges...": Rasmussen, p. 176, and from Twain: *Life on the Mississippi*, 1st ed., James R. Osgood, Boston, 1883, p 88.

READERS' COMMENTS

I take a different approach in quoting comments from readers. Most books place these comments on the back of the cover. These brief remarks offer little substance, such as the readers' experiences in relation to the book's topics. By having readers' comments in this section in the book, I can share with you their experiences, as well as more detailed thoughts and ideas about the book. I hope you enjoy and relate to them.

These comments (which I received in emails) do not have names attached. In some instances, I do not know who the sender is, as my material was later sent to unknown readers who responded only with an email address, or from a less-identifiable blog response.

If I do have names, for privacy purposes, I have deleted the name of the sender. If you would like to know the sender, if I have his/her identification (and I have domain names for most of these emails), I will contact the sender and ask for his/her permission. In this way, you can also verify the accuracy (pro and con) of this correspondence.

Unless a person included something personal, I have altered no words or grammar. I have used "——" in place of profanity or other words that a reader might find offensive. On a few occasions I must substitute a person's name with a noun or pronoun, in which case, I place brackets around my change. Any notes I add are also surrounded by brackets.

I have made the text the same font size and type, and changed minor formats. In some cases, an email was several pages. I took the liberty of shortening some of these emails, but I altered none of the words.

I look forward to your thoughts about my book and these readers' thoughts as well.

++++

Thanks for sharing your writing. Easley's Twin Lakes was such a wonderful part of our growing up. I can still hear all the "oh's and ah's" echoing around the lake as the fireworks were set off. We were so lucky. I remember the junior high class parties at the lake and the "walks" over the bridge. Keep sharing your stories.

++++

My grandparents moved to Hobbs when it was little more than a tent city. My granddad worked for Texaco at the time and moved from Roswell to Hobbs between 1935 and 1939. I have the date around here somewhere, but don't know where it is at the moment. My parents were married at my grandparents house on Linam Street in April 1939, and there was snow on the ground!

++++

The ranch [this reader's parents ran a ranch in the Little Texas' Lea County] is right on the city limits there just south of the football stadium. Mother and Daddy built our house right on the corner of Ark. Jct. road and the old main house with all the trees was 1/4 mile on down the road. That is where my grandparents lived. [My sister] and I inherited the ranch when Daddy died and we have kept it leased for grass to a couple of people all these years. We have had it since New Mexico was still a territory. Lots of memories tied up there.

++++

Thank you so much for *Light Side of Little Texas*. I had pulled Chapter 4 from your web site and shared it with my children who are city bred and reared. I could hear the noise and smell the smells and see [the] faces.

++++

I have begun a journey back in to time with you and can't resist commenting on your first chapter. It is just great, again can see and hear the people and places.

++++

I like the way [you] paced the story. I wanted to rush through it, being full of coffee, but I let myself go at the author's pace and it felt good. Brought back lots of Juarez memories, most of them incoherent, which tells you a lot about what I used to do in Juarez.

++++

I've just finished "Lips" and "Carnival" and enjoyed every word of both. You referred to "The Hunter and the Hunted" which I haven't seen yet - and hope to see soon.

++++

Took your story with me to baseball practice and sit in the car and read it. Brought back a lot of good memories.

++++

Keep the creative juices flowing - otherwise they all dry up!!

++++

This one was hilarious [The "Name that Name" story]. I practically spit hot chocolate all over my office when I read the question about [the University of New Mexico], "Why did you attend a foreign College?"

++++

Thanks so much U.D. ...... I am sure it will bring back wonderful memories! I sometimes wonder what my dad would have thought about Wal-Mart, Gibsons, and Target. It would have put him out of business. They all arrived on the scene shortly after he passed away. I believe Wal-Mart rules the world now.....haven't seen a Ben Franklin Variety Store in years!

I know I will enjoy a "trip down memory lane."

++++

The memoir is just terrific. I'm sure the day your mother sent you to school with [your brother] and the note is probably the day I met [your brother].

++++

I have read all of the stories that you have sent me, a half-dozen or so, and I look forward to reading "The Swimmer". They are very charming with a folksy wit. I also look forward to reading some of your policy essays. It is very understandable that your essays are less clear. It is hard to make something coherent, even a critic, out of something so haphazard.

++++

Thanks so much again for the stories. Your descriptions of Southeastern New Mexico make me feel like I was right there with you. I have never been to that part of the state yet feel now that I have. Do you think of it as beautiful?

++++

I loved your story, it made me cry and remember some of those times in my life. I love the way you write and I don't believe you should ever retire completely.

++++

I have loved the last story you sent "Thus Far It's Been a Good Life." Not finished with it yet, and a big part of that is that I don't want it to end. I love reading all about life in New Mexico in the 50's, and it dredges up many memories, mostly good, for me. I only allow myself to read a page a night - isn't that stupid? But this way, I can "savor" it.

++++

Loved your name game! (Note exclamation point!) Also, don't want to spoil your rantings, but it's not Peek-a-boo Street, it is Picabo Street, named after small town of Picabo, Idaho, south of Ketchum and east of Magic City. Honest. Am thoroughly confused about what to call you, so I guess you will be Harold!!

++++

I just finished your "Name that Name". How enjoyable! The twist at the end (Harold) is <u>great</u>.

++++

I loved your name story, but I would really love a longer story on your magical encounter with your turtle. It sounds to me to have been a very spiritual experience for you.

++++

First of all, it was funny! And that's the last bit of praise!

++++

Hal Raines, Harold Baines, Harold Carmichael, Hal McRae, Hal Holbrook, Harold Stassen, Hal Sutton, my uncle Harold etc. etc. They're everywhere. But to me there will only be one UD.

++++

I have read the Dog Catcher story and the one about [name deleted] shooting a crow in [a person's] orchard. I also read the story about [your son] and his music. I have enjoyed them all. The Dog catcher is my favorite to date.

++++

I've finally gotten to read this & I'm still laughing!!!!!! You're a NUT and I love it.

++++

I've already read "Thus Far" - and absolutely loved it.

++++

Oh My, [My husband] and I have sit and read this and laughed our heads off..................Thank you so much for the memories.......the laugh.......and for sharing with us your stories.

++++

Yesterday we received the last chapter of your book and last night [my wife] and I took turns reading it to each other. MOST ENJOYABLE!

++++

Ah, my tad pole Saviour. Loved your story...

++++

Beautiful story! The tadpole story is the only one I forwarded....so be sure I am on your list to get subsequent stories. I forwarded it to [name deleted] (his desk and computer are on the other side of the office) and I heard a lot of chuckles coming from him.

++++

UD... well written horse story. Dave Barry may not use the "figure" in his stories, but otherwise you're sure to be next in line for syndication (except that's a lot like work...) Thanks for sending it.

++++

Just finished your story. Very entertaining. I enjoy your way of inserting a couple of philosophical thoughts to accompany the base theme. Neatly done. Now, I know you have apologized (in the story) to a number of deserving people and "places" but I am wondering: Did you return the keys to Chief Robinson?

++++

I really admire and respect the stories you are writing. What a great idea they are!

++++

I have just read your Ed story; delightful! I have a warm feeling just thinking about the dialog between you two. You have such a way of entertaining yourself while making others feel good about themselves. But unlike most people of your reasoning level——you really do care for others and are interested in them. What a combination ! I read a description of what is " CLASS "——It said a classy person could walk with Kings and belong and sup with the common man and belong. That is you——I really think you would have been the greatest high- school teacher of all time!

++++

Weren't we all "Lost in Lea County" for about 10-12 years? And is that why our class song was "I wanna go home....."

Cute story....I didn't know "pistols" were allowed in NM, I thought the Texas cowboys had a corner on the market!

++++

Just read your yodeling account. Coincidentally, we were teaching the boys to yodel on our trip to New Jersey. "Grandma slid down the mountain on her Le-oh-laa-te-o." The boys loved it. I love country music of the old type, too. Brings back memories of my uncle who thought he could sing. He knew the words but his voice was grating. It provided amusement though.

++++

Thank you for the stories. I am looking forward to reading them.

++++

You write very well, and we would love to see any items you care to share.

++++

Loved your "Lost in Lea County." Very nicely done.

++++

I had to forward your Lea county story to my brother, even though he was not the country / western fan I was growing up (keep in mind I never have grown up).

++++

U (or Uyless or U.D. or Harold)...I read the first three chapters of Little Texas this morning and thoroughly enjoyed it. I thought your description of the evolution of your name was priceless.

Essays available at Blog.UylessBlack.com

America's Capital: Author's experiences in Washington, DC

America's Cities: Journeys and encounters in USA's towns and cities

America's Finances: A series on issues such as Medicare, Social Security, and debt

Computers and Networks: Essays on Internet net neutrality, copyright issues, and software complexity

Creatures and Computers: Drawing analogies to wildlife and Internet organisms

Customs and Cultures: A look at America and Americana

Eating and Drinking: Surveys of food fairs, cafes, and restaurants

Food Effects and Drug Defects: Reports on toxic foods and drugs' side effects

Foreign Affairs: America's relations with other countries

Foreign Places: Taking roads, ships, and trains through parts of the world

Immigration and Emigration: America's immigration practices and related problems

Politics in America: With several reports on National Press Club speakers

Presidential Places: Presidential homes, museums, and grave sites

Sports and Games: Essays on competition and the beauty of sport

The Deadly Trinity Trilogies: Two sets of essays to compliment *The Deadly Trinity* book

> **The Cepee Dialogues** (available 2013 as book; draft is available immediately to a requester)

> **Coming to You Live, from the Dead** (available 2013 as book; draft is available immediately to a requester)

Traveling America: Taking roads through America and America's cultures.

War Zones: Essays on cold, warm, and hot wars

These books, written earlier in Black's career, offer useful information for historians and researchers

IEEE Computer Society
Physical Layer Interfaces
X.25 and Packet Switching Networks

Prentice Hall
Data Communications and Distributed Networks
Computer Networks: Protocols, Standards, and Interfaces
Data Networks: Concepts, Theory, and Practice
The OSI Model
Data Link Protocols
Emerging Communications Technologies
Asynchronous Transfer Mode (ATM) Networks, Volume I
Wireless and Mobile Networks
SONET and T1
ISDN and SS7
Asynchronous Transfer Mode (ATM) Networks, Volume II
Second Generation Mobile and Wireless Networks
Asynchronous Transfer Mode (ATM) Networks, Volume IIII
Advanced Features of the Internet
Residential Broadband
Advanced Intelligent Networks
Voice over IP
The Point-to-Point Protocol (PPP)
IP Routing Protocols
Internet Security Protocols
MPLS and Label Switching Networks
Internet Telephony
Quality of Service in Computer Networks
Internet Architecture
Networking 101
Optical Networks
Multiprotocol Label Switching (MPLS) Networks

McGraw-Hill
The V-Series Recommendations
The X-Series Recommendations
TCP/IP and Related Protocols
Network Management
Frame Relay Networks

Made in the USA
Lexington, KY
02 November 2019